The Art of
Drawing

Holt, Rinehart and Winston

New York   Chicago   San Francisco   Atlanta
Dallas   Montreal   Toronto   London   Sydney

Bernard Chaet

Yale University

The Art of
Drawing

Editor   Rita Gilbert
Picture Editor   Joan Curtis
Manuscript Editor   James Hoekema
Project Assistants   Barbara Curialle, Polly Myhrum
Production Supervisor   Robert de Villeneuve
Designer   Marlene Rothkin Vine

Library of Congress Cataloging in Publication Data

Chaet, Bernard.
The art of drawing.

   Includes index.
   1. Drawing—Technique. I. Title.
NC730.C45   1978   741.2   77-24195
ISBN 0-03-089960-5

Copyright © 1978 by Holt, Rinehart and Winston
All rights reserved

Composition and camera work by York Graphic Services, Inc., Pennsylvania
Color separations and printing by Lehigh Press Lithographers, New Jersey
Printing and binding by Capital City Press, Vermont
8 9 0 1 2   138   9 8 7 6 5 4 3 2 1

*To the students whose talent
and enthusiasm motivated the experiences
described on the following pages.*

Preface

In preparing this second edition of *The Art of Drawing,* I have
held closely to the purpose that motivated the first: to share with
students and the general reader experiences I and my classes
at Yale have had in resolving certain "problems" encountered
in drawing. However, while the underlying themes remain the same,
new developments in my classes—and the implications of them—
have haunted me since the first edition, and these are
included here.

This book is intended as an introduction to drawing,
but it is not a manual of formulas for rendering, perspective,
or other technical devices. I hope that it will assist readers—
whether students, artists, or connoisseurs—to expand their
awareness of art, its processes and purposes. The book relates
the attempt I and my students have made to discover a general
rationale for the art and act of drawing. The resulting point of view
is that drawing from natural forms is basic to all personal
explorations in art, and that the assimilation into the artist's
memory of all forms of nature should provide the best support
for a search in behalf of individual expression.

To help those who are drawing for the first time, I have
prepared an opening section on some of the primary means and
materials of the art. Here, there are chapters on attitudes
and goals, on the properties of graphic expression in two dimensions,
on media, and on composition.

Following this, in Part II, is a much longer section
dealing with the process of visualization. This is the heart of the book,
offering chapters on various problems and the student response
to the challenges of each. The sequences were designed to be

flexible, so as to evoke the individual responses of students. Each one focuses on a specific form—such as a tree, a shoe, a paper bag—and requires the student to analyze in drawing the form itself, its surrounding space, and the adjacent forms. Through this section the forms become progressively more complex, so that the artist must constantly experiment with new and different attitudes toward form, new techniques, and new compositions. This series of chapters leads to a sequence at the end of Part II that traces independent study of chosen subjects. It is hoped that this will provide still greater expansion of visual vocabulary and the true beginning of personal development.

Part III concludes the book with an examination of master drawings and the very rewarding art of copying from works of great draftsmen of all ages. Here, too, will be found a chapter, new to this second edition, that makes the sometimes intimidating transition from drawing to painting. It is hoped that students will translate the concepts of visualization and personal response into a medium that presents different challenges in media and scale.

In more than twenty years of teaching drawing, I have been blessed with gifted and devoted students. Their work is liberally represented along with the master drawings reproduced throughout the book. The student drawings selected represent about half of all the works saved in my classes at Yale. Among them are drawings not only by professional art students—majors in painting, sculpture, printmaking, and graphic design—but also students in architecture and other fields. A great many of the student works, including all those in the "Drawing to Painting" chapter, are new to this edition. The student artists are identified in the captions, except where a missing signature or my failing memory have defeated attribution. Many of these same people are now professional artists and teachers. Nearly all the drawings are in the collection of the Yale University Art Gallery.

Readers familiar with the first edition of *The Art of Drawing* will notice one innovation in the rich, dark-brown duotone reproductions scattered throughout this book. It was not my intention to duplicate faithfully the appearance of the original works, but rather to convey the warm, very special quality unique to drawing.

As artist, teacher, and author my debts are many, and I want to acknowledge several of the most important sources of help I received in preparing *The Art of Drawing.* I must thank the many museums and individuals that granted permission for the reproduction of works from their collections. My special thanks go to Joseph Szaszfai, who photographed most of the drawings reproduced. I am indebted to Barry Nemett, a former student now at the Maryland Institute College of Art, for the idea behind the fascinating exercise of "masterwork into still life" on pages 296 to 301. Finally, as always, I must express my gratitude to the students who provide continual inspiration.

New Haven, Conn.   B.C.
August 1977

Contents

I Drawing: The Means and Materials of Vision

1 Directions

Since the Renaissance the art of drawing has come increasingly
to be considered a unique graphic experience rather than simply the
making of preliminary sketches to be translated into other media.
The working drawings of the Old Masters give us an intimate
glimpse of the artist's search and experimentation with ideas and
forms, for they often suggest the initial impulse that subsequently
gave birth to a fully developed artistic concept. Today we admire
not only the immediacy of these studies but also the individual
handwriting that the drawing itself reveals, which may later be
hidden or lost in the transposition to another medium.

Each generation invents new functions for drawing and
resurrects old ones. For example, some modern artists use drawing
to create an expressive division of space or to build spatial
relationships; for others it serves as a compositional search for the
unknown. Many artists still regard drawing as a rehearsal for more

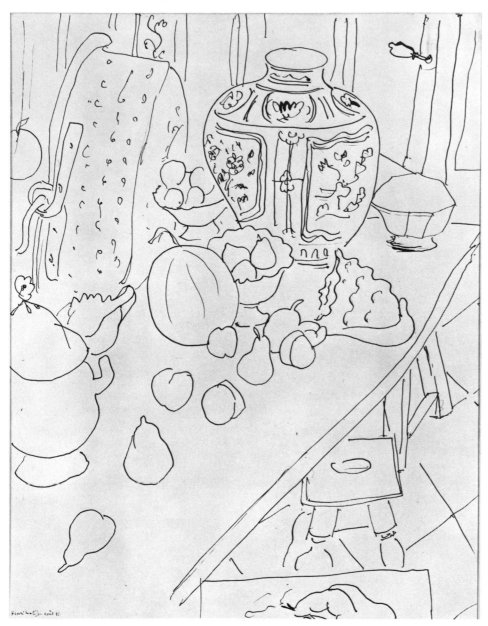

1. Henri Matisse (1869–1954; French). *Nature Morte, Fruits et Potiche.* 1941.
Pen and ink on paper, 20¾ × 16¾″. Musée Nationale d'Art Moderne, Paris.

formal works, while others consider it as simply form-making in black and white. In fact, drawing can be all these things and more, individually or in combination. Each artist's vision determines the function drawing will serve and the direction it will take.

The genius of Henri Matisse makes the line drawing in Figure 1 seem, at first glance, very easy to do. But careful study reveals that line has been manipulated skillfully to perform three functions: It projects the forms into space, and it both controls and energizes the entire composition. Obviously, this is a masterful use of line, and it is the result of long experience. The beginning artist cannot expect to acquire such ability instantly.

In a much earlier drawing by Matisse, *Antoinette* (*La Chevelure*) (Fig. 2), we can examine a part of the process by which a draftsman develops an individual style. One "invents" oneself as an artist by trying out many attitudes toward form. In this pencil drawing the incised features (eyes, nose, and mouth) testify to the study of works of such masters as Hans Holbein, who created simplified, individual, and seemingly rounded forms in drawing. Matisse combines this sculptural quality with a personal preference for arabesque rhythm, as in the flowing, continuous contours of the face, hair, and clothing. The plastic form is contained within these linear movements. Matisse often played such apparently contradictory styles against one another.

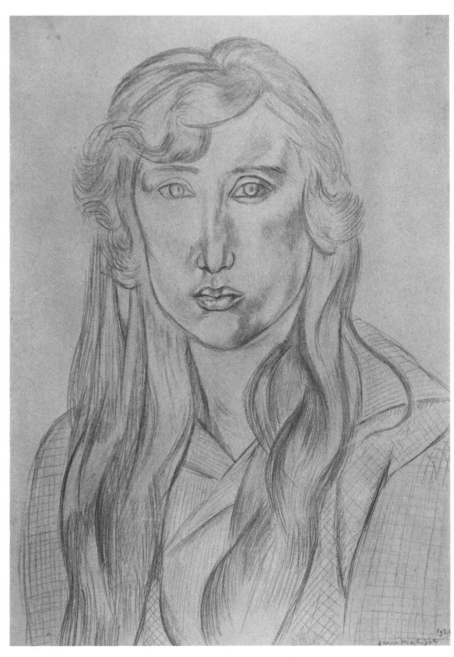

2. Henri Matisse (1869–1954; French). *Antoinette* (*La Chevelure*). 1919. Crayon on paper, 21 × 14½″. National Gallery of Art, Washington, D.C. (Rosenwald Collection).

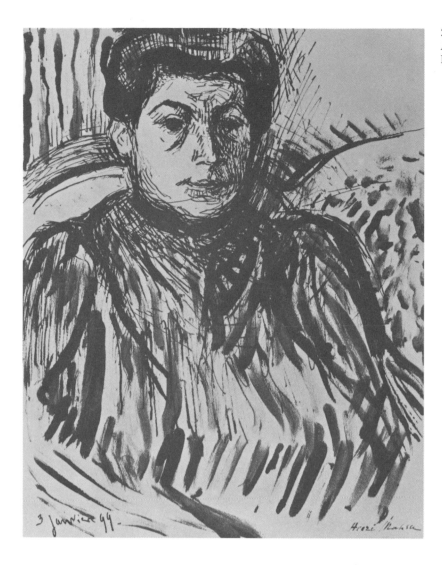

3. Henri Matisse (1869–1954; French).
Portrait of Madame Matisse. 1899.
Pen and ink wash. Collection Jean Matisse.

Another drawing, twenty years earlier, shows how Matisse' turn-of-the-century Fauvist attitudes determined his graphic means. In the portrait of Madame Matisse (Fig. 3), pen and brush strokes produce a variety of textures that together make an image of great intensity. This energetic grouping of contrasting strokes demonstrates the artist's interest in violent color interactions. A different graphic language, a pencil drawing of 1915, presents angular linear thrusts and overlapping planes, reflecting the fact that Matisse is here contending with a Cubist influence (Fig. 4).

From this brief Matisse series, which reveals a master changing techniques throughout his career, we discover a fact that will here be often reemphasized: Drawing is not a single technique; it is rather the personal choice of an appropriate graphic language to fit the demands of a particular concept.

Pier and Ocean (Fig. 5) by Piet Mondrian is a visual dance. The dancers, horizontal and vertical strokes (or shapes), interact in concert with the white space between them. This work shows that art deals with abstract ideas as well as with unique perceptions of the natural world. Mondrian evolved these motifs from his

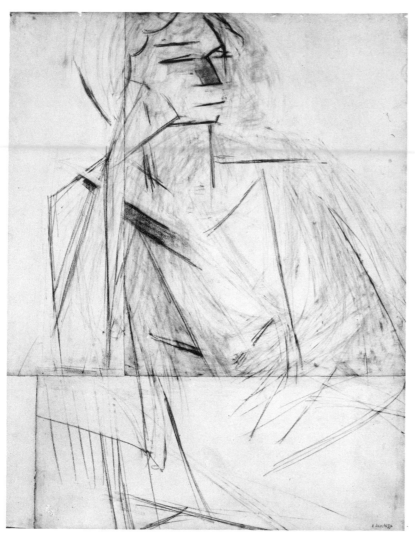

left: 4. Henri Matisse (1869–1954; French).
Portrait of Eva Mudocci. 1915. Pencil, 36½ × 28″.
Courtesy Pierre Matisse Gallery, New York.

below: 5. Piet Mondrian (1872–1944; Dutch).
Pier and Ocean. 1914. Charcoal, 19¾ × 24½″.
Gemeentemuseum, The Hague.

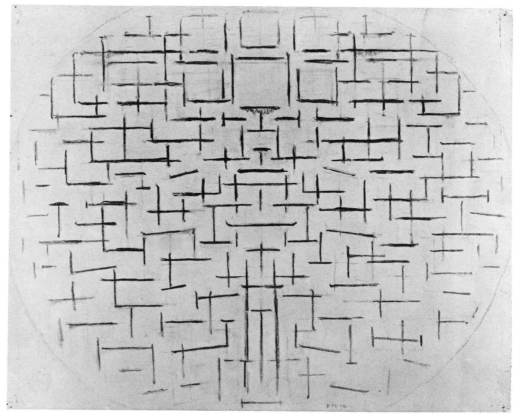

experience in drawing natural forms, as in *The Gray Tree* (Fig. 6). Here the major horizontal thrust of the horizon is countered by the gently waving verticals of the tree forms. These verticals spin a complete circle in space around the central core of the bending tree trunk to produce a volumetric structure that culminates in a pointed top. The cone thus formed suggests one of the functions of a tree—to act as an umbrella. Although Mondrian drew many of his ideas in this period from the Cubists, who were in turn influenced by Cézanne (Fig. 53), the form invention is a structure based on his own idea.

Jean Arp's *Automatic Drawing* (Fig. 7) reflects in visual terms an interest in an immediate, unrehearsed "stream of consciousness" performance. Yet this "automatism" is under the control of the artist's innate feeling for order and his previously selected form-shapes. The large black organic shapes (upper right) group and act together because of their proximity and similarity, while the diagonal line (upper left) anchors the whole composition and serves as a magnet to attract all the gently moving and changing shapes. This cohesion is possible because Arp directs it, whether consciously or subconsciously.

In Willem de Kooning's *Figure and Landscape* (Fig. 8) an effect of immediacy is produced by whiplash strokes speeding through the compositional space. The individual shapes of woman and landscape mirror each other within these pyrotechnics. Unlike Arp's *Automatic Drawing,* this work has no anchor to slow down its constant and allover motion.

6. Piet Mondrian
(1872–1944; Dutch).
The Gray Tree. 1912.
Oil on canvas, 30⅝ × 41¹⁵⁄₁₆″.
Gemeentemuseum, The Hague
(on loan from S. B. Slijper).

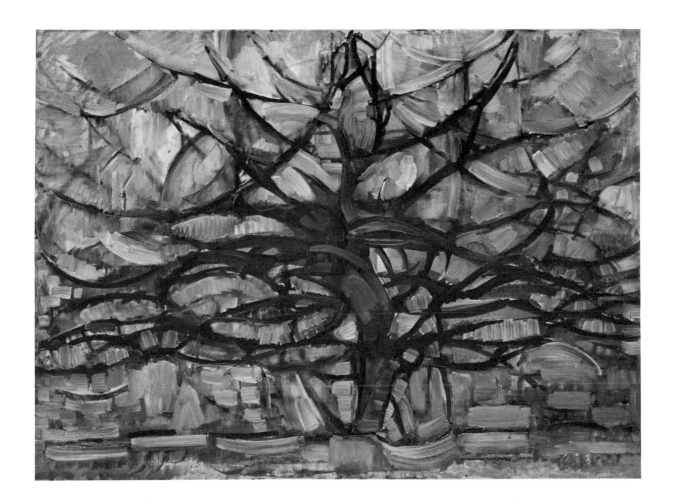

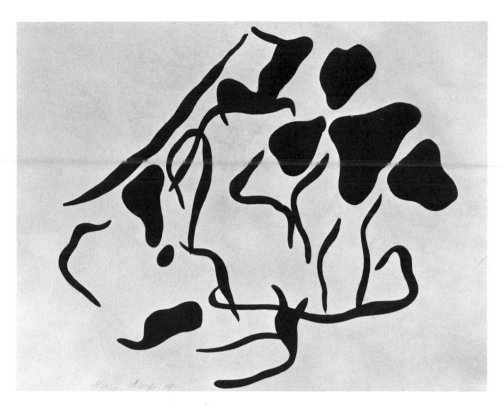

above: 7. Jean (Hans) Arp (1887–1966; French). *Automatic Drawing.* 1916.
Brush and ink on brownish paper, 16¾ × 21¼″. Museum of Modern Art, New York.

below: 8. Willem de Kooning (b. 1904; Dutch-American). *Figure and Landscape.* 1954.
Pen and ink, 16 × 20″. Courtesy Martha Jackson Gallery, New York.

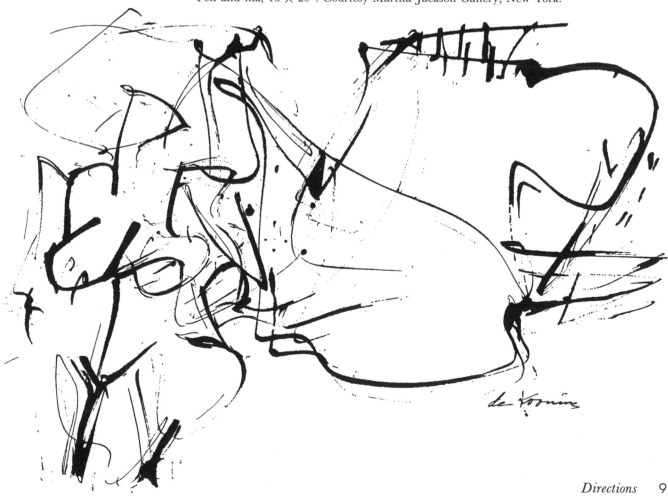

Pierre Bonnard is essentially a colorist, and in *Canaries* (Fig. 9) he alludes to this interest through his choice of materials. Using partly dried ink and a comparatively rough brush Bonnard produces a texture that suggests an atmospheric haze, an almost colorist effect.

In *Circus Interior* Alexander Calder uses economical means to create a vast space (Fig. 10). With a fine, continuous line that darkens and broadens very slightly, he establishes a deep space in the three circles that tip into the picture. The lines representing rope play against and ultimately fuse with the

9. Pierre Bonnard (1876–1947; French). *Canaries.* 1904. Brush, 12 × 7½″. Phillips Collection, Washington, D.C.

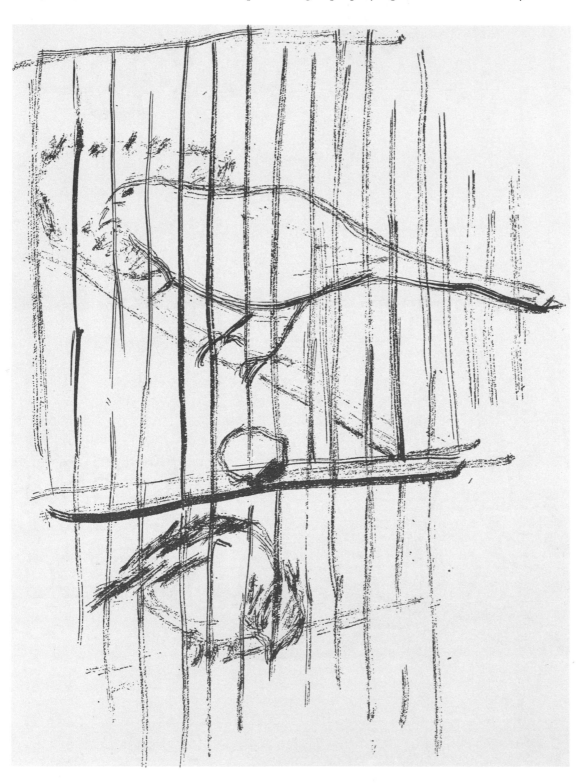

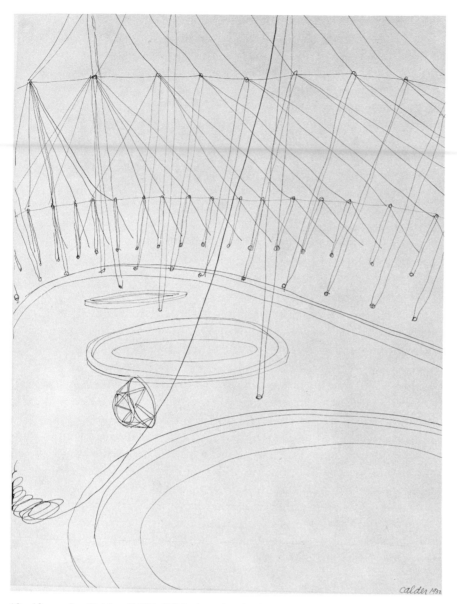

10. Alexander Calder (1898–1976; American). *Circus Interior.* 1932.
Pen and ink, 19 × 14″. Museum of Modern Art, New York
(gift of Mr. and Mrs. Peter A. Rübel).

circles in an overall arabesque. The combination of linear pattern
and coherent space seems almost magical.

The drawings that individual readers will find most
appealing are the ones that come closest to their own sense of what
is aesthetically satisfying. To those who strive for the perfect
adjustment of elements functioning simultaneously, Mondrian's work
will be of particular interest. To the colorist, Bonnard's suggestion
of atmosphere will invite study. The artist who believes in the
automatic release of subconscious impulses will be attracted to Arp,
while Calder will find his audience among students who see
economy and witty spatial ambiguity as goals. Those who prefer
speed and spontaneity will be moved by de Kooning's style.

Each of these illustrations exhibits the natural flow of a personally developed attitude. It is our hope initially to encourage the young artist first to become aware of personal preferences and then to keep them always in mind. At the same time, the student must realize that the art of drawing does not possess one set of principles that need only be learned to result in mastery. But an understanding of the expressive means of drawing (form, line, texture, composition, and so forth), as well as the mechanical tools artists use, is essential to the development of a personal vision, which in turn gives birth to an individual style.

The specific knowledge required for drawing depends upon the attitudes of the individual draftsman and the goals set forth as a personal commitment. The creative artist learns what is needed to fulfill that vision and discards the rest. In short, one absorbs only that which is personally meaningful. In learning to draw, one must address oneself to problems that can challenge one's image-making capacity.

At the same time, it is true that much basic education in the visual arts consists of game-problems that produce results without the conscious involvement of the participants. To speak about texture or line, for example, divorced from all other considerations within a work of art, can be misleading, for texture, line, value, and the rest are tools in the service of a vision and not an end in themselves. And to discuss these qualities without reference to a particular drawing leads to the inevitable pseudoscientific diagram that delivers generalities which may or may not be pertinent. Thus, in this preliminary consideration of means, materials, and composition in drawing, we will isolate and examine certain qualities in the drawings illustrated, but this will serve only to highlight for purposes of study elements that belong to a total artistic statement and have meaning only within the context of a specific work of art.

2 The Expressive Means of Drawing

Form, line, texture, value, and color are the plastic means by which
the artist can express graphic ideas. Although the term *plastic*
denotes something formed or molded, as in the three dimensions of
sculpture, the draftsman can, by a skillful use of line, texture,
and value, create a very real sense of plasticity within the two
dimensions of a flat surface. The "flat" arts of drawing
and printmaking are generally considered to be the *graphic* arts,
rather than the plastic one of sculpture. Color also is, in the pure
sense, often alien to these graphic arts, and while real color
certainly is used by some artists in their drawing, the effect of color
can be realized by exploiting in monochrome the variations that
are possible in line, value, and texture.

 Ground, support, page, and *sheet* are all terms that draftsmen use
in identifying the surface, or field, on which they place their marks.

 At the outset, then, we can say that drawing is a graphic linear
production in black and white on a paper support, but, as we have

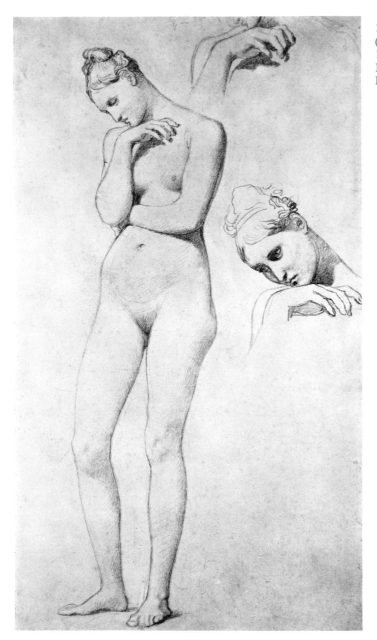

11. Jean-Auguste-Dominique Ingres
(1780–1867; French). Study for *Stratonice*.
1834–40. Pencil, 15½ × 8⅝".
Museum Boymans–van Beuningen,
Rotterdam.

seen and shall observe in the course of this narrative, the art
of drawing is almost infinite in its expressive range and in the
means that make this variety possible.

Line   By traditional definition, a *line* is the result of a dot moving
across the surface of a ground, such as paper. Once put down, the
line can establish boundaries and separate areas. It can, by
its direction and weight on the page, generate a sense of movement.
By applying lines in patterns of parallel and cross-hatched marks,
the draftsman can, with line alone, simulate texture on a
perfectly smooth paper surface. Indeed, using line exclusively—
that simplest and most subtle of graphic means—the artist
can realize almost any visual effect desired.

A frequent association with the verb "to draw" is the verb "to sketch," and within this definition the most common tool is the graphite pencil, familiar to everyone by the inaccurate term "lead" pencil. Pencils are available in various degrees of hardness and softness, and they can be made to produce both the long, clean, unbroken lines and the tonal shading seen in Jean-Auguste-Dominique Ingres' study for *Stratonice* (Fig. 11). Here, the line has great tensile strength, contouring the nude form with almost seismographic accuracy, but the line also becomes a subtle gray modeling of the form's volumes. Ingres has thus achieved a perfect marriage of two kinds of action: One is not conscious of where the line ends and where the forming tone begins.

In Auguste Rodin's *Standing Nude with Foot Raised* (Fig. 12) the pencil seems never to have left the paper, but rather gives the impression of a continuous, instantaneous gesture. However, in *Figure Sketch* (Fig. 13) Rodin carefully studies the volumes of the nude form as they tip into space. The use of line, then, like any action, depends on the function it is supposed to perform and not on a preconceived stylistic device. The artist's purposes determine the application of a particular drawing tool.

below left: 12. Auguste Rodin (1840–1917; French). *Standing Nude with Foot Raised.* Pencil and watercolor, 11¾ × 7½″. Rodin Museum, Philadelphia.

below right: 13. Auguste Rodin (1840–1917; French). *Figure Sketch.* Pencil. Rodin Museum, Paris.

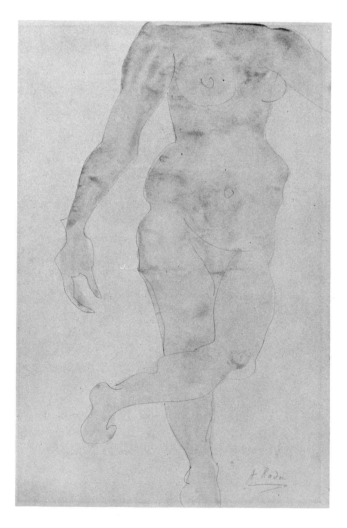

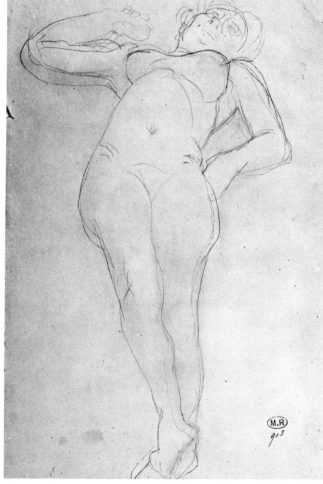

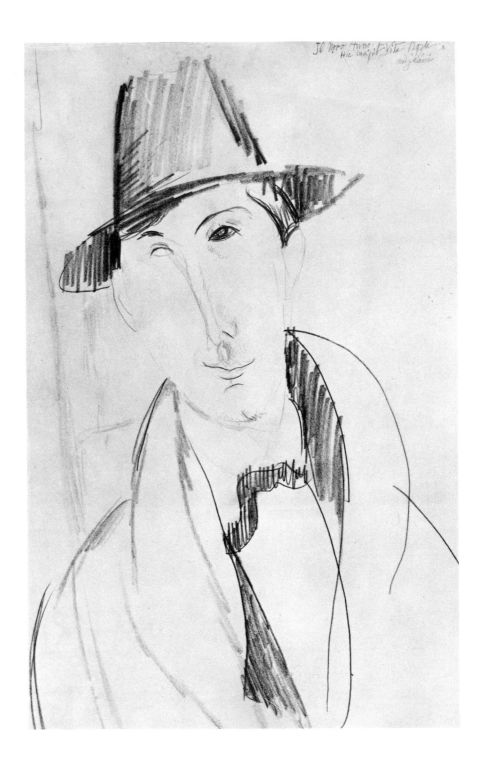

A similar contrast is evident in two drawings by Amedeo Modigliani. In *Mario the Musician* (Fig. 14) Modigliani's pencil expresses a quick, direct gesture, yet within this sketchiness the artist molds the planes of the hat around the head and those of the coat around the neck. The same instrument defines the contours of the forms in a more severe, self-conscious line in *Portrait of Jacques Lipchitz* (Fig. 15).

The drawings illustrated here were executed primarily in line and with the most ordinary, but most elastic, of tools—the graphite

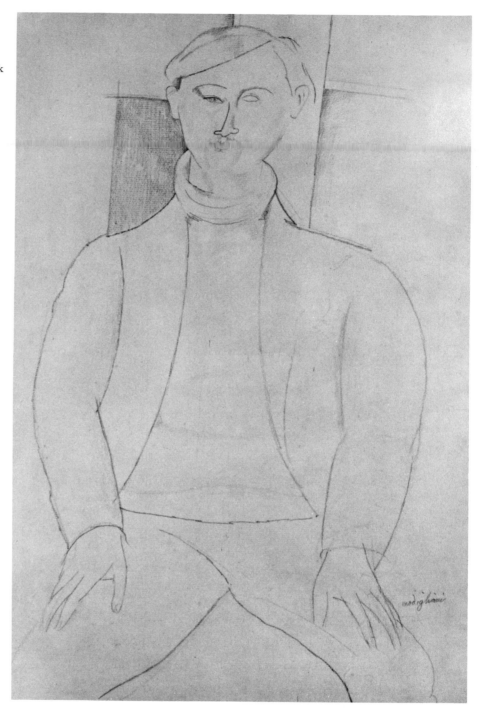

opposite: 14. Amedeo Modigliani
(1884–1920; Italian-French).
Mario the Musician.
Pencil, 19¼ × 12″.
Museum of Modern Art, New York
(gift of Abby Aldrich Rockefeller).

right: 15. Amedeo Modigliani
(1884–1920; Italian-French).
Portrait of Jacques Lipchitz. 1916.
Pencil, 10¾ × 9″.
Collection Lolya R. Lipchitz.

pencil—and in each example the means mirror the artist's intention.
Technique or style is simply a natural by-product.

Tone and Value   *Values* are the gradations of tone that the artist
can work from white to absolute black. Central as the line may be
to the draftsman's art, highly expressive work can be done
altogether in tone. Throughout this book, we will speak of
the various modes of graphic expression and the qualities they
produce in a work of art.

The academies of the past taught that each drawing should possess a full range of values from very light to very dark. In reality, it is the artist's vision that dictates the choice of a particular range of light, and not a set of rules. For example, in Holbein's *Portrait of the Wife of Bürgermeister Meyer* (Fig. 16) the very paleness of the drawing creates a unique mood— a particular light.

Lucas Cranach's *Portrait of Princess Elizabeth of Saxony* (Fig. 17) is a wash drawing on rose-colored paper, and here, too, there is an absence of a full range of values. The features are spotlighted: The darkest forms, the eyes, penetrate the soft pallor of the page, and the mouth, the next-darkest form, is seen after the eyes in a succession of focuses. This direction of focus makes the work unique.

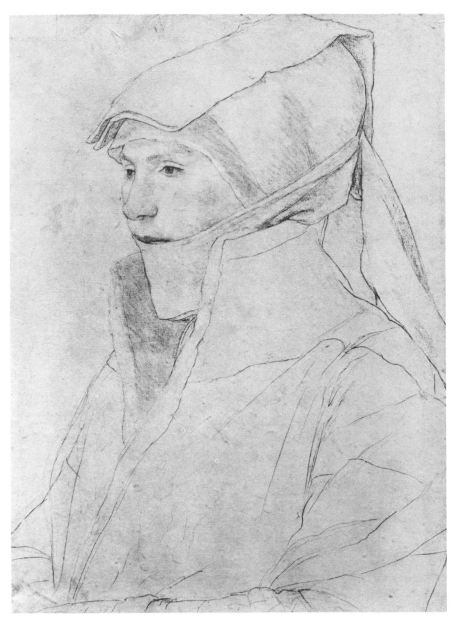

left: 16. Hans Holbein the Younger (1497/8–1543; German). *Portrait of the Wife of Bürgermeister Meyer.* 1525–26. Chalk, 15⅛ × 11″. Kupferstichkabinett, Kunstmuseum, Basel.

opposite: 17. Lucas Cranach the Younger (1515–86; German). *Portrait of Princess Elizabeth of Saxony.* c. 1564. Wash on rose-colored paper, 15½ × 11¼″. Kupferstichkabinett, Staatliche Museen, Berlin.

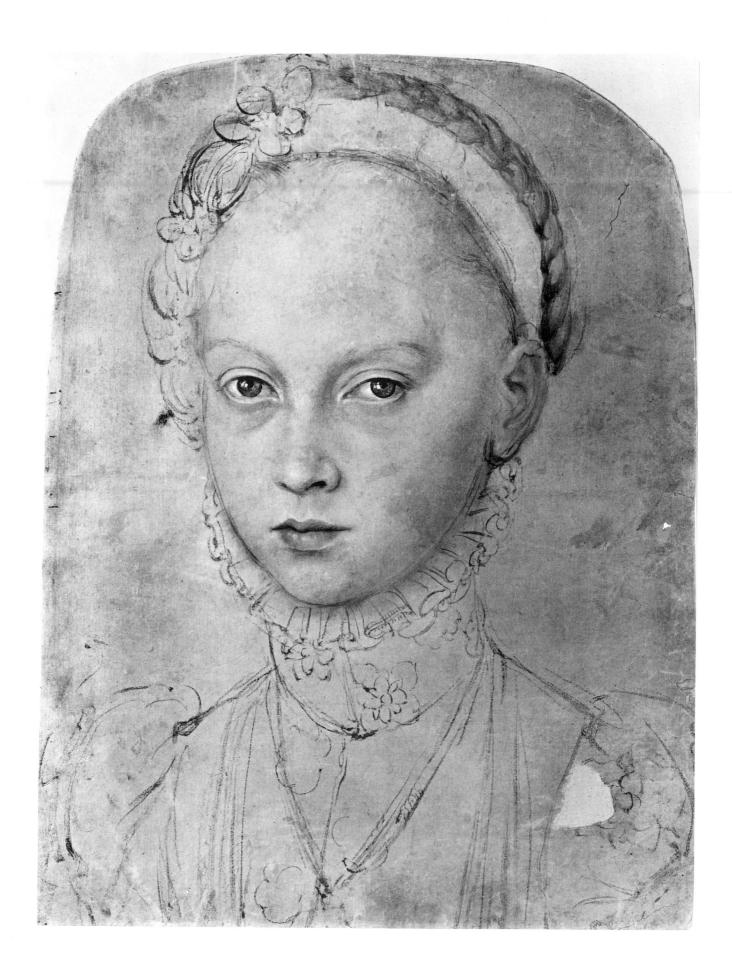

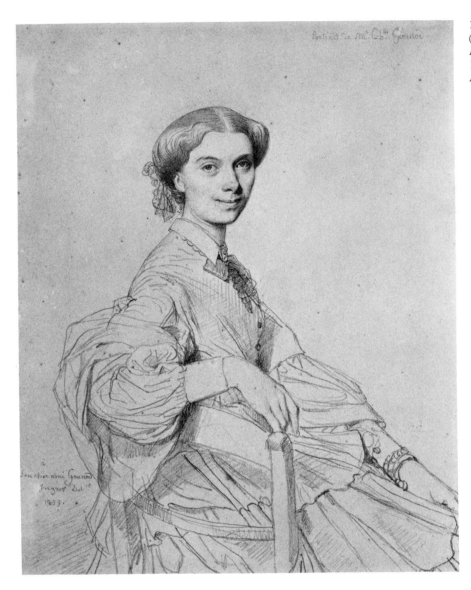

18. Jean-Auguste-Dominique Ingres
(1780–1867; French).
Portrait of Madame Gounod.
1859. Pencil, 10¼ × 8".
Art Institute of Chicago.

In the pencil drawing *Portrait of Madame Gounod* (Fig. 18)
Ingres uses a full range of values, but he does not distribute his darks
according to the actual appearance of the model. Ingres has
decided that in this work the head is the center of interest, and he
purposely keeps the greatest contrast of values in this area. The
range closes as the eye moves down into the drawing. At the bottom
we see clear but briefly stated notes, and yet these lowest areas
are solid and convincing. This is because the key has been
established in the head. These directed clues guide us and deceive
us into seeing that which is only suggested. Had Ingres used
equal contrasts in the chair, dress, and hands, the effect would have
been over-flattened, and the viewer would have been prevented
from participating in the experience directed by the artist.

Vision directs technique. In a drawing of the *Madonna and
Child* (Pl. 1, p. 23) Michelangelo uses the chalk marks in the same
way that he carves marble. Broad open strokes of parallel lines
are massed to form the Madonna, while in the Child's form

we witness a process of caressing and polishing the surface. The dialogue between the two methods of forming exists here as in Michelangelo's sculpture.

Texture   The term *texture,* quite properly, suggests the characteristics of rough or smooth. It is the tactile quality, the sense of touch, that we perceive in art. A textural effect can, as we have seen, be fabricated from the artist's use of lines and tonal values, or it can be the real physical nature of the surface the artist works on or of the drawing medium, such as grainy chalk.

Texture, like value, is more than just an added attraction in a work of art. Texture is automatically created when we draw a dark line across a page. The violent opposition of black and white creates a vibration similar to that caused by complementary colors. Texture, like any natural by-product of a process, must be absorbed into a larger context so that it enhances an idea.

Vincent van Gogh's *Cypresses* (Fig. 19) is conceived as one continuous rhythm of pen strokes which, although drawn in different widths and values, creates a vibrating pattern and a unified texture throughout the drawing.

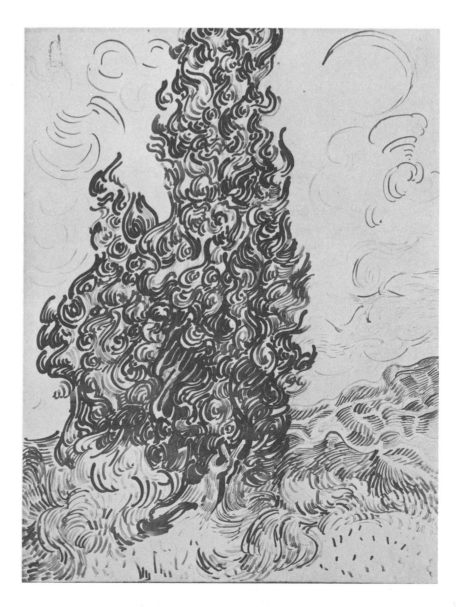

19. Vincent van Gogh
(1853–90; Dutch-French).
Cypresses. 1889. Reed pen and bistre ink,
15½ × 11¼". Brooklyn Museum
(A. Augustus Healy Fund).

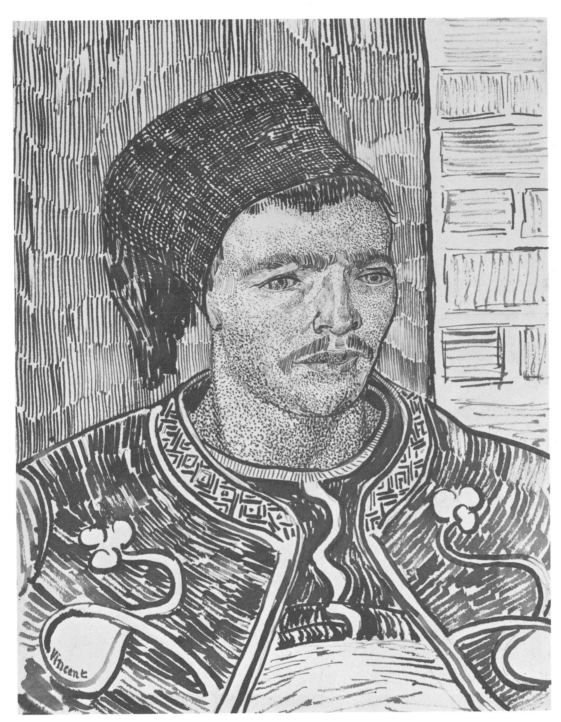

20. Vincent van Gogh (1853–90; Dutch-French).
The Zouave. 1888. Reed pen and ink, $12\frac{5}{8} \times 9\frac{1}{2}''$.
Thannhauser Collection, New York (Thannhauser Foundation).

In another Van Gogh drawing, *The Zouave* (Fig. 20), we
see an interaction of different kinds of marks (or groups of textures),
which create different wave lengths. Each group of distinct
marks acts upon its neighbors: The face composed of tiny dots plays
against the cross-hatching of the hat, and both interact with the
vertical strokes of the background. These separate textures

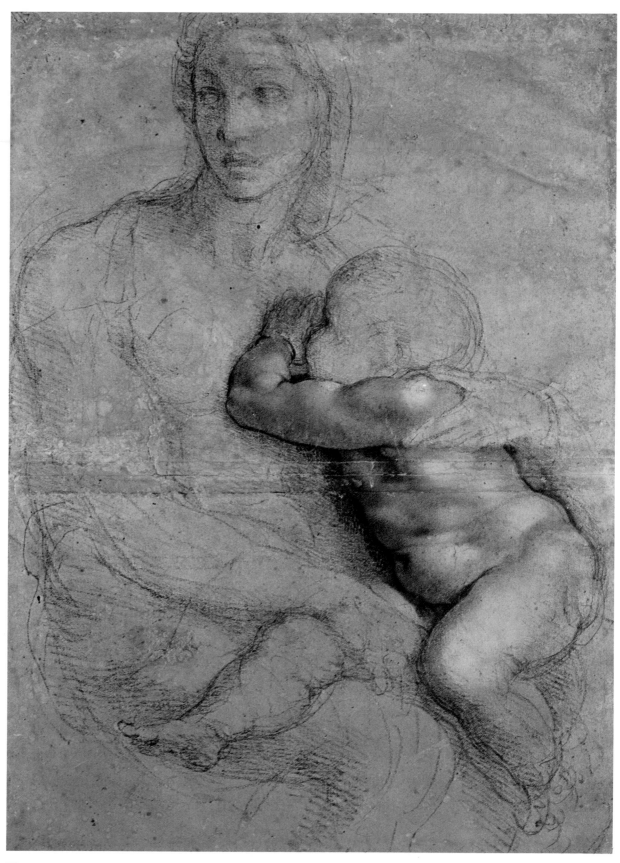

Plate 1. Michelangelo (1475–1564; Italian). *Madonna and Child.* 1535–40 (?).
Black chalk, red chalk, and white pigment on prepared paper; 21⅜ × 15⅝″. Uffizi, Florence.

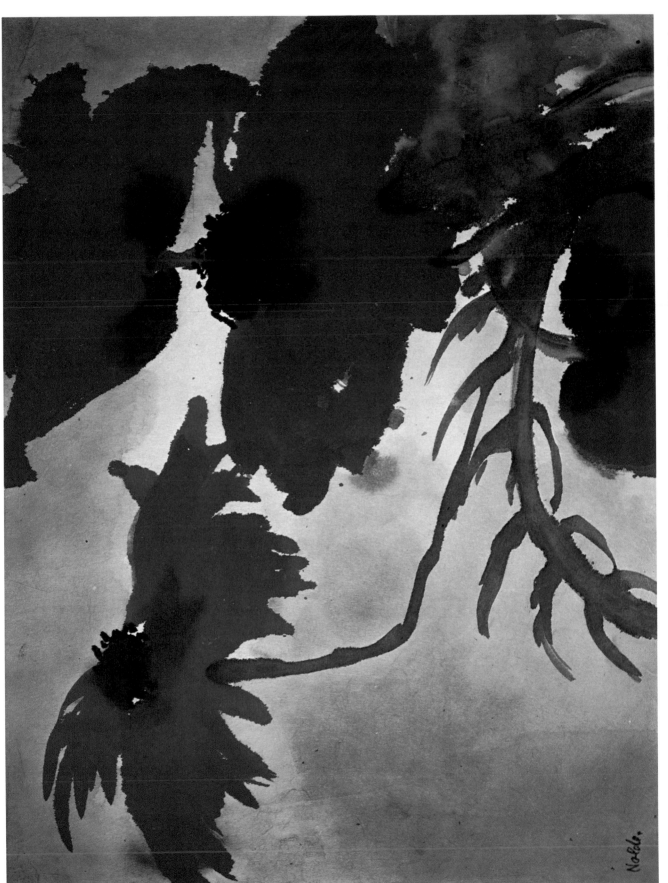

Plate 2. Emil Nolde (1867–1956; German). *Red Poppies.* c. 1931. Watercolor, 13 × 18″. Private collection, San Francisco.

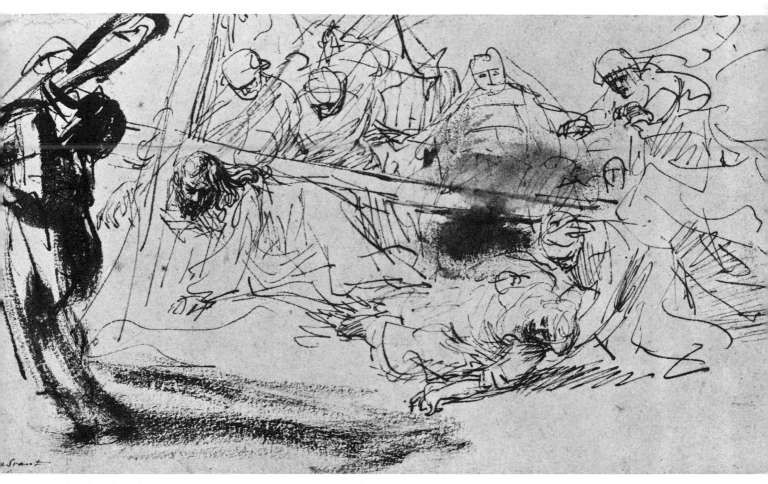

21. Rembrandt (1606–69; Dutch).
Christ Carrying the Cross. c. 1635.
Pen and ink with wash, $5\frac{5}{8} \times 10\frac{1}{8}''$.
Kupferstichkabinett, Staatliche Museen, Berlin.

are, in a sense, stand-ins for the color relationships in the painting
to which this study was ultimately applied. But the drawing exists
as a work of art in its own right. The interaction of textures
serves as a light-giving exercise, a concert of opposing marks that
create a unified vibration.

Similarly, in Rembrandt's *Christ Carrying the Cross* (Fig. 21)
different kinds of marks create different textures. Here, however,
two distinct instruments have been used—pen and brush. The
dry brush, which has been dragged across the rough paper, attaches
itself to the fluid wash figure on the left to create an L-shaped
frontal plane. The plane thus formed frames the center of interest,
the head of Christ. (The value of the pen strokes in the head
keeps it in place behind the frontal plane even though it
is the center of interest.) Finally, the rest of the drawing is
accomplished with lightly sketched lines, with but one spot of wet
wash to counter the dark figure pulling to the left. Texture, then,
not only creates a special light with the play of different kinds
of surface marks—wet, dry, sketchy, and loose strokes—but it also
indicates planes in space.

A sensitive visual concert of textural energies emerges from a range of very light to very dark pen strokes, combined with a light, delicate wash, in Claude Lorrain's *St. John in the Wilderness* (Fig. 22).

<u>Form</u>   Form is the shape of the images defined in an artist's work, whether they are "real" or abstract, two- or three-dimensional. The term can thus apply not only to the shape of recognizable

22. Claude Lorrain (1600–82; French). *St. John in the Wilderness.* Pen and brown wash, 8¾ × 8″. Norton Simon Inc. Foundation, Los Angeles.

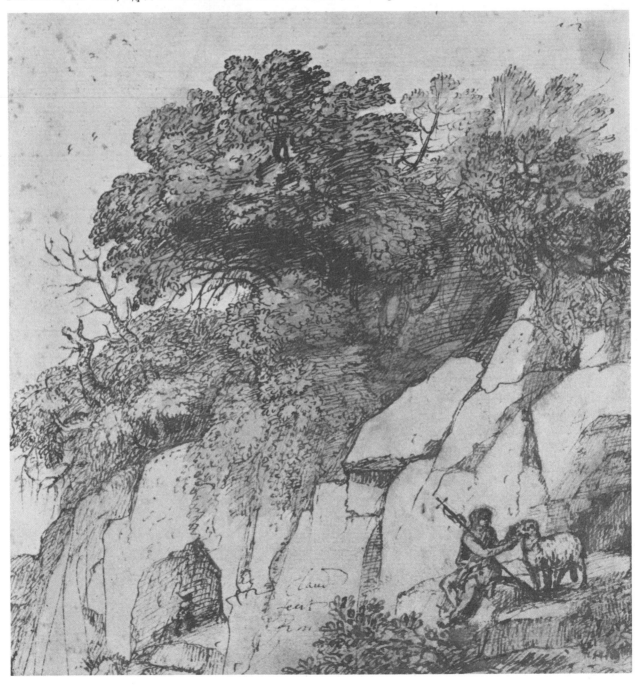

things but also to the form of particular areas or of the whole, the sense of volume created—even the shape of the surface on which the draftsman works. In addition, we often speak of the "formal" qualities in art, and this usually encompasses the full range of visual elements—line, tone, texture, color, and so forth—that may characterize an artist's overall style or performance in a given work. Through this comprehensive range of meanings, "form" denotes the visual substance of a work of art.

All levels of meaning can be brought to bear on Emil Nolde's *Red Poppies* (Pl. 2, p. 24), in which color acts as the major determinant of form. Brilliant wet light captures the postures of the flowers as they move in slow motion through the compressed space of the composition.

Space   Space is a still more complex factor in the graphic, two-dimensional arts than is form. There is the space on the surface of the draftsman's paper, which, in visual terms, is often referred to as the *picture plane.* There is also the deep space, or environmental space, that the artist knows to exist in the natural world, a space that contains forms and permits them to move about in it.

Through an experience of space and of the placement of forms in it, an artist works the surface of a drawing so as to give graphic expression to a personal vision of forms organized in spatial relationships. Forms are thus arranged in relation to each other, to the space "behind" them in depth, perhaps receding into the distance, and to the space "in front," that is, between the forms and the viewer. Of particular importance is the way in which forms are constructed in relation to the drawing itself, whose scale and shape define a powerful spatial field.

The relationship between form and space is the essence of composition, which will be dealt with in greater detail in Chapter 4, as well as throughout the book.

3 Media

Drawing is a unique art that employs special tools and materials.
The artist imagines future work in terms of these familiar materials,
but interest in them is not carried to the point of preoccupation with
"technique" as an end, separated from subject matter. If a tool or
a type of paper excites the artist, it is absorbed into the
whole concept of the drawing.

In our examination of line in Chapter 2, we saw the
relevance of the medium one chooses to this expressive purpose.
There, we considered primarily the graphite pencil, which
is a dry medium, but draftsmen work with a great many kinds of
substances, some dry and a number of them liquid. A feeling for
media, an awareness of their physical, sensuous qualities
and their expressive potential, is native to most artists, who savor
selecting and manipulating the materials they work with—the
silver gray of pencil, the velvety blackness of charcoal,

23. Albrecht Dürer ? (1471–1528; German).
Two Women with Mirrors.
Silverpoint with pen and ink, 13 × 8½″.
British Museum, London.

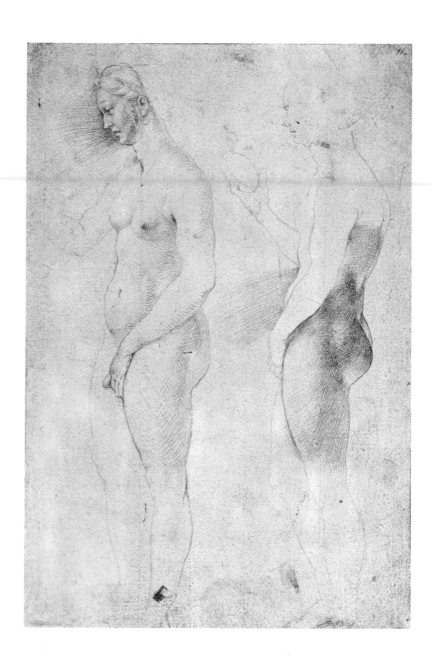

the intensity and brilliance of pastels, and the transparent fluidity
of ink wash. In this chapter, our concern will be for the marking
instruments—the media—of drawing, rather than the grounds
and surfaces the artist may choose to work upon.

Dry Media

Silverpoint   Each stroke shows in Albrecht Dürer's drawing
Two Women with Mirrors (Fig. 23). The medium here is silverpoint,
one of the oldest of the drawing media, surviving from antiquity.
It is closely related to etching in both its directness and
its grouping of lines to produce tones. Silverpoint cannot be used
on ordinary paper, but only on a surface that has been specially
prepared to "hold" the silver left by the draftsman's marking
action. The ground for silverpoint drawing is prepared by

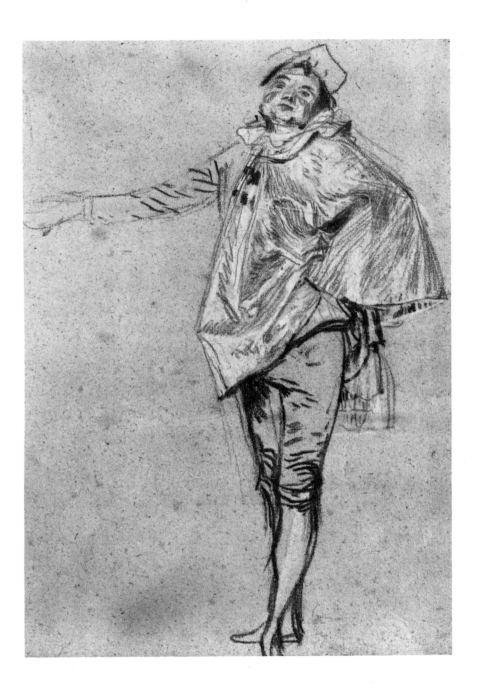

coating the surface with casein, watercolor (Chinese) white, or
a thin size of glue, mixed with a fine abrasive material,
such as bone dust. The medium itself is a long silver wire placed
in a modern mechanical pencil and shaped to a fine point. The
lines produced by silverpoint are uniformly delicate and gray,
oxidizing ultimately to a brownish color.

In this drawing Dürer has used the medium in a firm,
confident manner, with delicate contours and fully realized volumes.
The lines cannot be erased once they have been incised,
although corrections can be made by reapplying the ground.

<u>Chalk</u>   The term *chalk* as it is used today usually refers to conté
crayon, which comes in many shades, from red to brown to black.

Conté crayon can be sharpened with a sandpaper stick or left fairly blunt. (Chalk may also refer to pastel, a much softer medium. Because of its coloristic effects, pastel will be discussed separately.) Crayon includes the ordinary wax crayon and the greasy stick or pencil known as the lithographic crayon, so called because it works well in the water-and-grease technique of making prints by the process of lithography. In a study for *L'Indifferent* (Fig. 24) Antoine Watteau uses red chalk, called *sanguine*, combined with white and black chalks to achieve a directness of modeling. Watteau lets us see the individual strokes, and the effect is one of electric immediacy.

Jacopo Pontormo's *Study of Legs* (Fig. 25) was also drawn with sharpened chalk, but the touch is much softer, to the point of becoming a visual whisper. We can sense the artist delicately rubbing these fine tones (perhaps with his finger) into the fabric of the paper. Line blends into tone to bring out, in this case, a hint of the planar mass.

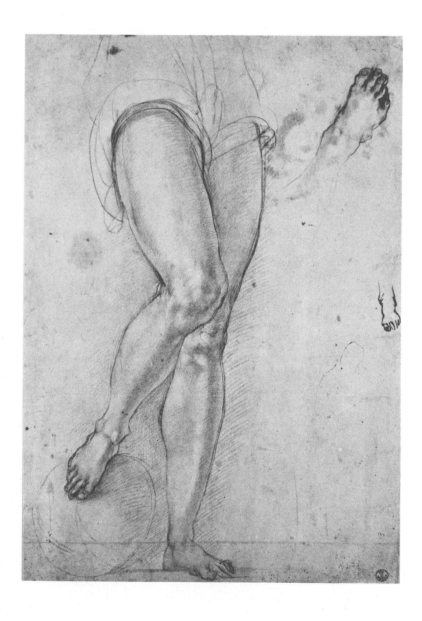

25. Jacopo Pontormo (1494–1556; Italian). *Study of Legs*. Chalk. Uffizi, Florence.

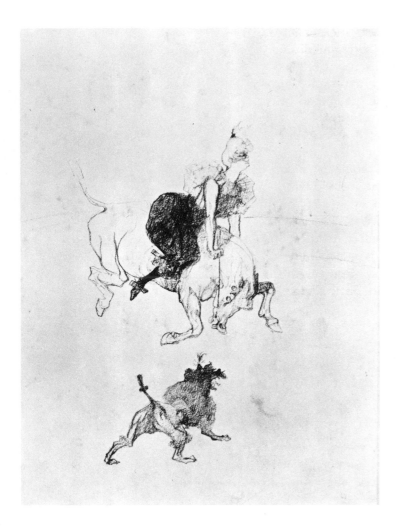

26. Henri de Toulouse-Lautrec (1864–1901; French).
Lady Clown. c. 1899.
Conté crayon in black with color, 13¾ × 9⅞″.
Collection Philip Hofer, Cambridge, Mass.

In Henri de Toulouse-Lautrec's *Lady Clown* (Fig. 26) line and plane are combined, and although the separation is a bit more distinct than in the Pontormo drawing, the artist's technical mastery does not let us see the separation. The horse is essentially linear, while the dog and rider are seen as masses that only secondarily reveal their linear substructure. The particular instrument—conté crayon—that the artist used was dictated by his form-conception, and he explores its possibilities to the fullest dimension.

Michelangelo used chalk in two manners. In Figure 27 comparatively dry, tiny strokes fuse at a distance to create a delicate, shimmering type of modeling that is almost impossible to reproduce. In Figure 28 he adopts a more fluid, painterly use of chalk, which we would normally associate with Titian and other Venetian draftsmen. Velvety rich darks at the center of interest gradually give way to planes produced by groupings of parallel lines, which in turn yield to pure line at the upper corners. The light areas of the chest and legs of the Christ figure and the back of the figure below are compressed and weighty; it hardly seems possible that they are formed simply by the white of the page.

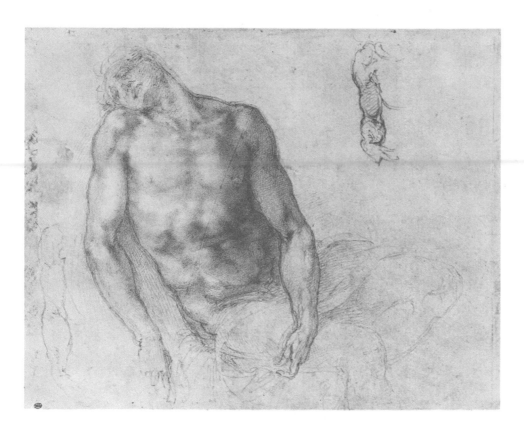

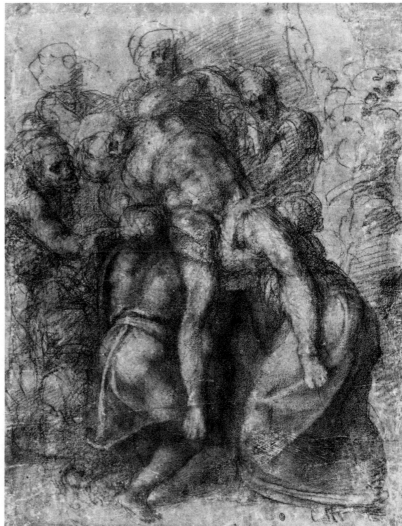

above: 27. Michelangelo (1475–1564; Italian).
Study of a Youth. Chalk, 10 × 12⁹⁄₁₆″.
Louvre, Paris.

right: 28. Michelangelo (1475–1564; Italian).
Compositional Study for a Deposition. c. 1550.
Chalk, 14¹¹⁄₁₆ × 11″.
Ashmolean Museum, Oxford.

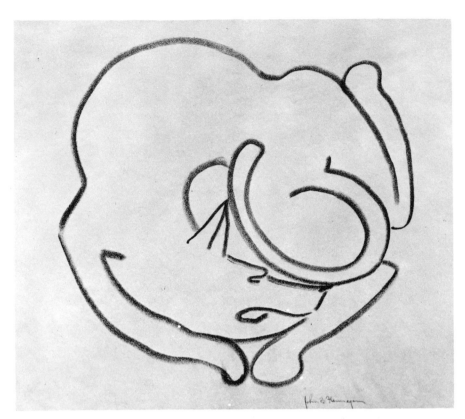

29. John Flannagan (1895–1942; American).
Dog Curled Up. Lithographic crayon, 11½ × 13″.
Addison Gallery of American Art,
Phillips Academy, Andover, Mass.

John Flannagan employs the blunt edge of a lithographic crayon in *Dog Curled Up* (Fig. 29). The artist, a sculptor, captures the dog's posture in one direct gesture. Although the planes are defined only in terms of contour, we do not feel cheated. The concept, again, dictates the use of the tool.

Patches of color electrify the dominant white of Arshile Gorky's drawing in pencil and wax crayon (Pl. 3, p. 41). Here the artist has carefully controlled the amount and placement of the color areas. The small stabs and soft tones of crayon fix the time it takes the viewer to scan the plunging rhythms that fill the composition.

A straightforward use of the conté crayon is seen in *Group of Old Trees* by Matheus Bloem (Fig. 30). There is no rubbed-in softness, as in the Pontormo. Rather, the tooth of the rough drawing paper picks up particles of chalk, which is applied in light, swift, free-moving strokes.

Francisco Goya's predilection for dark, dramatic, pressure-filled scenes receives a strong, full treatment in *La Tauromaquía, No. 8* (Fig. 31), a drawing in which the artist has used white paper to represent not only air but planes as well. The textured passage that fills the center of the drawing represents both the floor of the arena and its back wall, the change from one to the other suggested only by a slight and gradual shifting in value. In this reproduction, which reveals the texture of the paper, we can see the play of darks alternately filling in the grain of the paper and remaining on the surface.

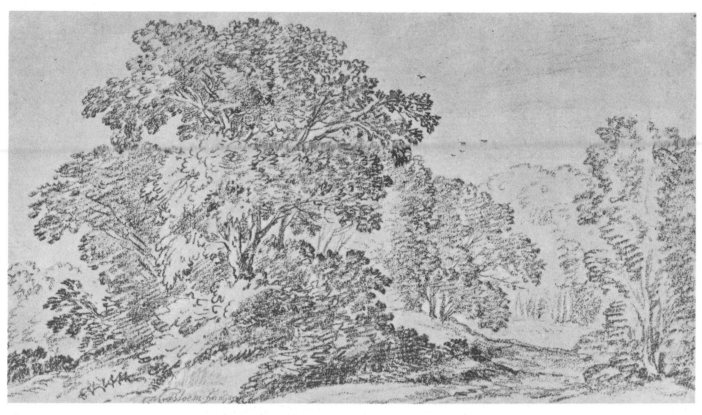

above: 30. Matheus Bloem (active 1640–64; Dutch).
Group of Old Trees. Chalk. Landesmuseum, Braunschweig.

below: 31. Francisco Goya (1746–1828; Spanish).
Cogida de un Moro Estando en la Plaza,
No. 8 from *La Tauromaquía.* 1815–16.
Chalk, $7\frac{1}{2} \times 11\frac{7}{8}''$. Prado, Madrid.

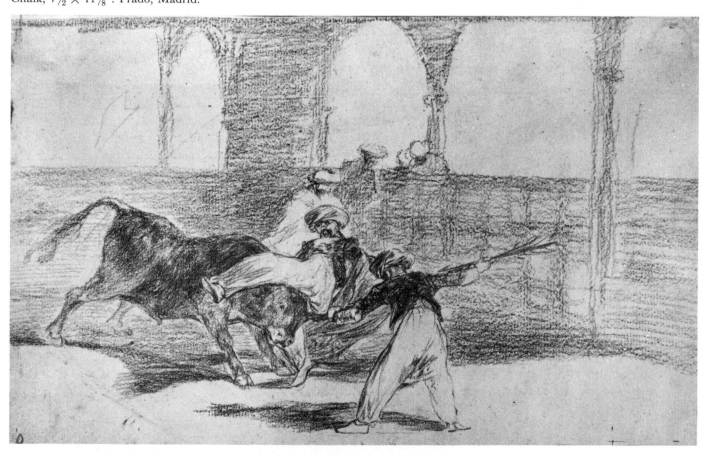

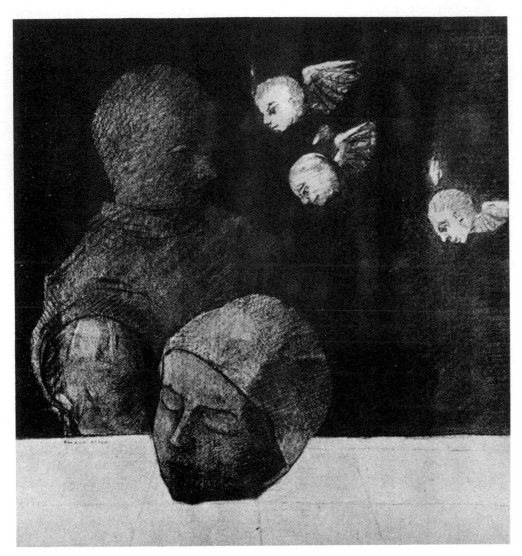

Charcoal   Charcoal comes in hard and soft varieties, the softer
producing the darker line. Compressed charcoal, which is much more
dense and black than the traditional kind, can be used to create
darks as rich as those in *The Prisoner* by Odilon Redon (Fig. 32).
Redon called his velvet-textured, highly personal drawings
"my blacks."

An anonymous student at the turn of the century produced the
charcoal drawing in Figure 33 from a cast of a Greek sculpture.
In this example we can observe the method of teaching that
was popular at most academies of the period. With a smooth
cardboard stump the student rubbed charcoal into the paper
to hide the individual strokes. The suppression of any personal
handwriting was a major goal in traditional academic training.

By contrast, Matisse, in *Head of a Woman* (Fig. 34),
incorporates into the finished drawing the erasures created by his
search for the correct location of forms on the page. The aura
provided by these erasures eventually becomes part of the head and
its environment.

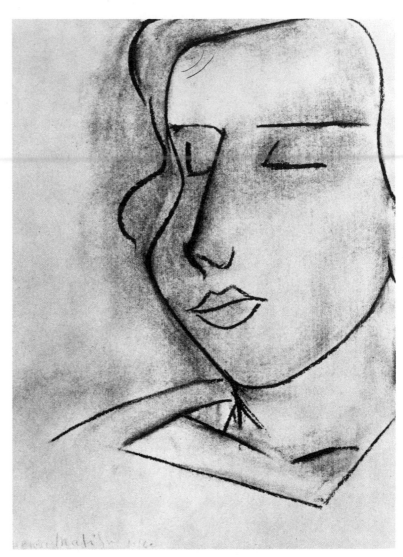

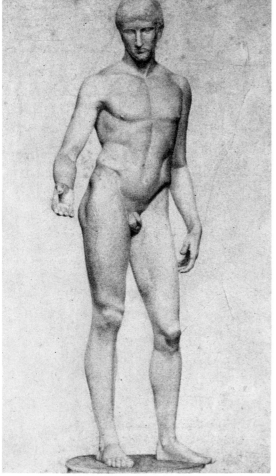

left: 33. Anonymous.
Cast of a Greek Sculpture.
Late 19th–early 20th century. Charcoal.
Collection the author.

above: 34. Henri Matisse (1869–1954; French).
Head of a Woman. Charcoal.
Whereabouts unknown.

Liquid Media

<u>Pen and Ink</u>   Among the most flexible of drawing media is pen and ink. A wide variety of effects can be obtained, depending upon the type of pen point, the amount and kind of ink, and the pressure exerted.

In Figure 35, Sandro Botticelli's *Inferno XXXIII* (illustrating a scene from Dante's *Divine Comedy*), an ordinary medium-weight steel pen point may have been used to achieve this fairly uniform, continuous line. The lines clearly define the shape and posture of each figure, and they also compress the whole space of the composition into a unified field. Forms do not project from, or drop behind, this uniform frontal plane.

Paul Klee employed the fine point of a steel crow-quill pen to produce a vibrating, blurred texture from the open-contoured line of *Up, Away, and Out* (Fig. 36), where the manner of drawing reinforces the title. Here again, technique is the by-product of concept.

35. Sandro Botticelli (1444?–1510; Italian).
Inferno XXXIII, illustration for Dante's *Divine Comedy.*
c. 1482–92. Pen and ink, $12\frac{3}{4} \times 18''$.
Kupferstichkabinett, Staatliche Museen, Berlin.

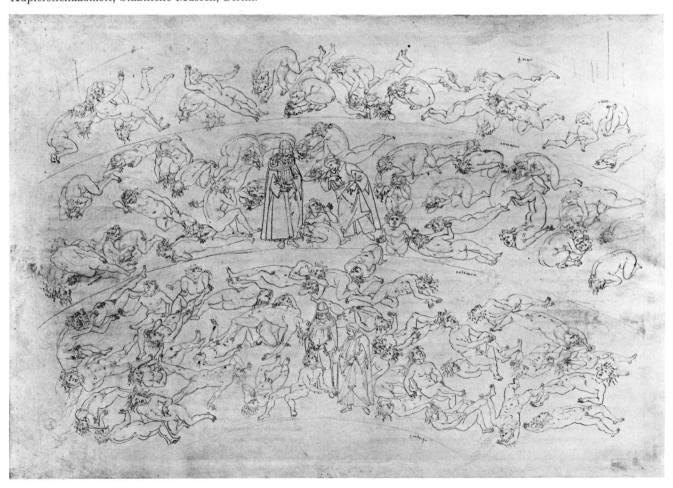

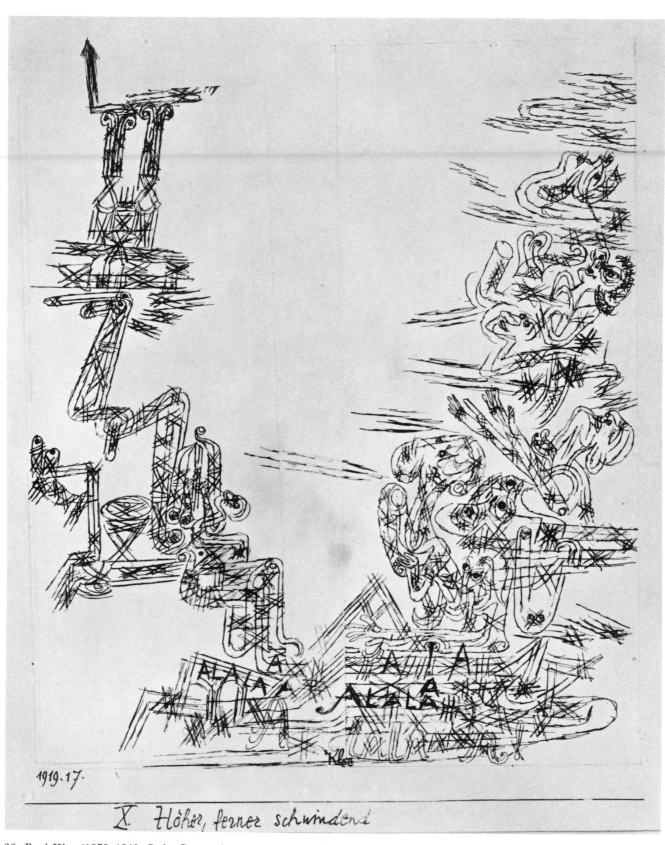

36. Paul Klee (1879–1940; Swiss-German).
Up, Away, and Out (*The Ascension of Termadeus*),
from Corrinth's *Potsdammer Platz*. 1919. Pen, 10¼ × 8⅝".
Paul Klee Foundation, Bern.

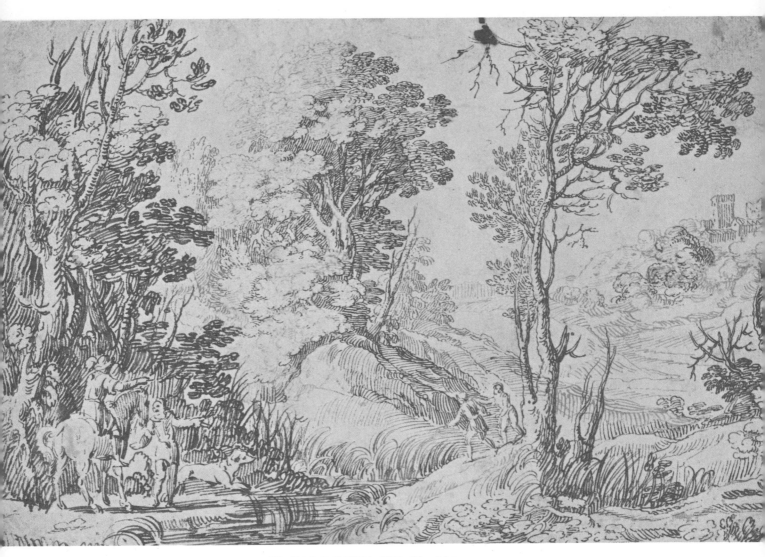

37. Paul Bril (1554–1626; Flemish).
Landscape with Horseman.
Pen and ink.
Landesmuseum, Braunschweig.

In Paul Bril's *Landscape with Horseman* (Fig. 37) a thicker
steel point has been used. Modern pen points come in many
sizes and shapes, and the artist should experiment with several
different kinds to find those that feel the most natural. In Bril's
drawing the ink has been watered down to keep the distant planes
pale in comparison to the foreground, thereby increasing the
illusion of depth, as well as the effect of light coming from the
left. The fluidity of the ink in these sections also tends to
heighten the airy feeling throughout the entire space. Notice,
too, that even the relatively heavy strokes seem rather
lightly and easily applied.

The length of a stroke of the steel pen point is limited by the
amount of ink it can hold in one dip. Not so with a new
instrument, the ball-point pen. The continuous, free-flowing line

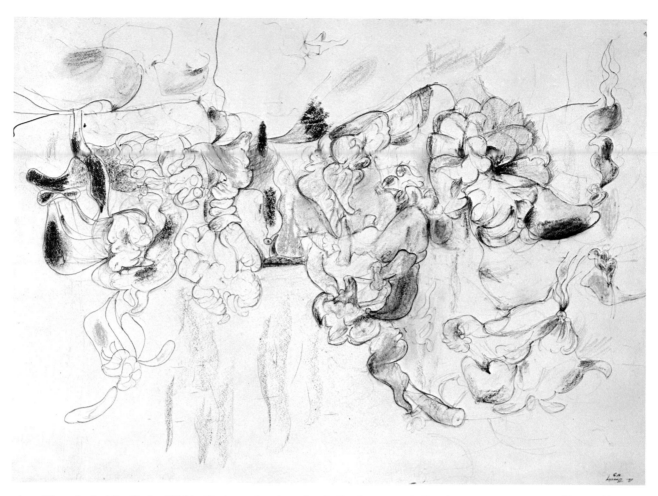

above: Plate 3. Arshile Gorky (1904–48; Armenian-American). *Landscape.* 1943. Pencil and wax crayon, 20½ × 27⅜″. Collection Mr. and Mrs. Walter Bareiss, Greenwich, Conn.

below: Plate 4. James Abbott McNeill Whistler (1834–1903; American). *Nocturne, The Riva, Venice.* Pastel, 5½ × 10½″. Yale University Art Gallery, New Haven, Conn. (Mary Gertrude Abbey Fund).

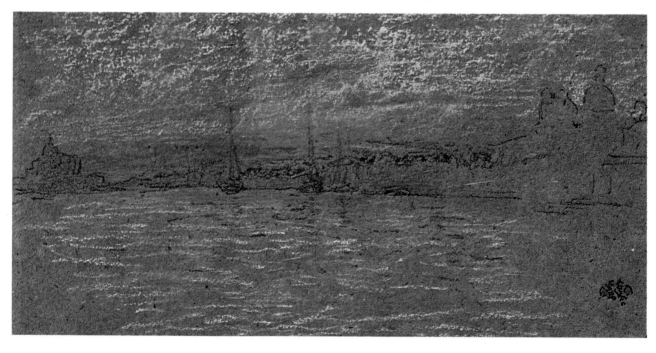

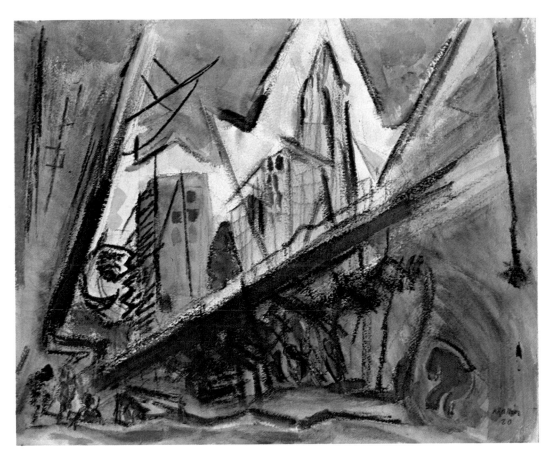

above: Plate 5. John Marin
(1870–1953; American).
Lower Manhattan. 1920. Watercolor, $21\frac{7}{8} \times 26\frac{3}{4}''$.
Museum of Modern Art, New York
(Philip L. Goodwin Collection).

right: Plate 6. Joan Miró
(b. 1893; Spanish-French).
Self-Portrait. 1937–38.
Pencil, crayon, and oil on canvas; $4'9\frac{1}{2}'' \times 3'2\frac{1}{4}''$.
Collection James Thrall Soby, New Canaan, Conn.

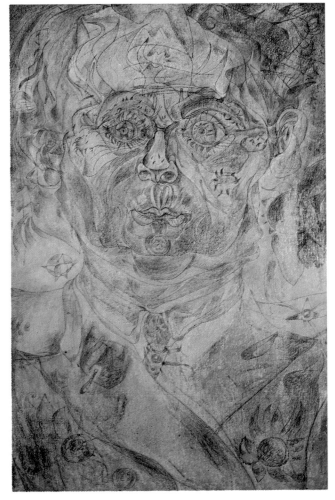

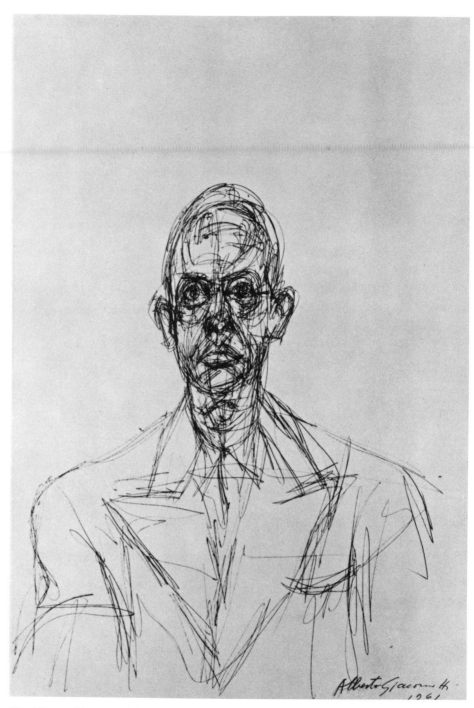

38. Alberto Giacometti (1901–66; Swiss).
Portrait of Herbert Lust in His Father's Topcoat.
1961. Ball-point pen.

in Alberto Giacometti's *Portrait of Herbert Lust in His Father's Topcoat* (Fig. 38) carves out the geometric core of the head and its location in the compositional space. This potential for unbroken line is the great advantage of ball point. However, the ink dyes used in ball-point pens may fade when exposed to constant light.

Each tool has its own kind of mark which becomes transformed in every stroke by the individual's personal sense of touch.

Cottages Among High Trees (Fig. 39), a quill-pen work by
Rembrandt, is a brilliant performance in the stretching of lines from
thick to thin. A light wash (ink diluted with water and applied
with a brush) has been added to give tone to the quill-pen
lines. One may prepare a quill (a turkey feather works well) by
first cutting a squarish angled point, convex on one side and
concave on the other. A slit down the middle of the point
helps hold the ink.

In Jacob de Gheyn's *Orpheus in the Underworld* (Fig. 40)
tiny pen strokes group together to create planes in both the
architecture and the columns of fanciful cloudlike forms. As in
Ingres' pencil drawing (Fig. 11), line moves imperceptibly
into toned plane. Yet each mark that builds the plane is visible.
A crow-quill pen, the tiniest available, could have been used
to produce this effect.

Still another type of pen is that cut from reed, which grows
in many locations. The artist should cut reeds with different kinds of
points to find a shape that works best. Van Gogh's reed-pen
drawings (Figs. 19, 54) are excellent examples of the
virtuosity of this tool. In the event that reed is not available,
bamboo pens (sold at all art-supply stores) make good substitutes.

Although we normally think of drawing in terms of dark marks
on white paper, Hyman Bloom's white-ink drawing *Fish Skeletons*
(Fig. 41) reverses this principle. The white forms set against a
dark maroon background have a tendency to move out toward the
viewer. Some of the large lines have actually been made with
a brush. The thin whitish film in the central portion of the drawing
is an especially interesting by-product of the white-ink
technique. Artists sometimes prepare an "ink" with white tempera

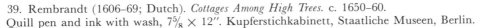

39. Rembrandt (1606–69; Dutch). *Cottages Among High Trees.* c. 1650–60.
Quill pen and ink with wash, $7\frac{5}{8} \times 12''$. Kupferstichkabinett, Staatliche Museen, Berlin.

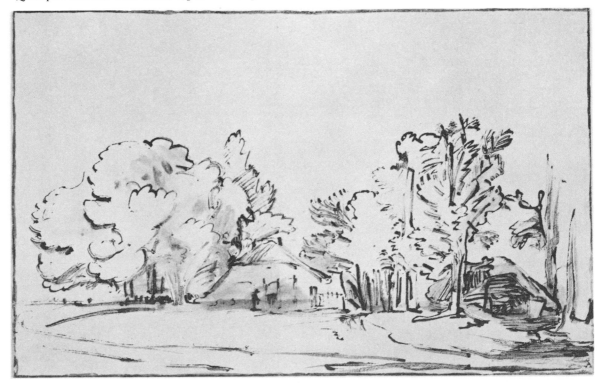

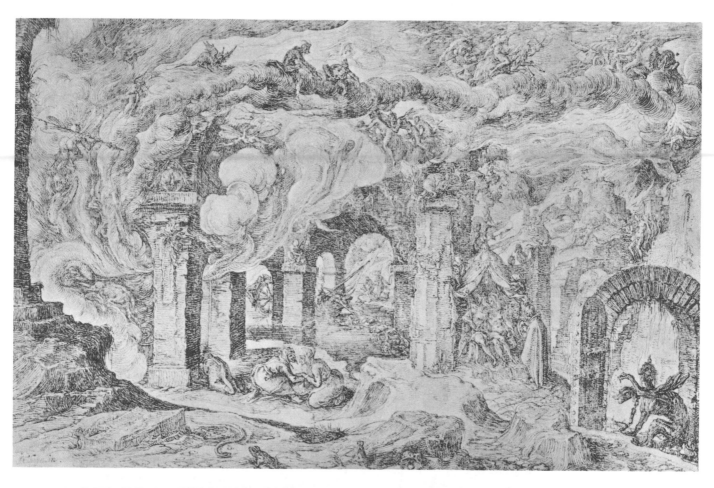

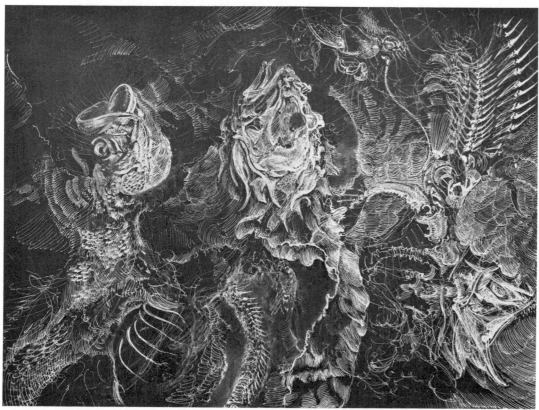

above: 40. Jacob de Gheyn
(c. 1530–82; Dutch).
Orpheus in the Underworld.
Pen and ink.
Landesmuseum,
Braunschweig.

left: 41. Hyman Bloom
(b. 1913; American).
Fish Skeletons. 1956.
White ink on maroon paper,
17 × 23″. Collection
Mr. and Mrs. Ralph Werman.

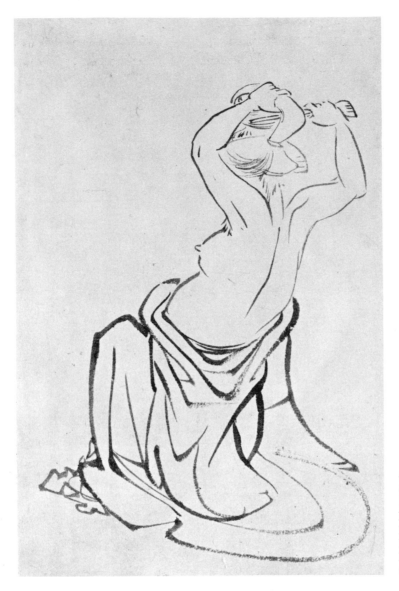

42. Katsushika Hokusai
(1760–1849; Japanese).
Woman Fixing Her Hair.
Early 19th century.
Brush and ink, $16\frac{1}{4} \times 11\frac{5}{8}''$.
Metropolitan Museum of Art,
New York (gift in memory of
Charles Stewart Smith, 1914).

paint and water, which makes it easy to blot out the pen strokes for correction. The residue of this blotting process produces ghostly white washes, which add to the mysterious quality of the work.

The examples of pen-and-ink techniques in this section are by no means a complete list of the possibilities in this medium. Rather, they are intended to show the potential variety of tools at the artist's disposal and the different effects that can be produced with these materials. There are no rules about what instrument is to be used, and there is no "best" instrument. As with linc—or any other component of drawing—the artist's aim determines the means.

Brush   Oriental artists write as well as draw with a brush, and this tool is as familiar to them as the pencil is to people in the West. The exquisite calligraphy that delights Western eyes is, for the Oriental, simply a natural use of the instrument. Even within

this context, however, there is mastery in a drawing by Hokusai
called *Woman Fixing Her Hair* (Fig. 42). Here bold brush
strokes of varying textures describe the folding drapery and activate
a spatial sweep around it.

   Matisse might have used a Japanese brush or a flexible
watercolor brush—either of which will produce a thick-to-thin
line—in *The Pineapple* (Fig. 43), a very large ink drawing. The
ink is unadulterated—that is, not diluted with water. With the

43. Henri Matisse (1869–1954; French).
The Pineapple. 1948.
Brush and ink, 41¼ × 29½".
Whereabouts unknown.

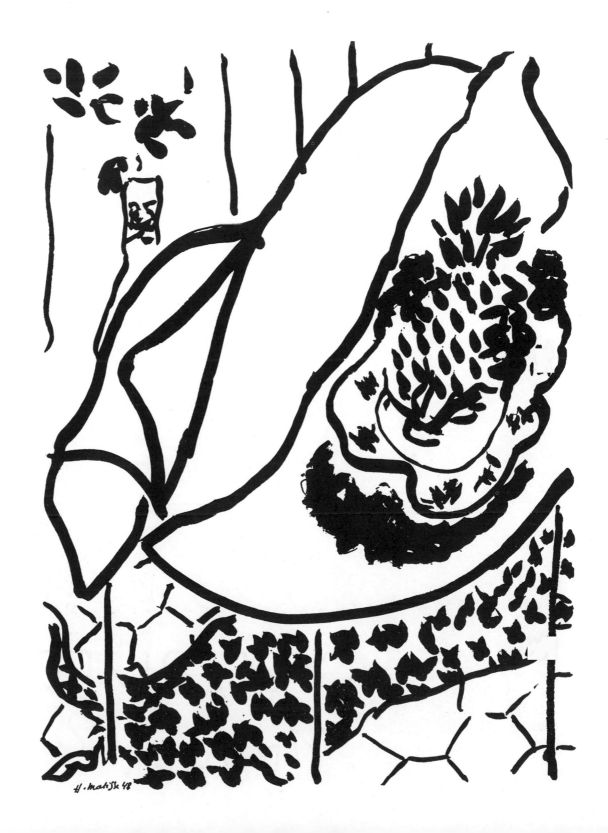

same kind of instrument, Paul Klee, in his *Self-Portrait* (Fig. 44), surprises us with the unique tilt of the head into the compressed space of the page. Klee, however, broadens the technique by slightly diluting his ink to give a broad wash effect and by applying some strokes (upper and lower left) with an almost dry brush.

In Willem Buytewech's brush drawing *Gentleman* (Fig. 45) the posture of the figure, with its turning head, torso, arms, and legs moving in opposing directions, is beautifully contained in the fluid wash. This effect can be accomplished with a fine-pointed watercolor brush and ink thinned with water.

44. Paul Klee
(1879–1940; Swiss-German).
Young Man at Rest (*Self-Portrait*).
Wash, 5½ × 7¾".
Private collection, Switzerland.

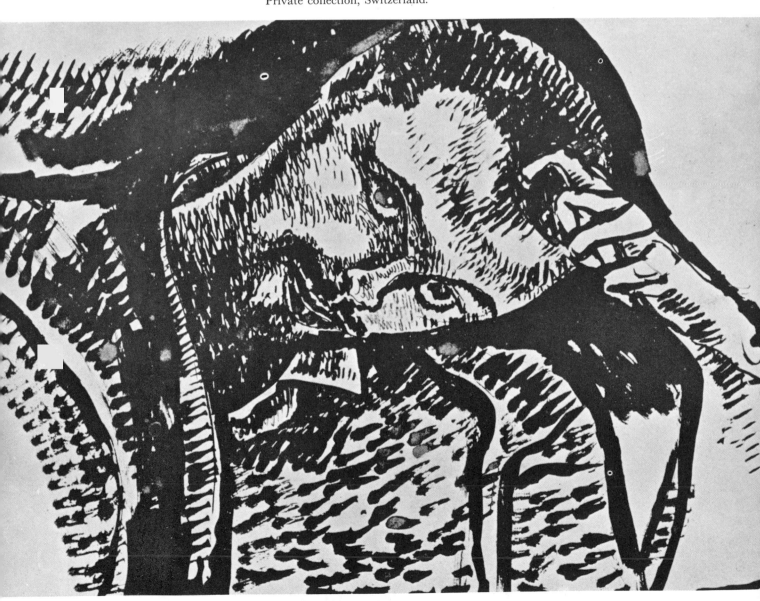

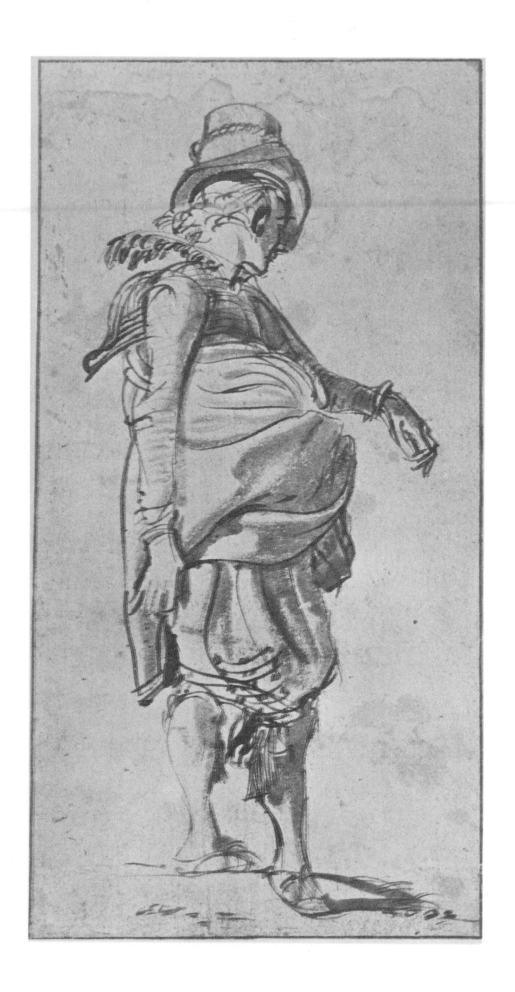

45. Willem Buytewech
(c. 1585–1626; Dutch).
Gentleman. Wash.
Kunsthalle, Bremen
(Destroyed in World War II).

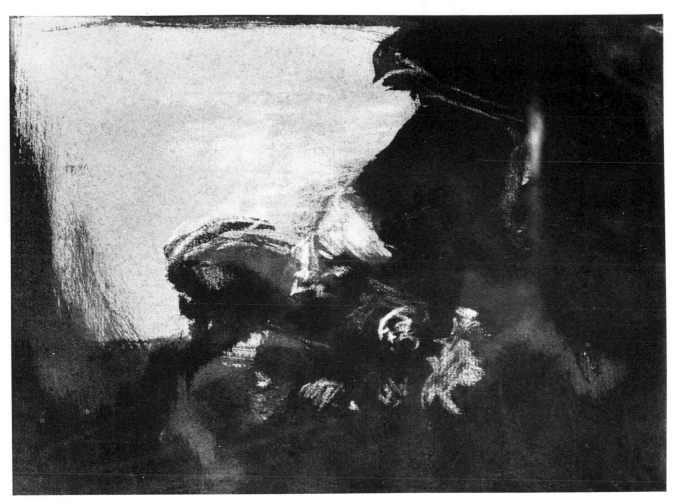

46. Francisco Goya (1746–1828; Spanish).
Nada, ello dirá, preparatory drawing for *The Disasters of War.*
Wash. Prado, Madrid.

Goya's preparatory drawing for one of his etchings in the *Disasters of War* series (Fig. 46) suspends a dramatically poised and frightening wave of darkness that is about to engulf the figure. This virtuoso performance seems to have been accomplished with one fluid stroke of the brush.

It should be evident from these examples that the brush is capable of producing unique and wide-ranging effects, and that the command of its use provides the artist with an extraordinarily expressive tool for the realization of a personal vision.

<u>Pastel and Watercolor</u>   We have defined drawing as a graphic linear medium and referred to it as "form-making in black and white." Painting, as a separate art, is concerned with color or, to stretch the definition, color-drawing. Within this terminology, it is difficult to classify pastel. As a form of chalk, pastels may be used to create individual strokes that are both graphic and linear. Yet they surely employ color at full intensity, without a wet medium to darken or change the colors.

The sensitive strokes, spots, and touches of Whistler's
Nocturne, The Riva, Venice (Pl. 4, p. 41) show a brilliant economy
of means in their suggestion of more colors, tones, and
actual description than are actually present. On the right
the brown paper ground, aided by a few deft black contours, acts
as both architecture and water. Sky and water are differentiated by the
varying lengths, groupings, and pressures of marks in the same color.

Both pastel and watercolor fall somewhere between drawing and
painting. John Marin's *Lower Manhattan* (Fig. 47), with its
textural contrasts and dynamic rhythms, performs as a drawing—when
it is reproduced in black and white. In color, however, the
spatial relationships are charged with the vibration and general
interaction of colors (Pl. 5, p. 42). The use of color, then,
changes the whole dimension of the expression and demands
separate sets of criteria.

47. John Marin (1870–1953; American).
Lower Manhattan. 1920. Watercolor, $21\frac{7}{8} \times 26\frac{3}{4}''$.
Museum of Modern Art, New York (Philip L. Goodwin Collection).

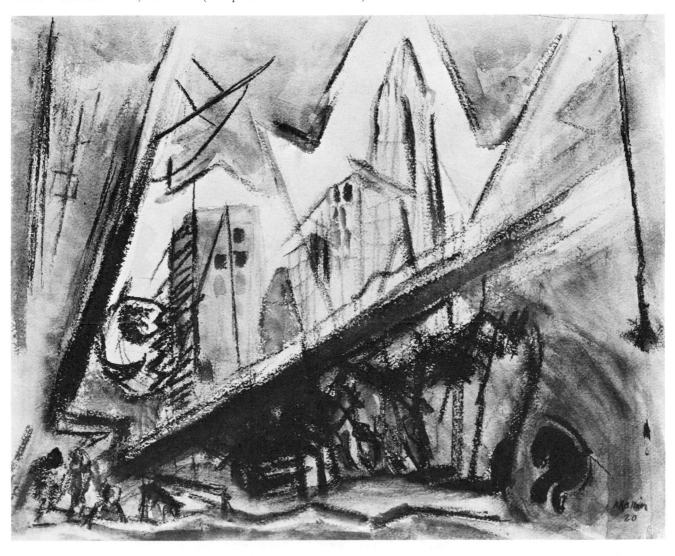

Though it may employ the broadest spectrum of colors, watercolor is linked to drawing in its general use of white as a ground for dark marks. *Tonal* watercolors—that is, those that stay in one color range—seem closer to drawing. But Goya's *Nada, ello dirá* (Fig. 46), which we labeled "wash drawing," could just as easily be called a watercolor. In the final analysis, establishing categories is the province of scientists and encyclopedists. Most artists do not concern themselves with this academic problem. In Chapter 13 we will return to this rich "border" area between drawing and painting.

Mixed Media

Mixed media is a loose term used to embrace the infinite combinations of materials and techniques that are possible in a work of art. Any of the tools and substances described above—plus others too numerous to list—might be combined to create a "mixed media" drawing.

Joan Miró's *Self-Portrait* (Pl. 6, p. 42), a graphic work done essentially in line, but with slight touches of tonal color, was produced by media mixed of pencil, crayon, and oil on canvas. Almost 5 feet high, Miró's drawing proves that there is really no size limitation for any medium. More important, it also reveals that the boundaries between drawing and painting are not absolute.

In our survey of media we have emphasized that the material, no matter how brilliantly employed, is merely a tool in the service of the artist's vision. If surface handling overpowers a work and "technique" is used for its own sake, the drawing is meaningless. It follows that if a particular drawing interests us primarily for this "how" of technique and only secondarily for its subject, it fails as a work of art. The beauty of drawing as an art is that all these qualities exist simultaneously and in balance.

4
Composition

Drawing shares with painting an interest in common visual phenomena
that we normally encounter in design courses. Perhaps the Italian
word *disegno,* which refers to both design and drawing, comes closer
to our meaning. These two acts—"to draw" and "to design"—are
indeed interrelated. We may call composition the act of
giving a unique sense of order, a life, to the forms we choose to
work with. This act of composing—or locating forms in concert
on a two-dimensional plane—does not mean merely enriching
the chosen forms by enveloping them in a nicely designed
arrangement. It is rather the transformation of a theme into a spatial
structure that finally merges with the content. A good example
of a compositional search is Delacroix' pen-and-wash study for
The Death of Sardanapalus (Fig. 48), in which the artist sets up a
flow of events in a special sequence on the page.

Artists should explore the perceptual phenomena that are
the engineering devices of the visual arts as carefully as they do the
various instruments and materials of their art. Both types of

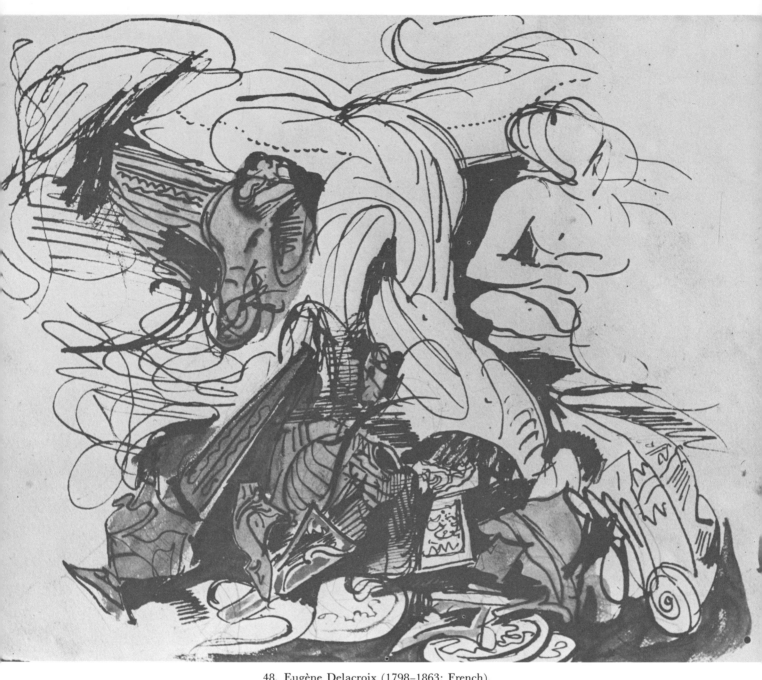

48. Eugène Delacroix (1798–1863; French).
Study for *The Death of Sardanapalus.*
Pen and ink with wash, 10 × 12⅝″.
Louvre, Paris.

experimentation give the young artist tools in developing a personal form vocabulary.

<u>Figure-Ground</u>   In Albrecht Dürer's *Adam and Eve* (Fig. 49) the white figures clearly exist in front of the dark background, which acts simply as a black curtain. The relationship of figure to ground is clear. However, in a series of compositions by Ralph

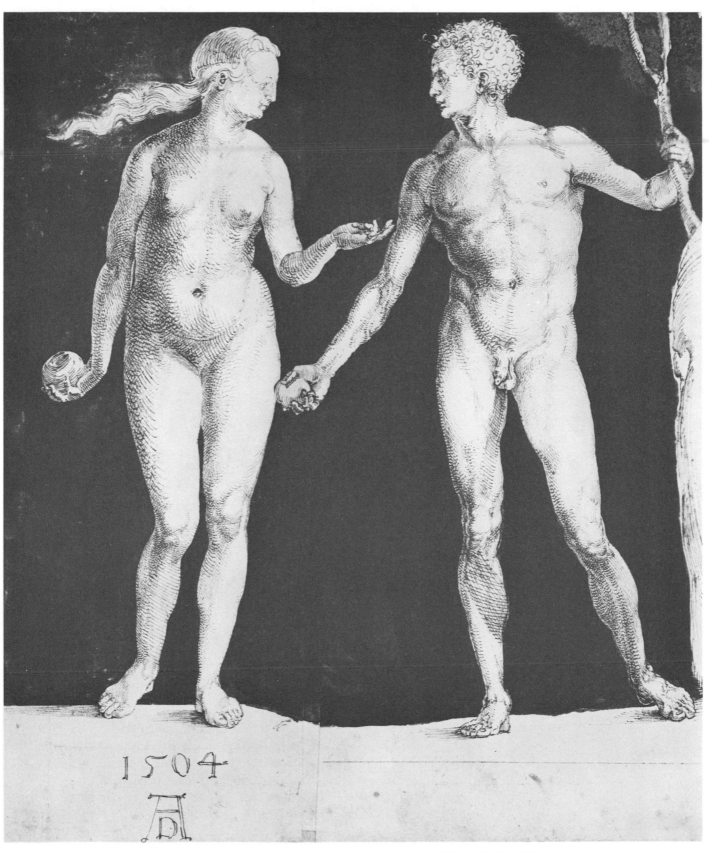

49. Albrecht Dürer (1471–1528; German). *Adam and Eve*. 1504.
Pen and brown ink with wash on white paper, $9\frac{5}{8} \times 7\frac{15}{16}''$.
Pierpont Morgan Library, New York.

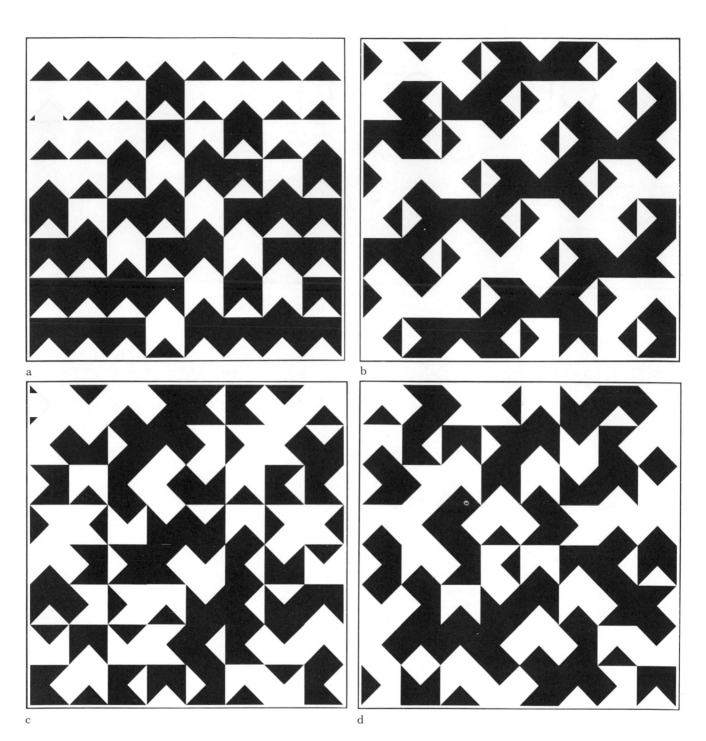

50. Ralph Coburn (b. 1923; American).
Variable I (four versions). 1968.
Plexiglas, each 16″ square.
Courtesy Alpha Gallery, Boston.

Coburn (Fig. 50) the distinction between what is figure (foreground) and what is ground (background) changes continually. In *Variable I(a)* the black triangles at the top read as black shapes in front of a white ground; but if we scan the whole composition, we notice that the white triangles along the bottom begin to appear as frontal shapes against a dark ground. Sections in between can be read either way, depending on how we focus. In *Variable I(b)* the play between what is figure and what is ground is more ambiguous. Both examples have a relatively simple order, *Variable I(a)* reading as distinct horizontal rows of

triangles and *Variable I(b)* reading as diagonal stripes. The
shift between figure and ground becomes more intense in
Variables I(c) and *I(d)* because the simple rhythmic order is
destroyed. In the latter two examples the eye moves more rapidly
from top to bottom over the broken pattern.

These four "variables" were not created with drawing materials,
but they fit the concept of drawing as form-making in black
and white. Each work is composed of 64 2-inch squares of
magnetized laminated plastic. The four compositions illustrated here
were all made from one design, which can produce more
than a million variations. What is important is the visual speed and
action of the figure-ground relationships—the possibility of more
than one reading from a single composition.

In Josef Albers' pen-and-ink *Structural Constellation* (Fig. 51)
the distinction between figure and ground, or foreground and
background, fluctuates constantly. Ruled, hard-edge lines make the
alternate "readings" possible, as the direction of the planes,
and thus our point of view, shifts back and forth. Pablo Picasso's

51. Josef Albers
(b. 1888; German-American).
Structural Constellation. 1954.
Pen and ink, 14½ × 11″.
Courtesy the artist.

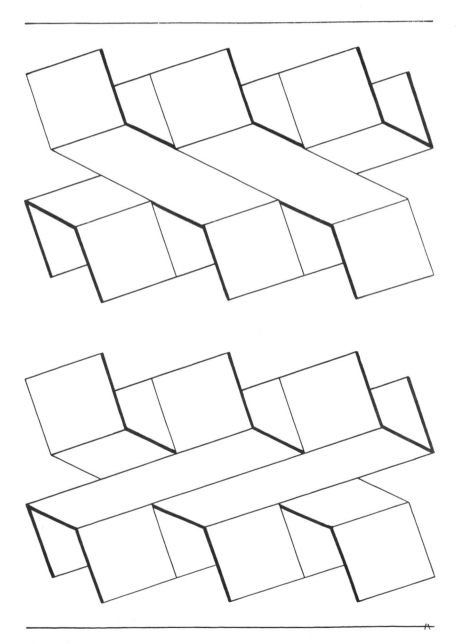

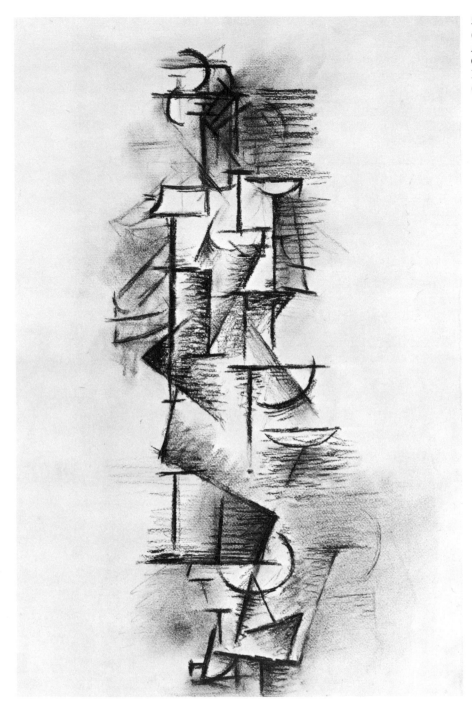

52. Pablo Picasso
(1881–1973; Spanish-French).
Female Nude. 1910.
Charcoal, 19$\frac{1}{16}$ × 12$\frac{5}{16}$''.
Metropolitan Museum of Art, New York
(Alfred Stieglitz Collection, 1949).

Female Nude (Fig. 52) also produces different readings, but not in purely graphic terms. The nude is buried in the overall structure of the composition, and we search, focusing and refocusing, to define the contours of the figure.

The idea of dual reading can be traced back easily to medieval illuminated manuscripts, border designs from earlier cultures, and some Renaissance compositions. It is clear that finding two or more visual solutions to one structure is an integral part of our way of perceiving pictorial space.

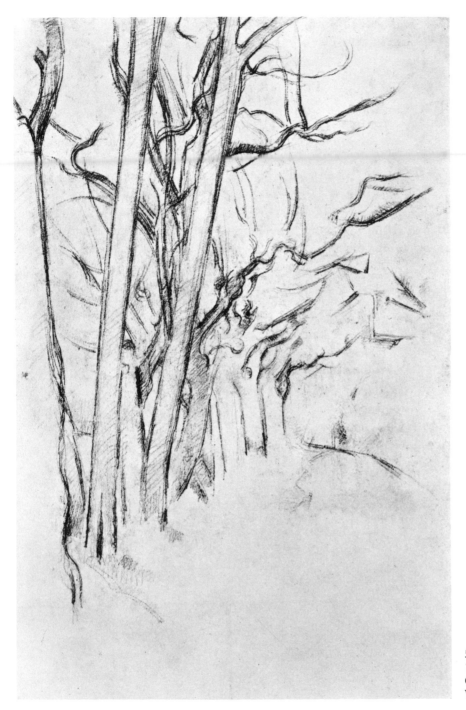

53. Paul Cézanne (1839–1906; French).
Tree and House. c. 1890.
Graphite pencil, 18⅜ × 12″.
Whereabouts unknown.

<u>Interspace</u>   The empty spaces between distinct forms are often
referred to as negative space, or interspace, as opposed to the
positive form-shape. Cézanne in his graphite pencil drawing,
Tree and House (Fig. 53), tries to shape and define the empty air
space between the trees. He considers this interspace to be
full and volumetric. The shapes of these spaces around the
forms are enclosed and released alternately by the sharp and soft
edges of the trees, so that space becomes an invisible but
seemingly flowing mass.

Van Gogh, in his letters, wrote about the resemblance between the movement of a field of grass and that of the ocean. In his *Landscape: The Harvest* (Fig. 54) the pen strokes change direction constantly—contracting and moving apart—as one follows them up the page. They become, in effect, a kind of visual inhaling and exhaling. It is clear that in this landscape the white ground (interspace) between strokes is an active participant in the vibration.

Rhythm   A sense of measured movement through time is a basic part of composition, especially in larger works. In a magnificently staged study for a *Crucifixion* (Fig. 55), Poussin produces a steady, even beat across the picture space. Each section and each actor within the larger movement is suspended, moving slowly at a regular pace through the whole space in perfect balanced harmony—the mechanism of a miraculous work.

Placement   We all seem to learn of the compositional tradition that warns against placing the main event in the center. But notice how Rembrandt moves us into the center of his invented space in Figure 56. He places us immediately behind the main figure with only a corner of a table, with its massive leg, to keep us at our distance. This table restrains the viewer; at the same time

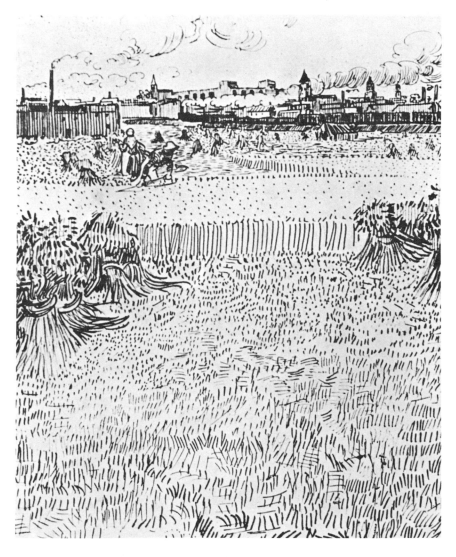

54. Vincent van Gogh (1853–90; Dutch-French). *Landscape: The Harvest.* 1888. Reed pen and ink, 12¼ × 9½″. Collection J. Hessel, Paris.

it connects the figure to the imagined floor plane by repeating the diagonal of the figure. These weights are balanced with a few quick, weightless lines to describe a head on the left and an interior room divider on the right. Notice, too, the implied connection between the two heads, which seem to be communicating.

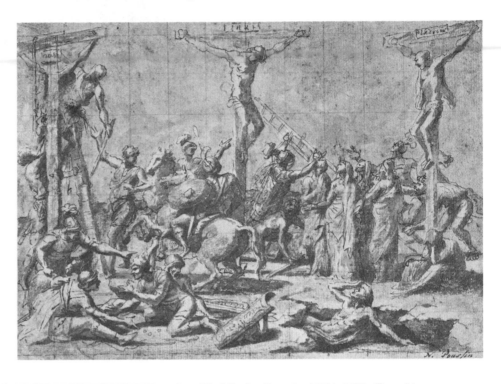

above: 55. Nicolas Poussin (1594–1665; French). *Crucifixion.* Pen and ink over chalk. Museum der bildenden Künste, Leipzig.

left: 56. Rembrandt (1606–69; Dutch). *A Woman in North Holland Dress.* c. 1642. Pen and brown wash, $8\frac{3}{4} \times 6\frac{1}{8}''$. Teylers Museum, Haarlem.

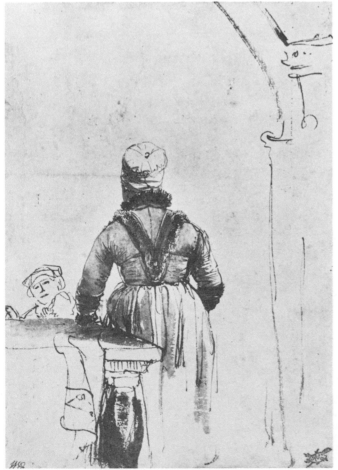

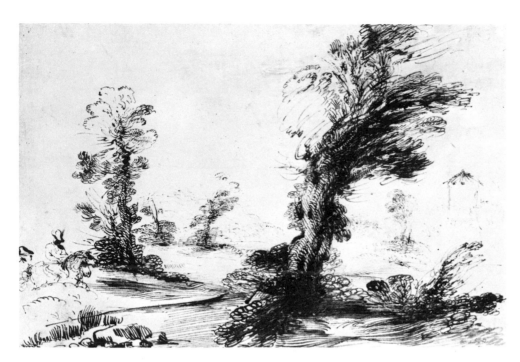

57. Guercino
(1591–1666; Italian).
Landscape.
Pen and ink, $8\frac{3}{4} \times 10\frac{1}{4}''$.
Teylers Museum, Haarlem.

Speed   In Figure 57, Guercino's rapid, circular strokes produce tree forms that seem to spin wildly in space. At the same time, the trees are placed like props equidistant from each other—a balancing action that almost cancels the intensely dynamic effect of the strokes.

58. Wassily Kandinsky
(1866–1944; Russian).
Untitled Drawing. 1932.
Pen and ink, $13\frac{3}{4} \times 9''$.
Collection Josef Albers,
New Haven, Conn.

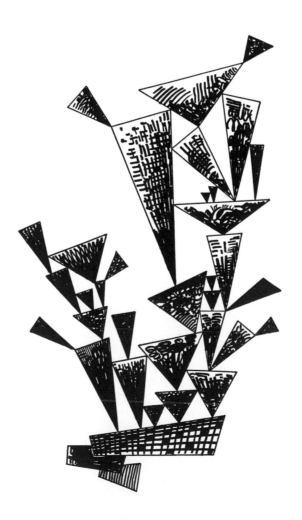

<u>Pressure</u>   The force or lack of force that one form exerts on another depends on the pressure at their meeting point and the angle of their meeting. In Wassily Kandinsky's *Untitled Drawing* (Fig. 58) the three bottom forms overlap one another to create a trio of pressure points at their intersection. These pressure points act in unison to form weights, which seem to hold up the "tree" of triangles. Because the triangles barely touch each other edge to edge, they form an almost weightless void compared to the weight at the base. Both kinds of pressure join in the total effect.

Two examples of another artist's work also demonstrate degrees of pressure. In Giovanni Battista Piranesi's *Construction* (Fig. 59) we sense the architectural members overlapping but not exerting much pressure on each other. However, in the sketch in Figure 60 we can feel the weight of the masses of these bisecting angles.

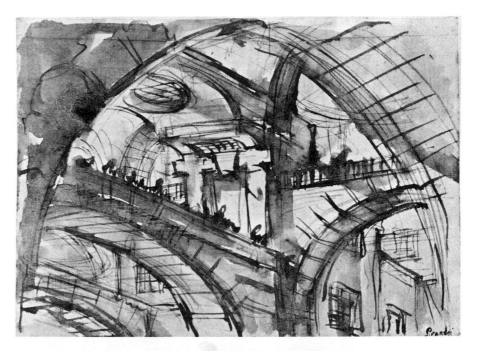

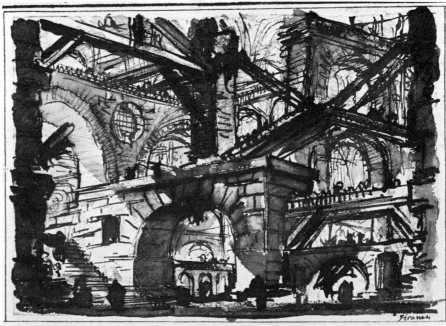

above: 59. Giovanni Battista Piranesi
(1720–78; Italian).
Sketch of a Construction.
Pen and wash over chalk.
Kunsthalle, Hamburg.

right: 60. Giovanni Battista Piranesi
(1720–78; Italian).
Sketch of a Construction.
Pen and wash over chalk.
Kunsthalle, Hamburg.

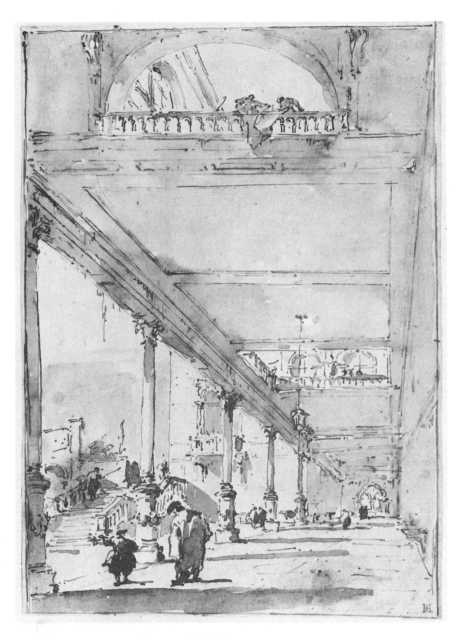

61. Francesco Guardi (1712–93; Italian).
Loggia of a Palace. Pen and bistre wash, $10^{13}/_{16} \times 7^{9}/_{16}''$.
Metropolitan Museum of Art, New York (Rogers Fund, 1937).

Bisecting forms appear also in John Marin's watercolor,
Lower Manhattan, (Pl. 5, p. 42), but they do not meet within the
compositional space. The point of their forceful impact,
which we follow by extension, is a loud visual shock off the left
corner of the page. This suggested crash, interrupted as it is,
is completed by the viewer, but at the artist's direction.
Marin experimented with such pressure-filled experiences many
times in his career.

<u>Perspective</u>   Instead of keeping us at a safe distance and guiding
us gently to the background, Francesco Guardi creates a magnetic

force strong enough to pull us into the space (Fig. 61). The logical system of perspective is here used to create an image— in this case, a strong physical sensation.

By contrast, in Bellini's *Flagellation* (Fig. 62) the system seems to overwhelm the drama of the subject. A stiff, self-consciously constructed perspective creates a firmly measured, architectonic space into which variously scaled figures and a prancing horse have been inserted. The occasional inconsistencies in Bellini's scaling of the figures can be compared to the perspectival distortion and spatial displacement intentionally and very knowingly employed to create a psychological mood in Giorgio de Chirico's *The Return of the Prodigal* (Fig. 63).

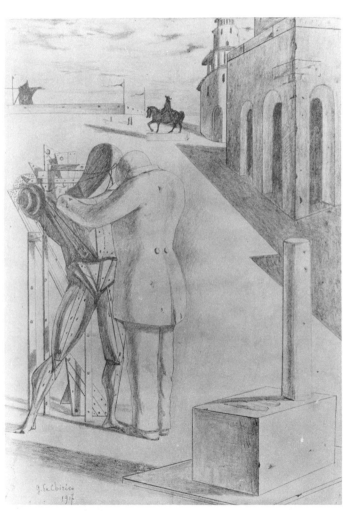

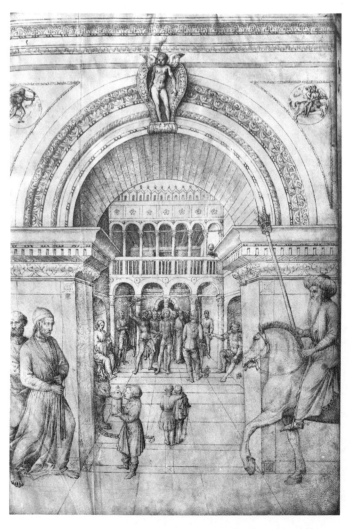

left: 62. Giovanni Bellini (c. 1430–1516; Italian). *The Flagellation.* Pen and ink. Louvre, Paris.

above: 63. Giorgio de Chirico (b. 1888; Italian). *The Return of the Prodigal.* 1917. Pencil, $11\frac{5}{16} \times 8''$. Private collection.

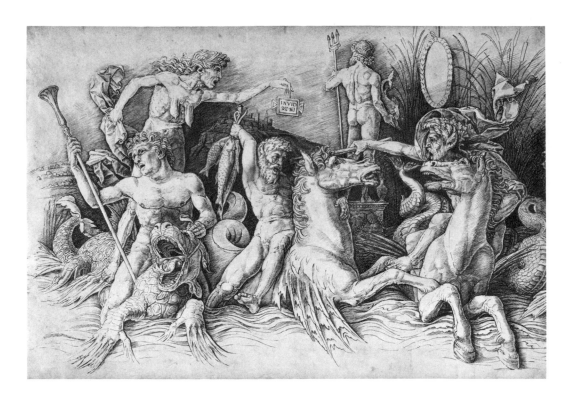

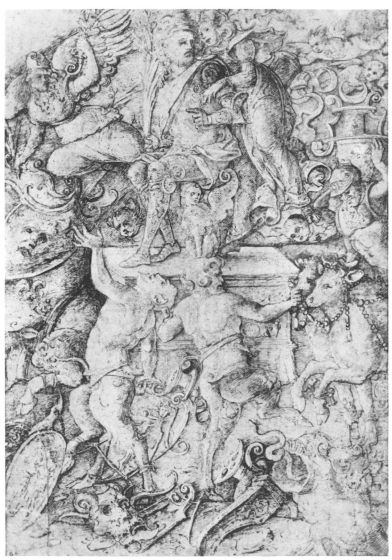

above: 64. Andrea Mantegna (1431–1506; Italian).
Battle of the Sea Gods. c. 1490.
Engraving, 11⅝ × 17¹/₁₆".
Museum of Fine Arts, Boston
(gift of Francis Bullard
in memory of Stephen Bullard).

left: 65. Bernardo Parentino (1438–1531; Italian).
Triumphal Procession. Pen, 15⅝ × 10½".
Teylers Museum, Haarlem.

66. Jan van Eyck (1390–1441; Flemish).
Maelbeke Madonna. Silverpoint, 11½ × 7".
Albertina, Vienna.

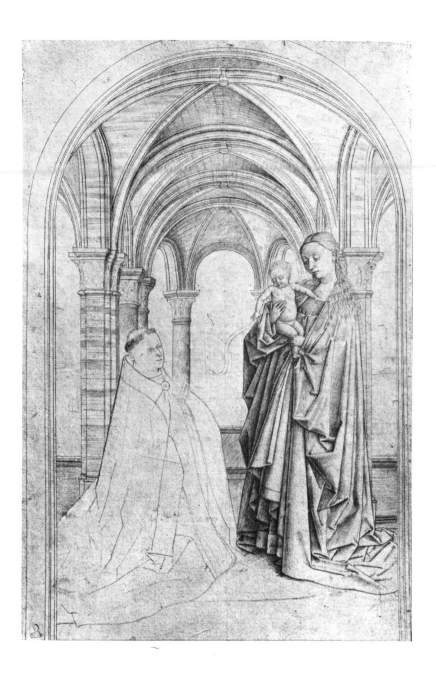

Overlapping planes recede to a shallow backgound in Andrea Mantegna's *Battle of the Sea Gods* (Fig. 64). The cramped space is equivalent to a sculptured relief, and the violent action of the figures and horses makes them seem to erupt from their crowded stage. Piling one form over another, Bernardo Parentino also creates a low-relief-like, vertical space in his fantasy, *Triumphal Procession* (Fig. 65).

The placement of figures in an architectural environment necessarily affects their volume as they relate to the setting. A moment's study of Jan van Eyck's *Maelbeke Madonna* (Fig. 66) reveals that the sense of volume in the figures comes almost entirely from the detailed spatial rendering of the architecture. Taken by themselves, the figures seem flat and two-dimensional, rather like paper cutouts set in front of a deep space.

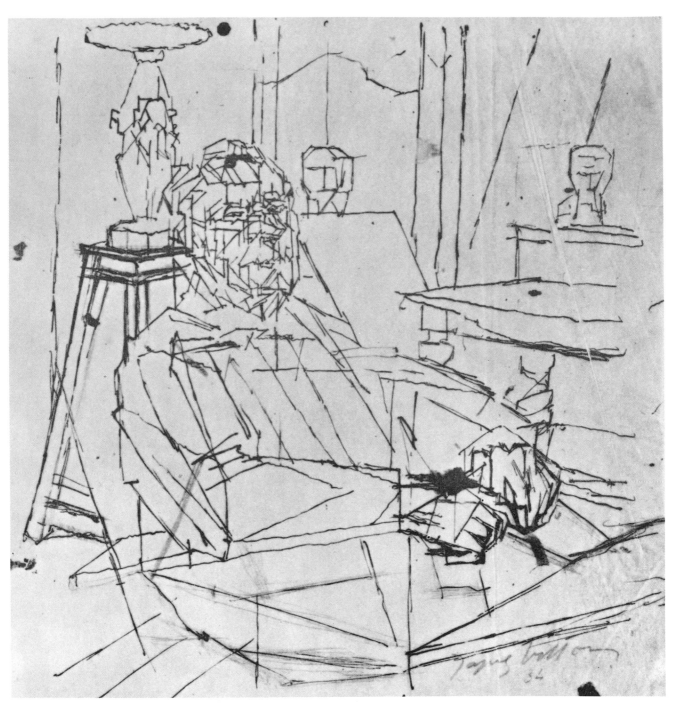

67. Jacques Villon (1875–1963; French).
Self-Portrait. 1934. Graphite pencil with pen and ink, $9\frac{11}{16} \times 8\frac{7}{8}''$.
Courtesy Galerie Louis Carré, Paris.

Two 20th-century drawings will demonstrate that pictorial
space always remains subject to individual invention, for the way
in which space is organized is itself expressive. Jacques Villon
in his *Self-Portrait* (Fig. 67) diagrams and dissects the
whole space of the drawing. Lines that establish planes locate the
figure and relate it to its surroundings. A strong oblique line just

below the hands sets up a system of planes that tilt back into
space, while the furniture behind the head counters this movement.

Like Mantegna, Fernand Léger in a study for *The Smoker*
(Fig. 68) establishes a narrow spatial field. There is very little space
from the circles that represent smoke to the head behind the
circles, to the strong vertical stripe behind the left shoulder, to the
horizontal stripes, to the final white wall plane. In this structure,
with its tension between circles, horizontals, and verticals, space
moves back in planes parallel to the picture plane. We can
compare this to the oblique cutting into space in Villon's drawing.

68. Fernand Léger (1881–1955; French).
Study for *The Smoker*. c. 1921. Graphite pencil, 12⅛ × 9⅜″.
Musée National Fernand Léger, Biot, France.

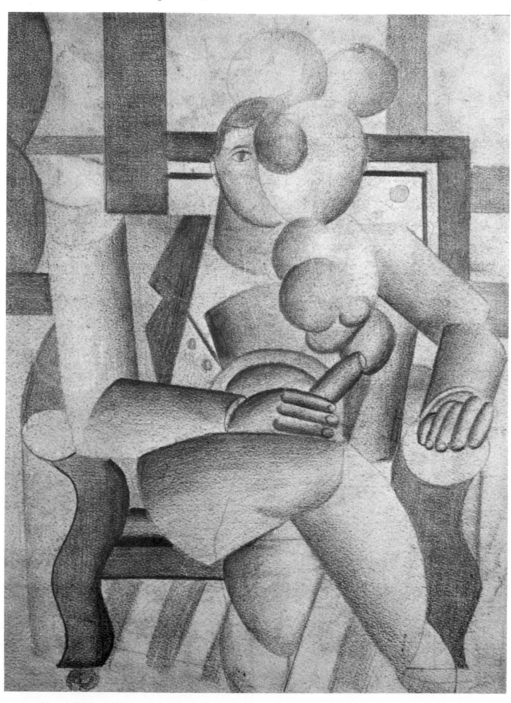

Scale   The scale of any object or structure is usually defined in terms of some other object or structure. In *Landscape with a Fort* (Fig. 69) Dürer gives the rock formations the scale of a mountain by juxtaposing them against smaller forms representing boats, houses, and trees. However, even without these details, the mass of rock dominates the page, and thereby assumes scale. We will explore this problem of scale in Chapter 6, when we attempt through drawing to transform rocks into mountains.

"Real" Space and Picture Space   The space at the bottom of Van Gogh's *Starry Night* (Fig. 70) is clear and logical: Trees overlap the view of the town, buildings exist in normal relationships to one another, and mountains recede into the distance. But as we look upward to his principal forms, the stars, the enormous scale of these celestial giants overpowers the scene below. The negation of "real" space is a by-product of Van Gogh's dramatic psychological vision.

In Nicolas Poussin's pen-and-wash *Death of Meleager* (Fig. 71) vibrations of light move through the tree forms and penetrate the clouds to form continuous vertical movement. This pattern, which produces a true visual drama, nevertheless decreases the "normal" planar relationships of foreground, middleground, and background. The visual reality in this drawing is a two-dimensional

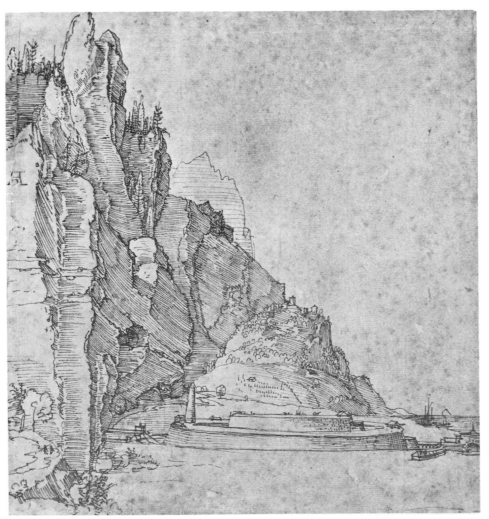

69. Albrecht Dürer
(1471–1528; German).
Landscape with a Fort Near the Sea.
1526. Pen and ink.
Biblioteca Ambrosiana, Milan.

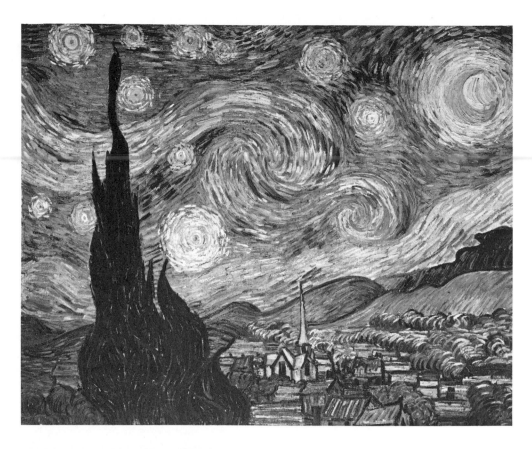

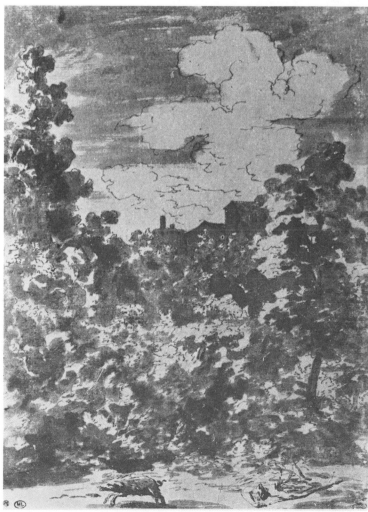

above: 70. Vincent van Gogh
(1853–90; Dutch-French).
Starry Night. 1889. Oil on canvas, 29 × 36¼″.
Museum of Modern Art, New York
(acquired through the Lillie P. Bliss Bequest).

left: 71. Nicolas Poussin (1594–1665; French).
The Death of Meleager.
Pen and ink with wash, 9⅞ × 7¼″.
Louvre, Paris.

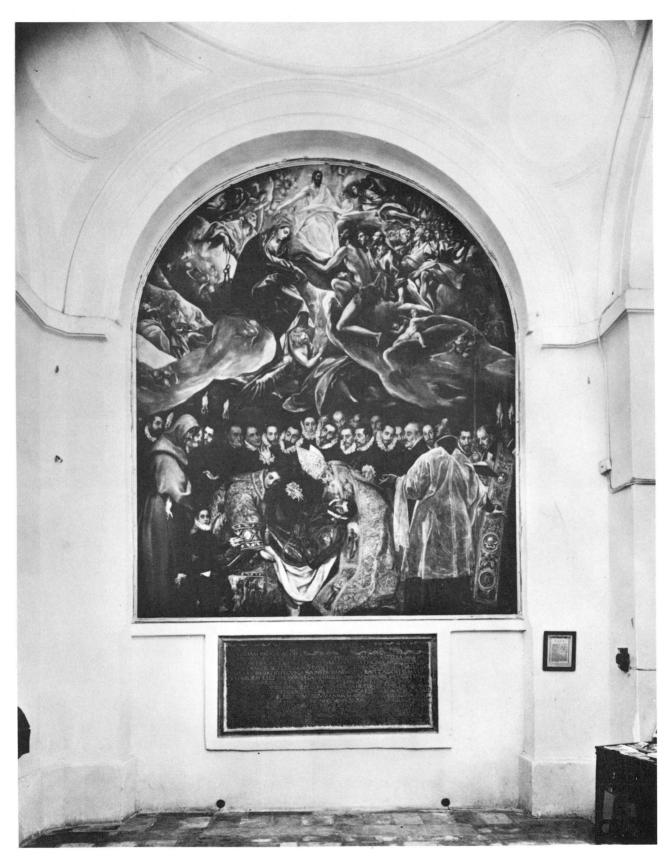

72. El Greco (1541–1614; Greek-Spanish).
The Burial of Count Orgaz. 1586.
Oil on canvas, 16′ × 11′10″. San Tomé, Toledo.

73. El Greco (1541–1614; Greek-Spanish).
The Holy Family. 1592.
Oil on canvas, 4′3⅞″ × 3′3½″.
Cleveland Museum of Art (gift of the
Friends of the Cleveland Museum of Art
in memory of J. H. Wade).

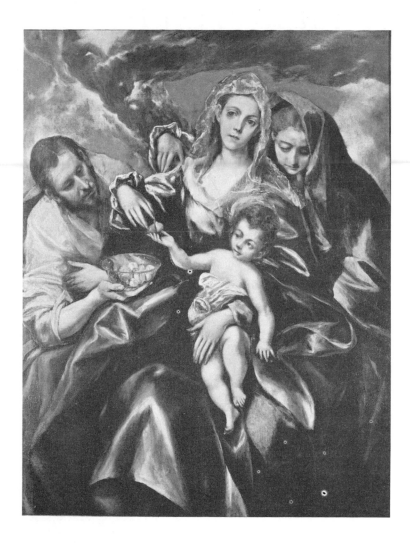

wall of light. Needless to say, our implication here is that
faithful imitation of nature, however much it may require genuine
skill, is not a criterion for measuring artistic ability.

<u>Distortions</u>   When one views El Greco's mural-size painting
The Burial of Count Orgaz (Fig. 72) installed in the place for which
it was designed, the effect is quite different from seeing it in
reproductions. The painting was conceived to be observed from a
particular viewing height, with the viewer's eye-level well down in
the bottom third of the picture. As one looks up into the
arched top section of the painting, the Christ figure, the angels, and
the flowing drapery all form a vivid spatial thrust. But in a
reproduction these forms seem distorted and awkward in relation to
the rest of the painting.

The same can be said of El Greco's *Holy Family* (Fig. 73).
Standing directly in front of the painting, one is forced to
use peripheral vision to contain the forms that bulge and
stretch out at either side. The viewer becomes physically involved
with the painting. Again, the reproduction, with its distorted
cheeks and heads, its pulling arms and draperies, can only hint
at the effect the artist intended.

The distortions in Cézanne's *Clockmaker* (Fig. 74) are oddly similar to El Greco's, and, in some ways, they serve the same purpose. As in the two El Greco paintings illustrated, the proportions of the figure change depending on the viewer's position in relation to the canvas. However, in addition to this, Cézanne's drawing gives the effect of many different viewpoints from the *same* eye level. The pulling out of the clockmaker's right shoulder, the sloping away of the far side of the figure, and the stretching, contradictory planes of the head all combine to create the impression that the figure is seen from several angles simultaneously, even when the viewer is standing directly in front of the painting.

Throughout this introduction we have extracted and analyzed specific qualities in the drawings and paintings that are illustrated in order to understand better the form-life that makes each a work of art. In the following chapters we shall examine some "problems" representative of age-old concerns of serious draftsman-artists and the responses of selected students to these problems. If, in these examples, we continually point to the underlying visual logic of the drawings, it is only to emphasize that the way in which an artist structures space is, in itself, an expressive art.

74. Paul Cézanne (1839–1906; French). *The Clockmaker.* 1895–1900. Oil on canvas, 36¼ × 28¾". Solomon R. Guggenheim Museum, New York.

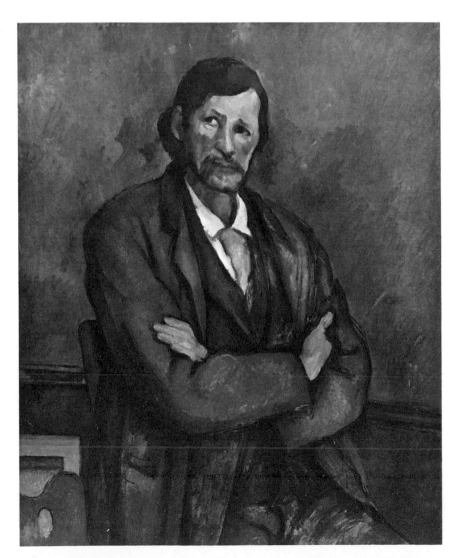

II Drawing: The Process of Visualization

5 Landscape

Two drawings of trees attributed to Leonardo da Vinci can be used to represent the major ideas to be explored in this chapter: the structure of a form itself and the same form as part of an environment. These viewpoints are not necessarily contradictory. They can be combined at will.

The pen-and-ink drawing of a tree reproduced in Figure 75 exaggerates the point of juncture where one branch grows out of another to suggest a joining and growth similar to that in bone and muscle. The gentle, gradual swelling and stretching as one form pulls out of another is constructed almost as if the tree were a human figure. No clear line marks exactly where the tree emerges from the ground. Instead, we feel the roots pulling loose from the earth and spiraling upward. This sense of pulsation is fostered by clusters of rounded pen strokes at the point where the branches sprout outward into three-dimensional space, suggesting an inverted cone. The same modeling

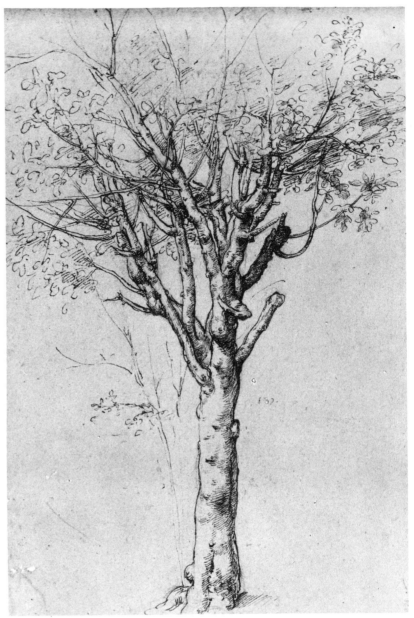

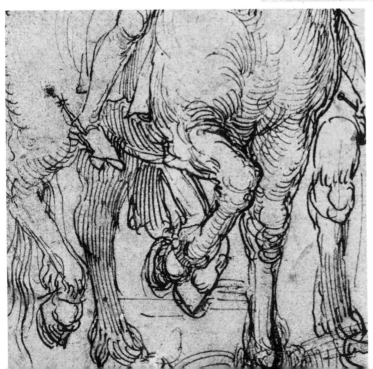

above: 75. Leonardo da Vinci (1452–1519; Italian)
or Cesare da Sesto (1480–1521; Italian).
Tree. Pen and ink over black chalk
on blue paper, 15 × 10⅛".
Royal Collection, Windsor (copyright reserved).

left: 76. Albrecht Dürer (1471–1528; German).
Two Young Riders, detail. c. 1493–94.
Pen and ink, 7 × 6½".
Staatliche Graphische Sammlung, Munich.

attitude exists in a detail of Dürer's drawing, *Two Young Riders* (Fig. 76), at the point where the front leg of the horse pulls out of the body. Both examples suggest that drawing is concerned with discovering, then understanding, and finally expressing an attitude toward form.

The second Leonardo drawing, *Copse of Birches* (Fig. 77), is not an idle, unfinished sketch. The apparent haze through which the trees are seen is intentional, as is the placement of the forms at the top of the composition. The heavy mass set high on the page produces a particular *spatial experience,* which is another role for drawing. When this work is reproduced in books, the empty space at the bottom is usually eliminated, thus robbing the drawing of its distinctive spatial effect.

77. Leonardo da Vinci (1452–1519; Italian). *Copse of Birches.* c. 1508. Red chalk, 7½ × 6″. Royal Collection, Windsor (copyright reserved).

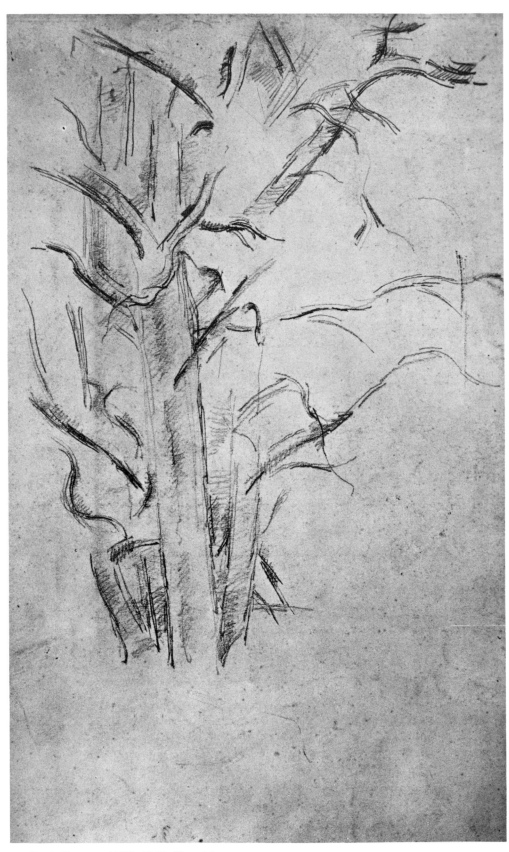

78. Paul Cézanne (1839–1906; French).
Sketch of a Tree. Graphite pencil.
Whereabouts unknown.

Volume is also defined in Cézanne's *Sketch of a Tree* (Fig. 78), but instead of stressing a sculptural swelling as Leonardo did, Cézanne breaks up the volume of the tree by controlling the contours of its form, opening and closing them at will. Because of this fragmentation, the air around and between the volumes seems as fully modeled as the tree; that is, the empty space becomes as substantial as the object.

In Leonardo's drawing (Fig. 77) the horizon is suggested by the lower edge of the dark mass, and the sky is revealed only between the top of the page and the upper branches of the trees. By contrast, in John Constable's *Study of Clouds* (Fig. 79) the horizon hugs the very bottom of the space. Gravity is established at the lower right, where the darkest, clearest, heaviest masses rest. The artist counters this downward pressure by anchoring a large and broken-edge cloud mass to the opposite corner. Between these two opposing masses the amorphous cloud forms, weightless by designed contrast, glide freely in the space of the page.

79. John Constable
(1776–1837; English).
Study of Clouds. 1830.
Graphite pencil and watercolor, 7½ × 9″.
Victoria & Albert Museum, London.

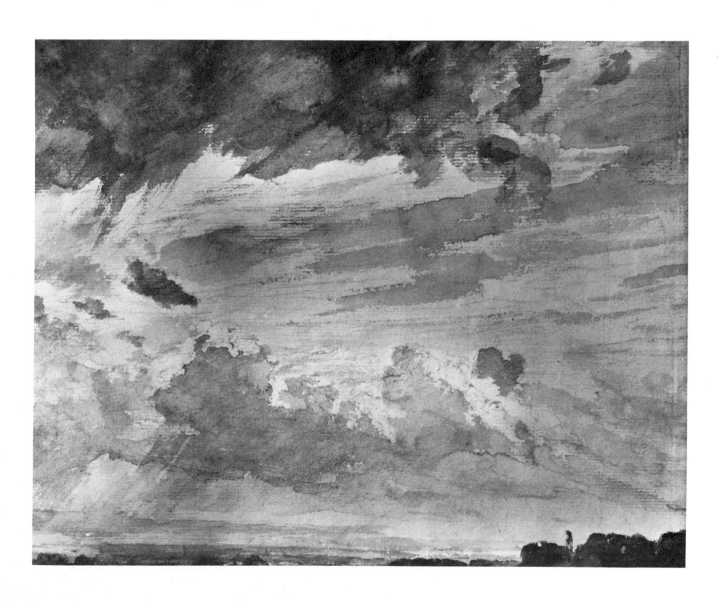

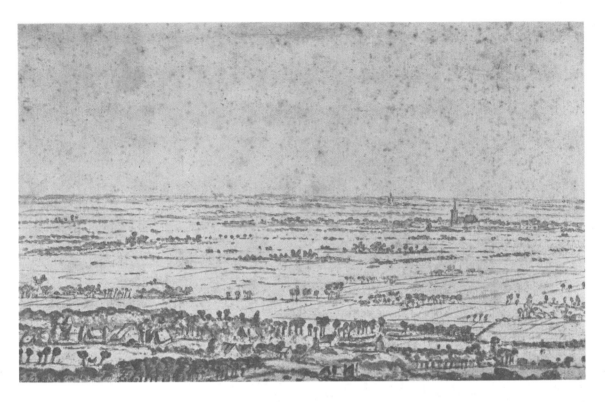

above: 80. Hercules Seghers
(c. 1589–c. 1638; Dutch).
Landscape with Churches.
Black pencil with brown wash.
Kunsthalle, Hamburg.

right: 81. El Greco
(1541–1614; Greek-Spanish).
View of Toledo. c. 1604–14.
Oil on canvas, 47¾ × 42¾″.
Metropolitan Museum of Art,
New York (bequest of
Mrs. H. O. Havemeyer, 1929;
the H. O. Havemeyer Collection).

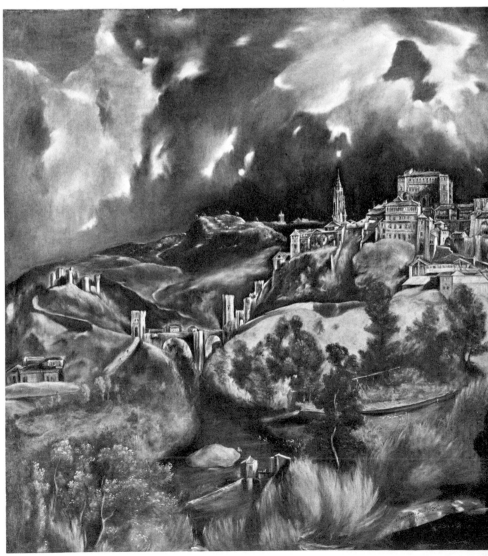

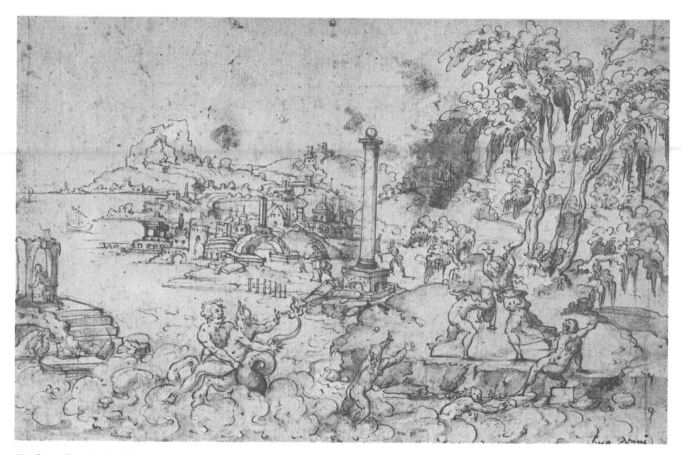

82. Jean Cousin the Younger
(c. 1522–c. 1594; French).
View of a City by the Sea, with Abduction of a Nymph.
Pen and brown ink. Louvre, Paris.

Yet a third variation in the placement of a horizon is seen in
Hercules Seghers' *Landscape with Churches* (Fig. 80). Here the
horizon line is a fraction above the center, and the trees,
constructed in irregular layers, recede gradually to this boundary.
By controlling the amount of sky that is visible, the artist
constructs an open, pressureless space. But, as in the Constable
drawing, the heavier weight at the bottom establishes gravity.

The location of the horizon in these three examples is not an
accident. In each case the artist has made a calculated decision in
order to provide the viewer with a particular experience.

In El Greco's *View of Toledo* (Fig. 81), the rhythmical shapes
that intertwine throughout the canvas eliminate the horizon
as a prime focal point. Instead, planes move *through* the
horizon to the light and dark masses in the sky. The dramatic clouds
are engineered to give the illusion of moving over one's head,
thus engulfing the spectator in the picture space.

Jean Cousin's *View of a City by the Sea* (Fig. 82)
clearly presents three planes in space: foreground, middleground,
and background. The artist chooses and constructs his space,
moving it logically, step by step, to the horizon. Another

approach is used by Raoul Dufy in *Wheat* (Fig. 83). Dufy places large, casually spaced pen strokes in the foreground and lets the white of the page establish a frontal plane. He then gradually reduces the size of the strokes to lead the eye backward to the dominant mass of the trees, which vibrates with textural change. The sky behind serves as a backdrop, yet the whole space is quite shallow.

Receding space can also be presented by dark frontal masses, as in Seurat's conté drawing, *Place de la Concorde, Winter* (Fig. 84). The one dominant vertical is echoed in a casual rhythm throughout the work and is set in tension against the horizon line and other horizontals, thus giving order to the composition. This central vertical, then, is the focus that tightens and particularizes space.

In a pen-and-ink landscape by Claude Lorrain (Fig. 85), trees and foliage press and stretch against the sides of the page to draw us into the large open ground before us. As the artist opens this space, he takes us on a rolling ride through the hillside—a beautiful, exhausting trip.

In *Low Tide, Beachmont* by Maurice Prendergast (Pl. 7, p. 91), the rocks are modeled sculpturally, yet the figures are fairly flat. This mixture of flat and volumetric forms is held together by the use of the same color for dresses and water, and by the allover rhythmic distribution of rocks, people, boats, and water.

83. Raoul Dufy (1877–1953; French). *Wheat*. Pen and ink. Whereabouts unknown.

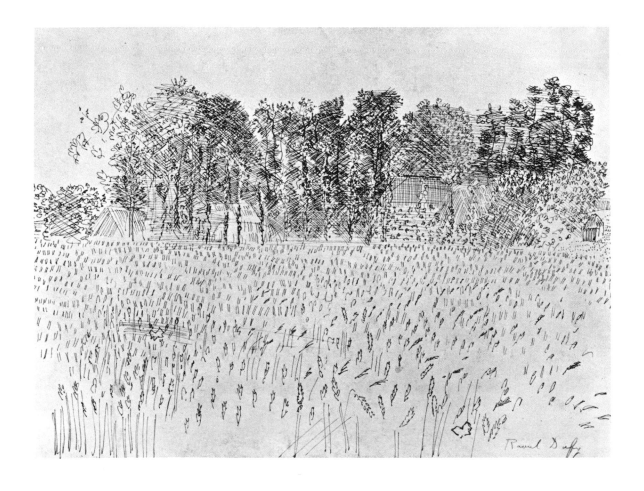

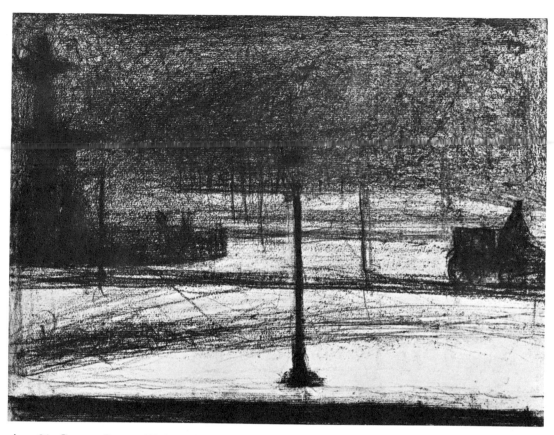

above: 84. Georges Seurat (1859–91; French).
Place de la Concorde, Winter. 1882–83. Conté crayon, 9⅛ × 12⅛″.
Solomon R. Guggenheim Museum, New York.

below: 85. Claude Lorrain (1600–82; French).
A Clearing in a Wood. 1640–45.
Pen and pale brown wash, 7¾ × 11⅝″.
Teylers Museum, Haarlem.

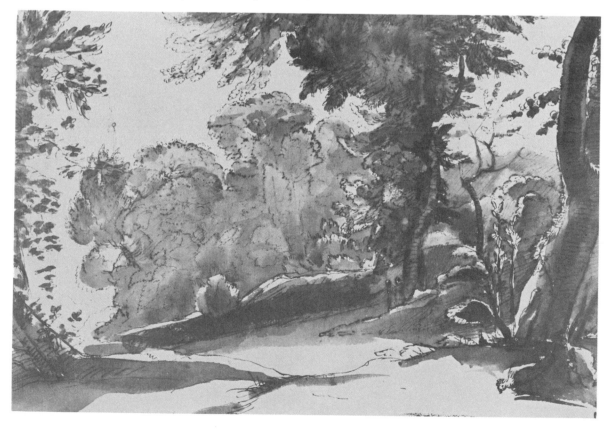

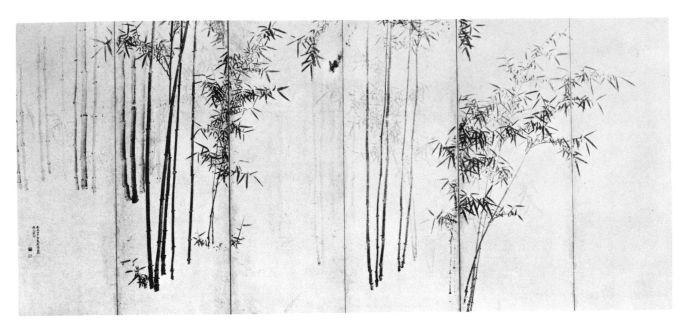

86. Maruyama Okyo (1733–95; Japanese).
Bamboo. Six-panel screen, brush and ink.
Kyoto National Museum.

All elements are locked in a frontal position, and the forms
move logically into space in clear stages.

As its title implies, the main event in Edward Hopper's
Captain Strout's House (Pl. 8, p. 92) is the house, but it is the
staging, the visual manipulation of the whole page, that
gives form-life to what could have been merely picturesque
description. The tipping fence plays a game of angles with the
pitched roofs and strong shadows at both ends of the picture space.
These roof forms frame and hold the composition. In addition,
the large, strongly modeled cylinder of the lighthouse creates
another pressure that helps define the spatial position of the house.
Finally, we get to the house itself and its more subtle play of
shadows and expressive window shapes.

The space in *Bamboo* (Fig. 86), a Japanese folding screen
in six panels by Maruyama Okyo, is carried smoothly from
one panel to another by the white interspaces between the vertical
tree forms. These intervals lead the viewer's eye across the
surface of the screen in a directed time sequence from left to right.
Short, casually spaced, parallel brush strokes and their
interspaces (panel one) become long, assertive strokes and are
used to introduce scattered leaf forms in the second panel.
In panel three the leaf strokes hover near the top of the composition
only, but they assert themselves on the white space and the
ghostlike trunk forms below them. The long, slender verticals of the
trees are echoed again in panel four, this time more delicately,
and a few leaf forms are repeated at top and right. In panel five the
dancing leaf strokes define a diagonal upward thrust, and the
composition is brought to a close in a final spray of feathery strokes
in the last panel.

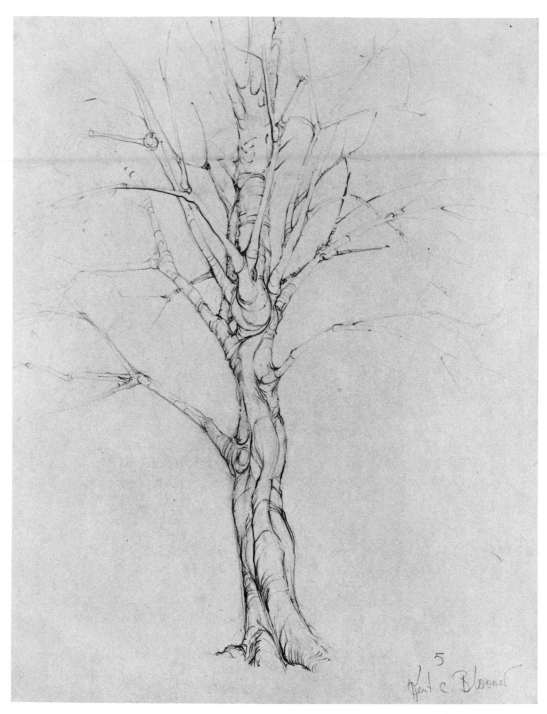

87. Kent Bloomer. *Sculptural Tree*. 1960. Graphite pencil.
Collection Yale University Art Gallery, New Haven, Conn.

Student Response

<u>The Individual Tree Form</u>   The drawing in Figure 87 presents a tree
stripped of its surface bark. The extremities pull and stretch
in a sculpturally conceived attitude toward form. Each section seems
cut, welded, and fitted into place. The student, who is a
sculptor, translates the object through his own form preferences.

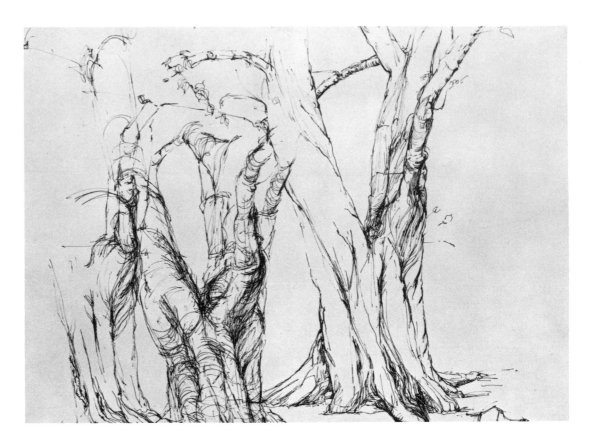

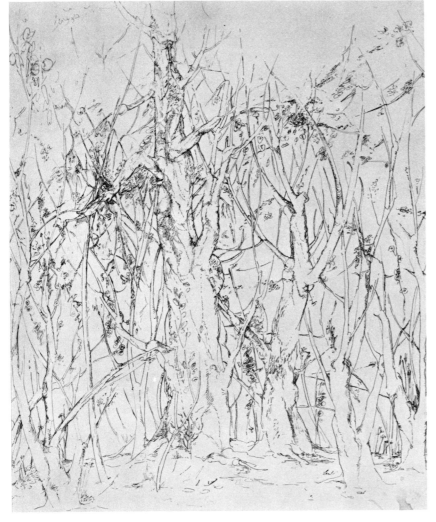

above: 88. Student drawing.
Trees Intertwined. Pen and ink.
Collection Yale University
Art Gallery, New Haven, Conn.

left: 89. Donald Lent.
Trees: Tension and Rhythm.
1960. Pen and ink.
Collection Yale University
Art Gallery, New Haven, Conn.

Pulling and stretching are also evident in the pen drawing in Figure 88. An accompanying theme is found in the insistent intertwined forms that house volumetric projections. Notice that the artist hides human figures in the trees.

Landscape Space   Two attitudes, rhythm and volume, exist in the complex study in Figure 89. Branch forms entwine to create tension and interlocking rhythms in a space that is relatively shallow. On closer examination we discover one major articulated volume, the large tree form, which is studied as an individual structure, yet exists as part of the allover composition. This sculpted volume merges into the total rhythm of the work. The artist directs his viewer to see first the rhythms and then the sculptural volumes that compose them.

The drawing in Figure 90 hurtles us directly into its space. The cut-off wall at the lower right, a sharp diagonal tipped into space, moves swiftly to the counter-tipped horizon. Its headlong rush is slowed only by dark, amorphous shadows. The high angle of vision, coupled with the tilted horizon and wall, throws us off balance, and to restore our equilibrium we must complete the motion in our minds. By projecting us directly into the composition, the artist makes us create a total environment beyond the picture.

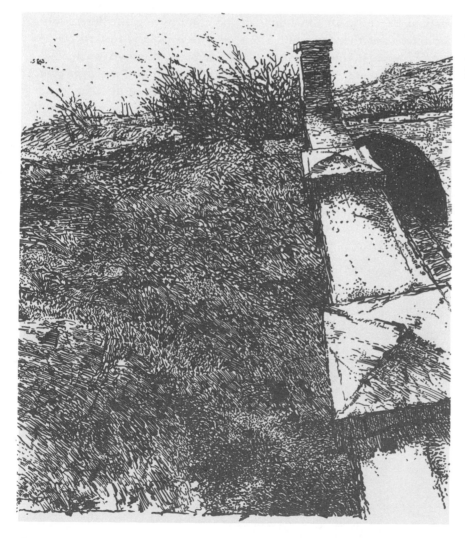

90. Robert Birmelin.
Landscape with Oblique Horizon. 1955.
Pen and ink.
Collection Yale University Art Gallery,
New Haven, Conn.

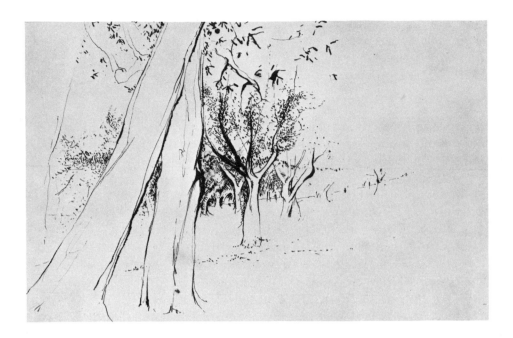

The leaning diagonal tree in Figure 91 also pushes us into the drawing, but, by comparison, it is only a tentative projection. The form cut off at the top inhibits our passage, and, more important, the projection is immediately counterweighted by a crowding vertical mass. To reinforce this counterweight another vertical tree form in the center of the composition further reduces the tension of the diagonal. The space itself presses toward the viewer, because the horizon is visible between the two vertical trees and thus seems closer than it should be. The total impression creates sufficient tension to fill the large white area at the right.

Unlike the last two examples, the wash drawing in Figure 92 makes us detached observers of a calm, panoramic scene. The brush strokes start almost halfway up the page and move back in a relatively tensionless retreat. The large white area at the bottom serves as a frame and also keeps the viewer at a safe distance from the first row of black spots, the symbols of vegetation.

above: 91. Joanna Beall.
Landscape with Diagonal Tree.
1956. Pen and ink.
Collection Yale University
Art Gallery, New Haven, Conn.

below: 92. John Frazer.
Panoramic Landscape. 1959. Wash.
Collection Yale University
Art Gallery, New Haven, Conn.

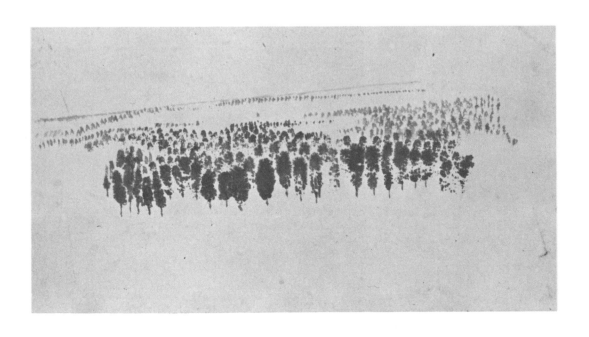

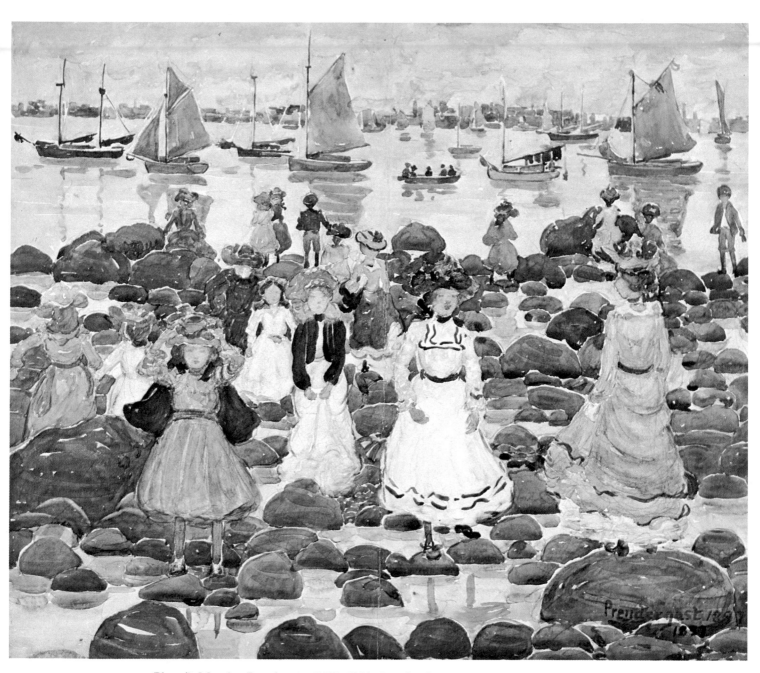

Plate 7. Maurice Prendergast (1859–1924; American).
Low Tide, Beachmont. 1897.
Pencil and watercolor, $19\frac{1}{2} \times 22\frac{1}{8}$″.
Worcester Art Museum, Worcester, Mass.

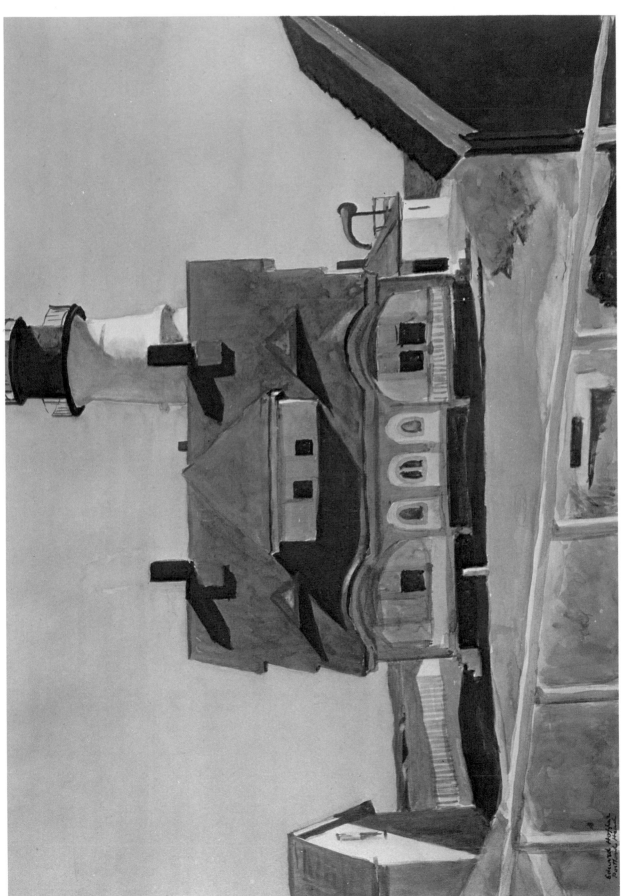

Plate 8. Edward Hopper (1882–1967; American). *Captain Strout's House, Portland Head.* 1927. Watercolor, 14 × 19½". Wadsworth Atheneum, Hartford, Conn.

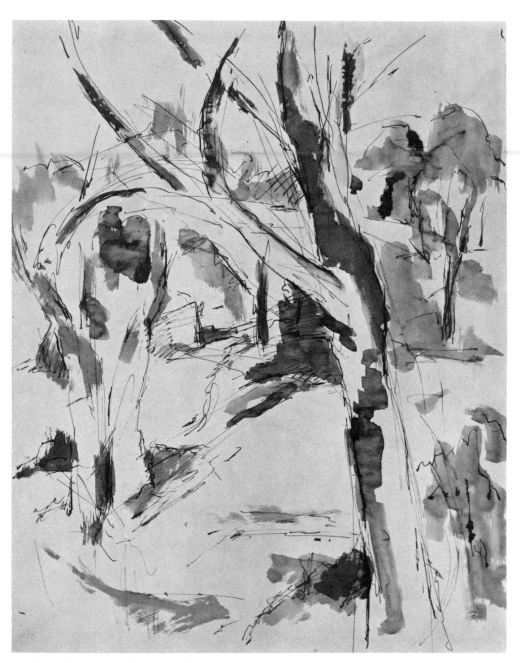

93. Barry Schactman. *Landscape Conceived Geometrically.*
1959. Pen and ink with wash.
Collection Yale University Art Gallery, New Haven, Conn.

The broken light in Figure 93 derives from shapes (grayed,
soft-edged washes) which, at first sight, do not organize themselves
spatially. One notices first the geometric shapes—the dark
triangles behind the tree at the extreme left and the same shape
repeated on the right. Punctuating the space, they set up
what we can term spatial stations, similar shapes answering one
another, and the eye tends to group these corresponding
shapes. Yet if we deliberately do not concentrate on the triangles,
the allover broken light appears as the main interest. Thus,
by focusing differently, the viewer may get two readings.

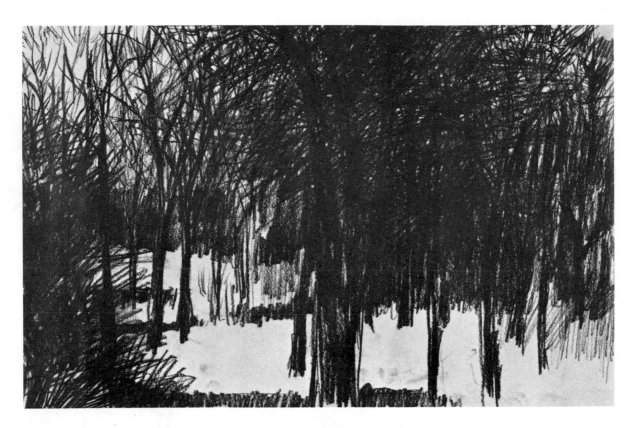

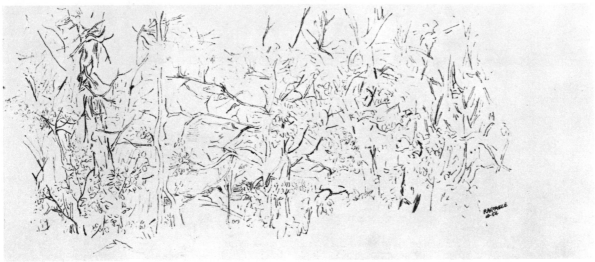

94. *top:* Paul Covington.
Textured Landscape.
1961. Charcoal.
Collection Yale University
Art Gallery, New Haven, Conn.

above: 95. Joseph Raffael.
Landscape with Dancing Rhythm.
1954. Pen and ink.
Collection Yale University
Art Gallery, New Haven, Conn.

The light in Figure 94 creates space much as in Seurat's drawing (Fig. 84); that is, the shapes in the foreground recede logically but with no tension-producing diagonals. The simple shapes of the opposing horizontal and vertical masses carry the weight of the composition. The lines that define these masses are always exposed, even in the darkest areas. They are neither blurred nor rubbed. These lined planes produce a texture that is a by-product of constructing the masses, not a decorative afterthought. And the vibrating lines, in turn, become a light-giving force.

In the pen-and-ink drawing in Figure 95 the white of the
paper is used to establish a long horizontal wall of light.
This is punctuated with a delicate, economical calligraphy that
does not violate the white but, rather, creates a dialogue with it.
These strokes define a slow, tensionless dancing rhythm.
The drawing was produced by a careful observation of linear
patterns directly in front of the motif and the selection of these
elements from an actual landscape. However, this does not
necessarily mean that the artist must study nature directly to produce
such a visual action. At the time this drawing was done,
the student's paintings were quite abstract, but the kinds of rhythms
and shapes he preferred in painting he purposely sought in
nature and presented in drawing.

Figure 96 presents a drawing from the end of a long series
concentrating on a group of trees. The earlier drawings,
not reproduced, were individual studies of one or two trees;
a second group dealt with the tonalities of the whole space.
Gradually, as the series developed, the artist drew upon
both attitudes simultaneously. Of course, either attitude is enough
for a successful motif, but in this example the artist sought to
explain each individual structure at the same time that he
controlled the total space and light.

96. Justus Pearson. *Group of Trees.*
1974. Conté crayon.
Collection Yale University
Art Gallery, New Haven, Conn.

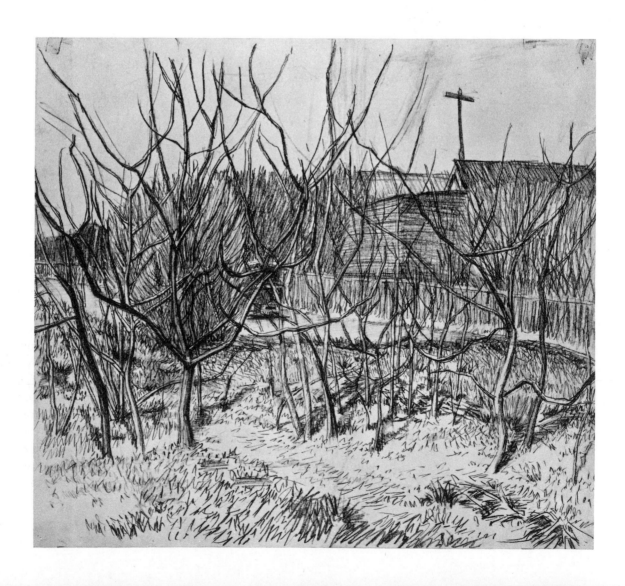

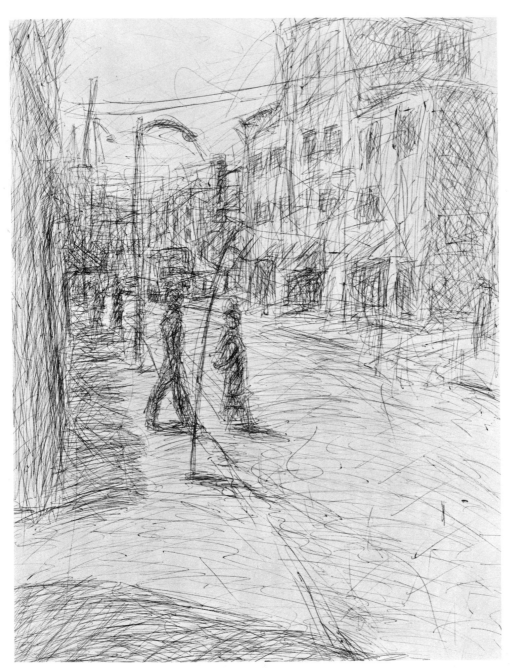

97. Sam W. Dunlop. *Urban Landscape.* 1976. Ball-point pen.
Collection Yale University Art Gallery, New Haven, Conn.

Landscape need not be concerned solely with unspoiled nature.
A whole new family of forms and space can be discovered
in urban themes. In Figure 97 the figures are poised as if they are
moving, yet they seem as firmly rooted as the buildings.
The open strokes (in ball-point pen) are constantly moving, weaving
a delicate light that engulfs and silences the steady parade
of verticals representing lampposts, signposts, figures, and
buildings. A contrasting example, the large wash drawing in Figure
98, is at first hard to read in reproduction. We are on the seventh

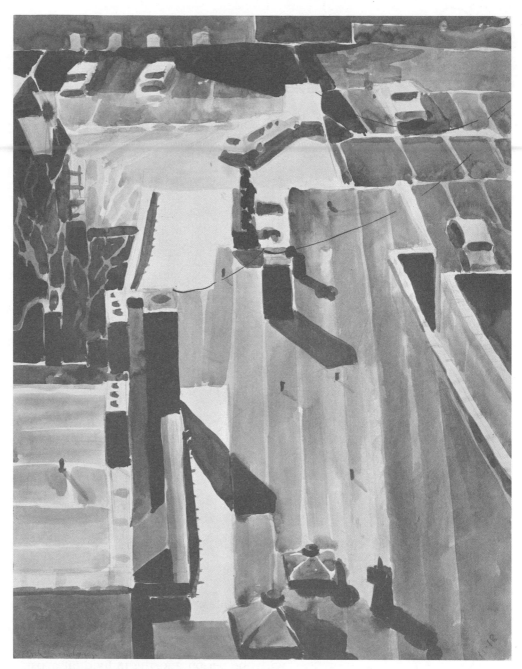

98. Eric Sandgren. *Aerial Cityscape*. 1974. Ink wash.
Collection Yale University Art Gallery, New Haven, Conn.

floor looking down at a roof below; gradually we perceive
automobiles at the top. The simple, abstracted masses were
achieved after several tries at boiling down the actual shapes
to their simplest geometric equivalents.

In summary, we must emphasize that each form should be studied
from two points of view: the object regarded as a particular
volumetric structure and the object used as a compositional tool
for a particular spatial expression.

6 Forms from Nature

For centuries artists have been bringing natural forms into the studio for study. As we might expect, the kind of study varies with the period and the individual artist. Renaissance artists studied twigs and rocks to re-create trees and mountains. Picasso and Braque used still life subjects as a basis for the shallow, flickering planes of their Cubist paintings, and artists ever since then have often started from natural forms even when the final work is entirely abstract.

The idle sketching of these natural forms for the sake of play is not wholly worthless. But for this studio problem the uniqueness of the form, its quality of being an *actor* was stressed. The students were asked to assume an attitude toward the forms and to study their character and their volumetric structure as a basis for future interpretation. This was to include an analysis of the artistic use they could make of the forms, as well as a testing of themselves by drawing the forms from memory.

The memory drawings are nearly always the best. Memory brings out the essential attitude; unnecessary detail (unnecessary for the particular attitude) is simply forgotten. More important, memory drawing helps one to realize that drawing is more what is known than what is seen.

Natural forms were introduced to reinforce the ideas expressed in Chapter 5—the creation of landscape space and the articulation of individual objects in the landscape. However, the individual forms have become more complicated, presenting more issues and discouraging the development of a "one style, one medium" approach.

Plants

The difference between Antonio Pisano Pisanello's pen drawing of lily bulbs and other plants (Fig. 99) and a rendering in an encyclopedia is that the latter is concerned with the characteristic contour-shape for the purpose of identification. Pisanello assumes another approach: the forms seem to be bending, moving, and blossoming sculpturally. The form at upper left, for example, flexes like metallic drapery. The flower form at the center of the page suggests the presence of a bud moving up through the central cylindrical volume, spreading the protecting leaves apart. In short, each form on the page has an exaggerated characteristic.

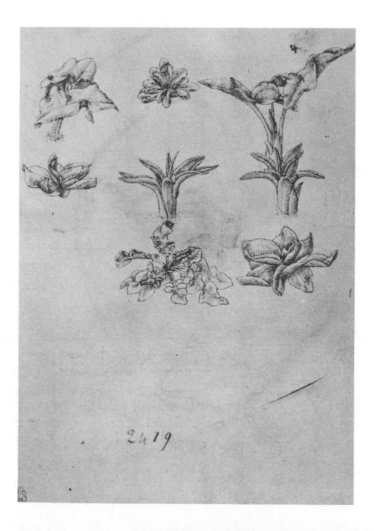

99. Antonio Pisano Pisanello
(1397–1455; Italian). *Studies of Flowers.*
Pen and ink. Louvre, Paris.

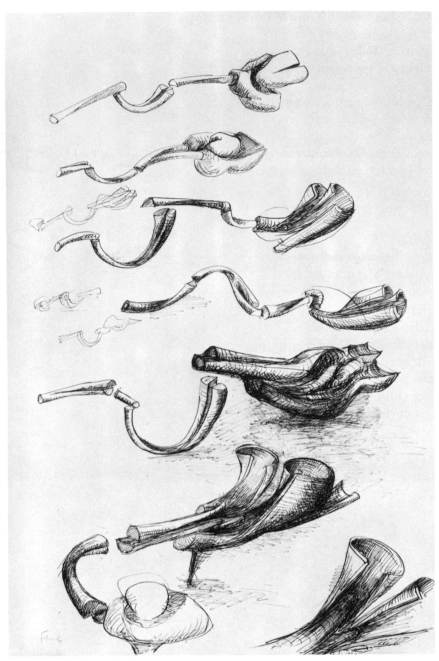

100. Lawrence Fane (b. 1933; American). *Page from a Sketchbook.* 1974. Pen and ink. Courtesy the artist.

In Leonardo's *Lily* (Pl. 9, p. 109), each section of the plant is clearly diagramed and articulated, and the viewer's focus is distributed fairly equally throughout the composition. This drawing probably was intended for translation into another medium, for the surface has been punctured with tiny needle holes along the edges of the form. This would allow the design to be transferred, for example, to a wood panel.

A page from a sculptor's notebook, in Figure 100, lets us read a plant form in terms of the artist's own vocabulary. We witness a form in nature going through an evolution of invention: the plant is dissected, cut into sheets, and bent to suit the materials he has in mind. Materials and invention are placed in the service of a particular image.

It is not only the projected volumetric character of each form that may be essential to the artist. Composing the page itself can be the crucial task, as in Ellsworth Kelly's *Rubber Plant* (Fig. 101), in which the shapes and interspaces coalesce to make us see this plant in a new way. Both attitudes may be stressed together or separately in varying degrees, since a drawing can serve equally as a rehearsal for translation into another medium, or as a complete work in itself (Pl. 2, p. 24).

In Charles Demuth's plant study (Pl. 10, p. 109) the strongest forms are the dark brown background shapes set into the page in a vague diamond arrangement. As we view this drawing, the brown shapes gradually melt, and the farthest edges of the diamond shape merge with the page, so that we begin to recognize the two pale green stems of the flowers moving in front of them. At this point we explore further to discover the delicacy of the flowers. Demuth has structured a particular experience, an initial scattering of attention, which gradually reveals the soft forms within the composition. At the end of this process we discover the brilliant technical handling of the medium.

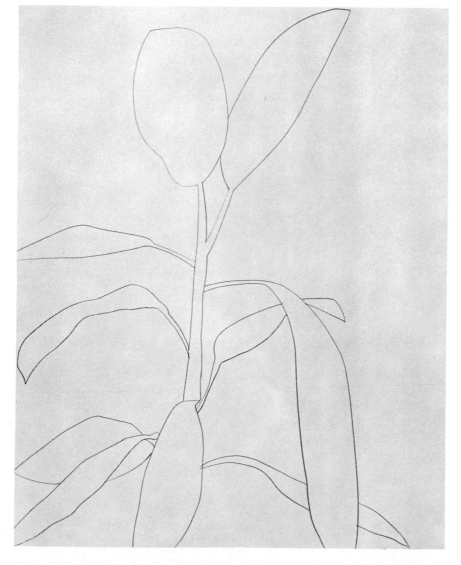

101. Ellsworth Kelly (b. 1923; American). *Rubber Plant*. 1958. Pencil, 29 × 23″. Collection Pierre de Croisset, New York.

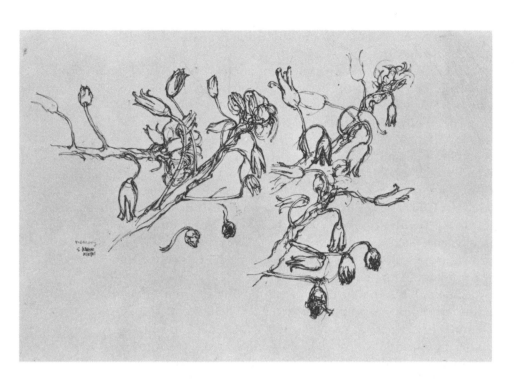

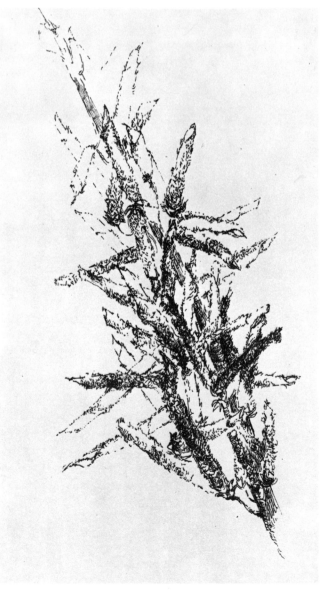

above: 102. Sandra Whipple.
Drooping Flower Forms. 1961.
Pen and ink.
Collection Yale University
Art Gallery, New Haven, Conn.

right: 103. Mark Strand.
Cylindrical Growth. 1958.
Pen and ink. Courtesy the artist.

104. Mark Strand. *Texture and Volume.*
1958. Pen and ink. Courtesy the artist.

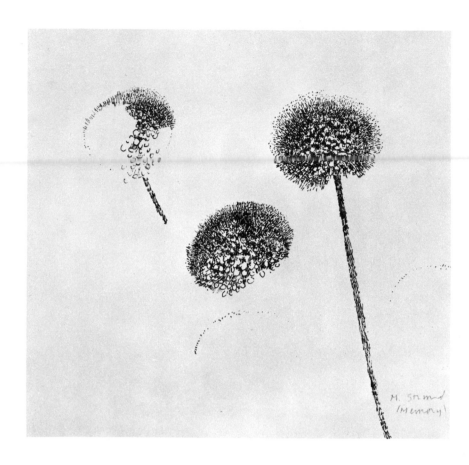

Student Response

Figure 102 is a memory drawing completed in less than two hours. The attitude is evident: The broken-line contours of the form are obviously exaggerated; they droop, float, hang, twist, turn, and seem to die in slow motion in the center of the page. The continuous white border holds them in the space and at the same time serves as a barrier between the viewer and the scene.

The contours in Figure 103 (also a memory drawing) are predominantly open. The modeling was achieved by thinking of the forms as growing from the inside. Although the whole form has been constructed within a gently pointed, diagonal cylinder, the broken light hides this construction and suggests, instead, lazily spiraling forms. This broken light and the dark patterns are organized to move around the volume. We should note, too, that the light source is invented, not imitated.

Figure 104 (a memory drawing) is not merely a texture study. The texture is used in the service of both light and volume. It is part of the modeling, not a decorative effect. The very tiny pen strokes at the outer edges of each ball form vibrate and act upon the space around them, suggesting energy moving outward. Note, too, the larger white units in the centers, which gradually get smaller. Here again, the leftover white paper acts as a unit within the modeling, not as mere passive space surrounding a form.

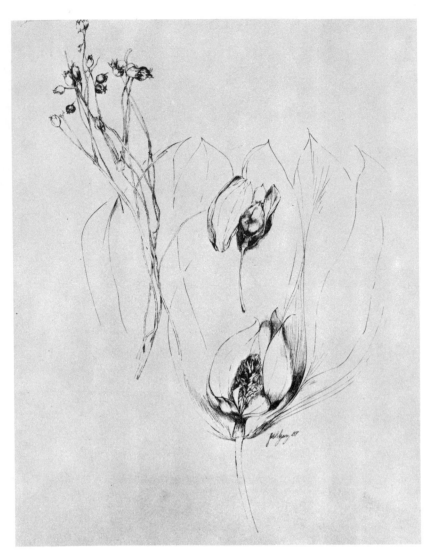

105. Joel Szasz.
Flowers: Space and Interspace. 1957.
Pen and ink.
Collection Yale University Art Gallery,
New Haven, Conn.

The same medium—pen and ink—was used in Figure 105 as in the previous two drawings, yet the instrumentation is quite different. The hand seems to have moved simultaneously through the modeled forms and the surrounding space. There is a reciprocal action: both the forms and the space around them seem to be moving together at the same tempo.

The intersections studied in the drawing in Figure 106 attempt to articulate the way in which one form grows out of another. The irregular sequence of these articulations in space, coupled with the peculiar posture of the lower form, gives life to the idea. But the instrumentation here also contributes to the effect: The swiftly drawn pen lines darken sharply at the intersections for further dramatization.

In the pen-and-ink drawing in Figure 107 the individual form gives way to a study of how a group of forms interact. The placement of the darkest mass establishes both gravity and the plane that is farthest back in space. (If we were to block out the dark, the page would seem to slide.) The pattern of light in the jars suggests solidity, and this is accomplished without enclosing the forms in firm contours. In order to achieve the diffuse light that pervades the drawing, it is essential that the lines be left open. If the jars had been firmly outlined, the vibrating, irregular forms of the plants would have taken on a different pattern of light and shadow.

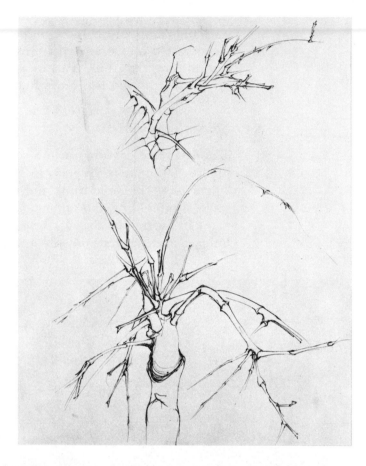

right: 106. Student drawing.
Patterns of Growth. Pen and ink.
Collection Yale University
Art Gallery, New Haven, Conn.

below: 107. Vaino Kola.
Interacting Flower Forms. 1962.
Pen and ink.
Collection Yale University
Art Gallery, New Haven, Conn.

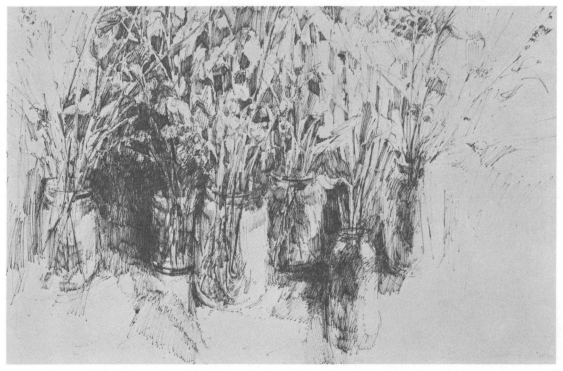

Roots

By examining root forms at close range we are permitted
many kinds of investigation. For some the roots suggest distorted
animal-like configurations; others are interested in the velocity
at which the forms unexpectedly travel; still others examine
the sculptured weights, thrusts, and counterthrusts into space. Yet
no matter which attitude or combination of attitudes is stressed,
one consideration should be borne in mind: All the extremities that
were twisted into strange patterns underground derive from a
central core, the trunk. This idea has a parallel in figure drawing,
in which arms and legs move from the cylinder of the body.

Student Response

The first three drawings in this section suggest animal imagery.
Figure 108 presents the roots in a dramatically staged composition.
The actors—the large trunk and root forms—gesticulate at center
stage. The lighting and ambiguous background add to this effect.

    In Figure 109 the root branches resemble claws, and the
bulging mass suggests organic matter that seems capable of

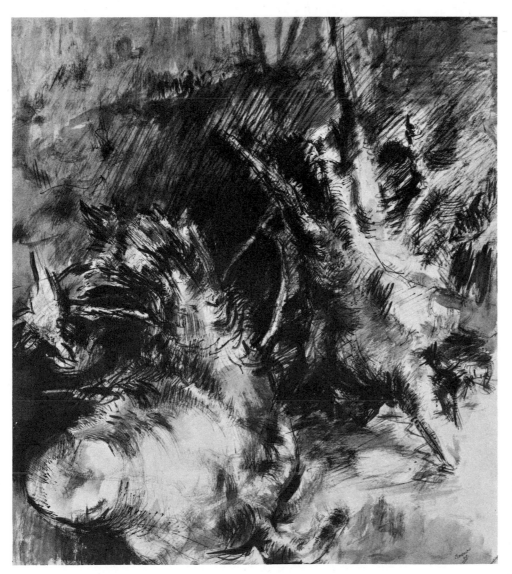

108. Michael Economos.
Gesticulating Roots. 1960.
Pen and ink with wash.
Collection Yale University
Art Gallery, New Haven, Conn.

109. Frederic Felton.
Writing Branches. 1959.
Pen and ink.
Collection Yale University
Art Gallery, New Haven, Conn.

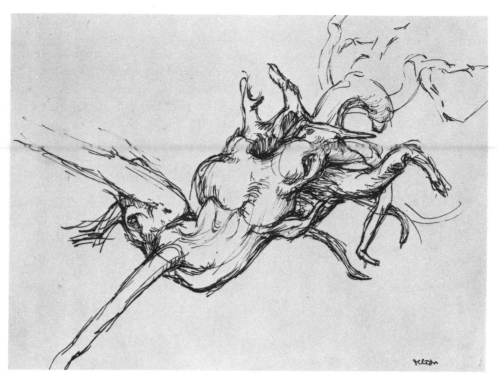

crawling. The swelling shape writhes and twists diagonally across the page.

Each form in the wash drawing in Figure 110 applies weight and pressure on its neighbor in a reciprocal action. The complicated structure is interpreted as a heavy sculpture.

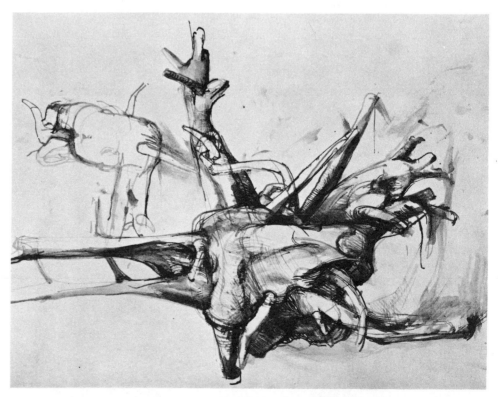

110. Michael Mazur.
Reciprocal Pressures.
1960. Wash.
Collection Yale University
Art Gallery, New Haven, Conn.

The brush drawing in Figure 111 focuses on speed. Specific
details are articulated by the fast line that contains the
modeled sections within its flow. Long, looping brush strokes play
upon the carefully chosen details. The most detailed areas are
the intersections where forms meet in tension.

The pen-and-ink drawing in Figure 112 uses techniques
similar to those in Pisanello's work (Fig. 99) to express the actions
of roots by accenting their postures. It is a study of poses—the
dancing movement of a whole form—and the artist repeats
the action across the page to underscore the theme.

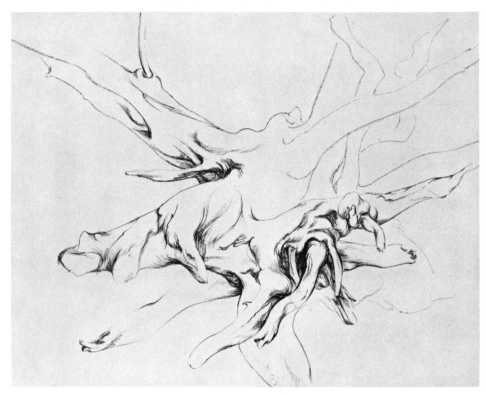

111. John Cohen.
Roots in Tension. 1954.
Brush and ink.
Collection Yale University
Art Gallery, New Haven, Conn.

112. Louis Klein.
Postures of Roots. 1959.
Pen and ink.
Collection Yale University
Art Gallery, New Haven, Conn.

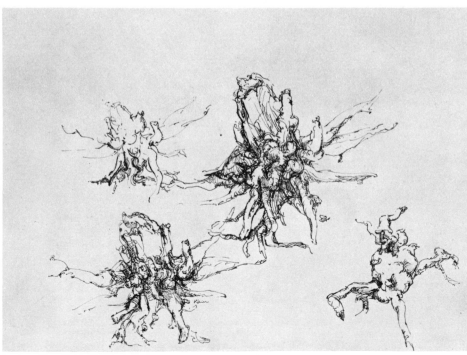

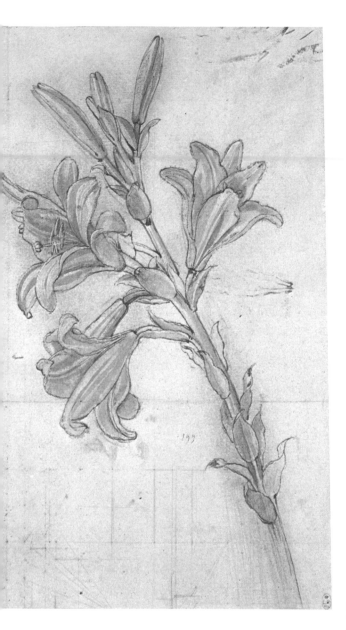

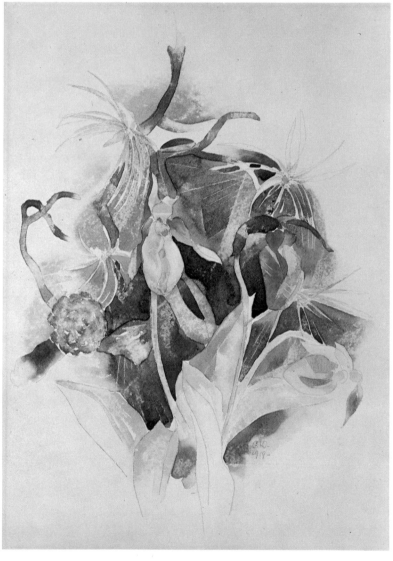

left: Plate 9. Leonardo da Vinci
(1452–1519; Italian). *Lily.* c. 1479.
Pen and ink with sepia wash,
heightened with white over black chalk; 12⅜ × 7″.
Royal Collection, Windsor (copyright reserved).

above: Plate 10. Charles Demuth (1883–1935; American).
Flowers. 1919. Watercolor, 13¾ × 9¹¹⁄₁₆″.
Columbus Gallery of Fine Arts, Columbus, Ohio
(gift of Ferdinand Howald).

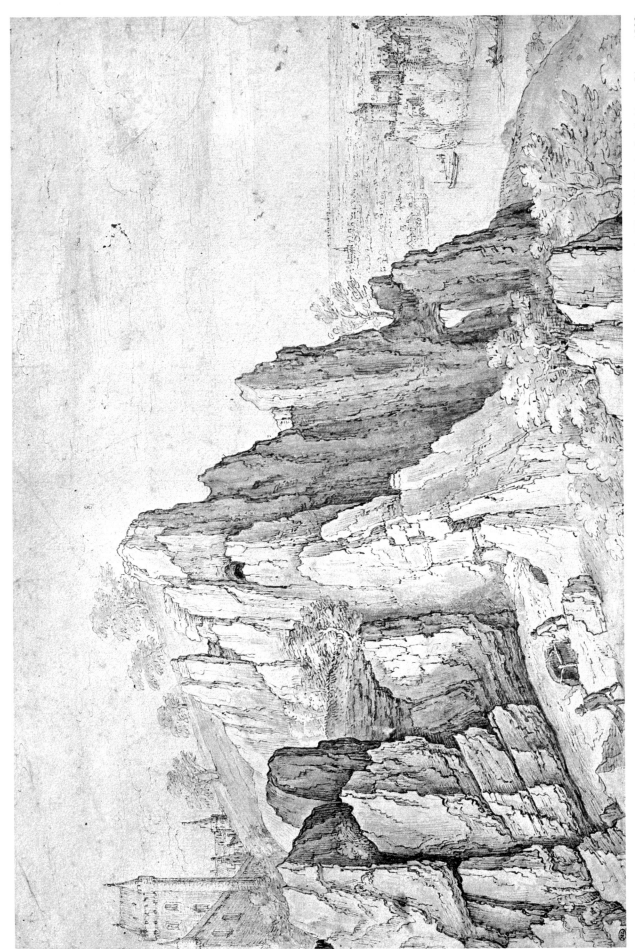

Plate 11. Lucas van Valckenborch (1530/35–97; Flemish). *Rocks Overlooking a River.* c. 1582. Pen and watercolor, 11½ × 17¼″. Louvre, Paris.

Rocks as Mountains

For this problem the students arranged rocks on a table to simulate mountain ranges. The study was related directly to the landscape space ideas that the students were working on independently at the same time. The concept to be examined is scale and the problem of constructing large masses within that scale. A person must be considered as an ant in this context. If one merely imitates rock texture, the translation of scale is lost. The models—the rocks—are meant to suggest infinitely greater mass.

Pieter Bruegel presents his *Alpine Landscape* (Fig. 113) from a high vantage point, so that we look over a level plain far below us toward craggy, tilting peaks of dizzying scale. The masses are simplified, but a winding road leads us partway into the picture, to a point opposite a deep, serpentine ravine in the distant slope. Some students prefer to construct a definite path, while others present the rock forms in a more generalized landscape environment.

Lucas van Valckenborch's *Rocks Overlooking a River* (Pl. 11, opposite) is probably an invention, to judge by the regularity of the spacing and the rather too convenient view of buildings and trees at the upper left, as well as the panorama on the right. The graded regularity in the construction of the mountains reinforces this impression. Although invented, the space conveys a strong sense of scale.

113. Pieter Bruegel the Elder (1525/30–69; Flemish). *Alpine Landscape*. Pen and ink. Louvre, Paris.

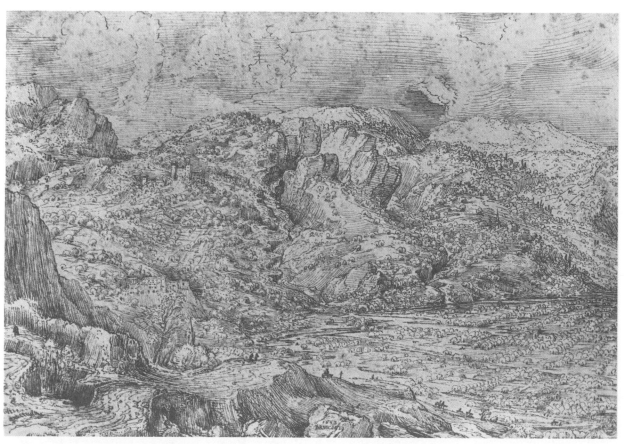

The proportions of the masses, plus subtle accents where forms overlap, give *The Coming of Autumn* by Hung-Jen (Fig. 114) a feeling of tremendous scale. The winding S-shape trail along the bottom weaves a path that ultimately unites the road and mountain into a consistent rhythm. The vertical trees at lower left are repeated many times as a counterpoint to the rounded, solid mountains, and the tiny house directly behind the trees adds to the illusion of depth and scale.

114. Hung-Jen (1610–63; Chinese). *The Coming of Autumn.* Hanging scroll, ink on paper; 48⅛ × 24¾″. Honolulu Academy of Arts (Wilhelmina Tenney Memorial Collection, 1955.)

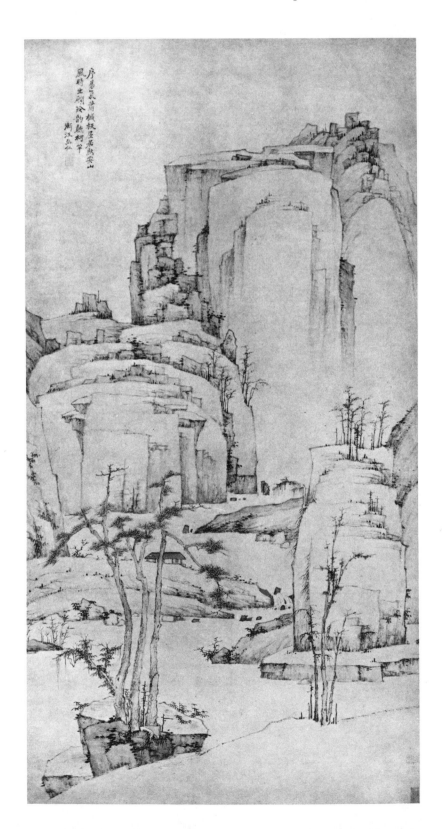

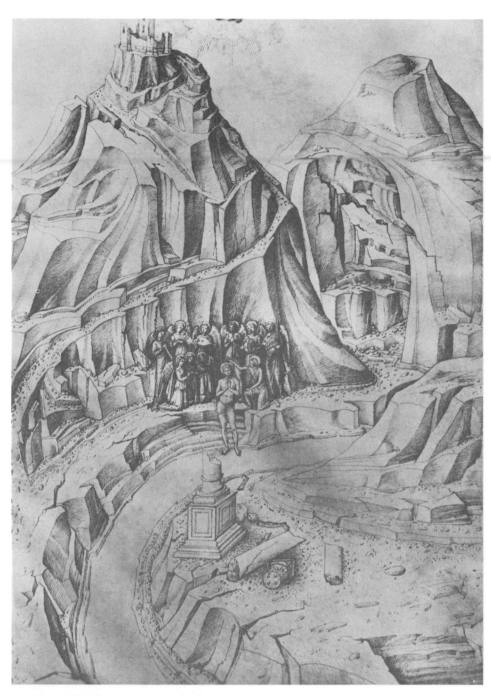

115. Jacopo Bellini (c. 1400–70; Italian).
Baptism of Christ. Pen and ink. Louvre, Paris.

In Jacopo Bellini's *Baptism of Christ* (Fig. 115) the sharp,
angular mountains seem as architecturally designed as the
broken column in the foreground and the castle at the top.
As in the Chinese drawing, a sweeping curve leads us into space
and winds to the summit. The whole creates a stage for the
magnificent drama that unfolds in the center of the composition.
The chorus of angels directly behind Christ is delicately
and deliberately woven into the rock forms.

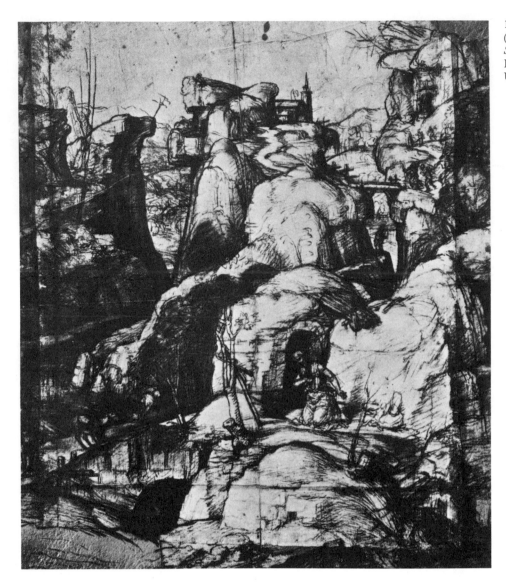

116. Piero di Cosimo
(c. 1462–1521; Italian).
Saint Jerome in a Landscape.
Pencil, 24¾ × 21⅛".
Uffizi, Florence.

In Piero di Cosimo's drawing *Saint Jerome in a Landscape* (Fig. 116), we have the opposite kind of structure: dark solid masses play against loose linear movements to produce domelike mountains. Careful scrutiny reveals bridges, buildings, and perhaps caves carved into these large, piled-up forms.

Student Response

The viewer's vantage point in Figure 117 is from a high peak overlooking another mountain form. We are invited to inspect the large masses, the possible paths for climbing, and hidden details. Like the crevices and points on the mountain, the tree on the central form contains a variety of rocklike details. These details are not strictly ornamental; they do not divorce themselves from the overall mass. The structure to the right, bare by comparison, still reveals all its steps and turns. The whole drawing is composed of gently tilting masses.

Unlike Figure 117, the drawing in Figure 118 (a memory
drawing) invites the viewer's eye to rest on the heavy weights of the
central plane. Having been forced to look at this dark, weighted
mass, we discover within it a rhythmic, linear theme that
moves through to the forms behind. The artist's skill in making us
follow this path gives a particular sequence to the drawing.

right: 117. Harry Keshian.
Mountains in the Distance.
1955. Pen and ink.
Collection Yale University
Art Gallery, New Haven, Conn.

below right: 118. Jeanette Lam.
Weighted Mountain Forms.
1955. Pen and ink.
Collection Yale University
Art Gallery, New Haven, Conn.

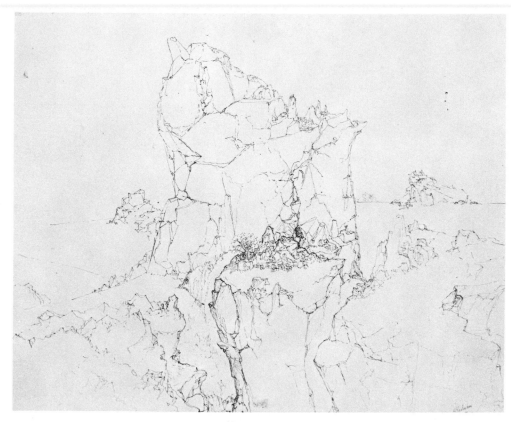

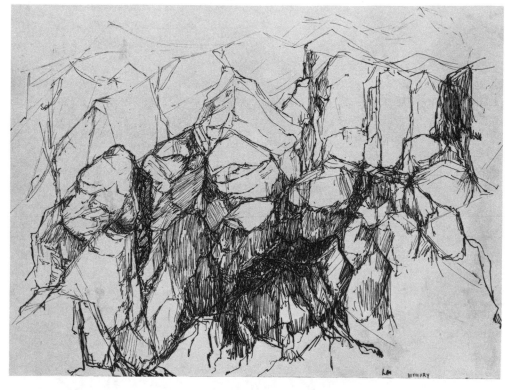

In the memory drawing in Figure 119 the shapes are mountainlike, yet they appear to be more elastic, more organic than those of the previous drawings. We seem to be very close to the forms, yet the undercut portion at the center pushes sharply into the page. We have, therefore, more than one reading. We might choose to take the trip underneath and then return to the main form, pressed against a sky mass that seems to be advancing. This drawing, with its fantastically conceived shapes, provides the viewer with many visual actions and counteractions.

119. Robert Birmelin. *Fantastic Mountain Landscape.* 1954. Pen and ink. Collection Yale University Art Gallery, New Haven, Conn.

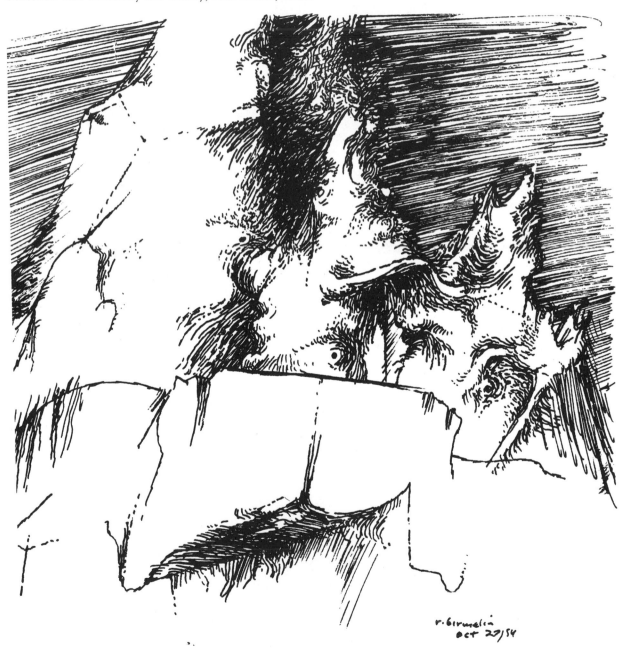

7 Interiors and Objects

Interiors

The artist's reaction to human environments—the settings
in which we spend much of our lives—has been a popular subject
for centuries. The character of a particular place obliges
the artist to perceive definite relationships of scale and light,
which in some ways parallel landscape space. For example, it is
a common error to identify individual objects at the expense
of a total spatial organization. But architectural interiors and the
inanimate objects that fill them are obviously constructed
in different ways. The objects tend to be sharp-edged and geometric,
and the direction of light falling on the objects may not be clear.

The work of beginners underlines these problems. Student
artists have a tendency to make every object in an environment
the subject of a separate portrait, instead of constructing
the whole space and forcing the objects to articulate it.

Van Gogh's reed-pen and ink *Bedroom at Arles* (Fig. 120)
is composed of furniture and a strongly patterned floor. It is this

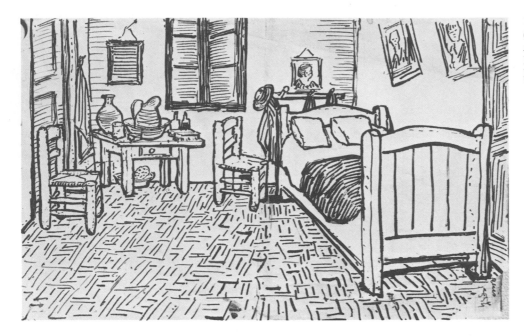

120. Vincent van Gogh
(1853–90; Dutch-French).
Bedroom at Arles. 1888.
Pen and ink, 5⅛ × 8¼".
National Museum
Vincent van Gogh, Amsterdam.

strong visual vibration of pattern that prevents the description
of bed, chairs, and objects from coming into individual
focus. The rhythmic lines weaving the floor space are echoed
in the objects and make us see the whole drawing simultaneously.

Red chalk (which was employed initially as a layout)
combines with a sepia wash to give Piranesi's architectural fantasy
a red-gold glow (Pl. 12, p. 143). The light thus produced
softens all the edges and unifies the whole composition. When
the drawing is reproduced in black and white, this softening
effect shows up as a much harsher series of staccato rhythms, and
this distorts the artist's intention. The darkest tones appear only in
the lower portion of the drawing—the angular stairs at the
left and the various figure groups. These darks give a weight
to the floor plane and gradually blend into the lighter, airier washes
at the top. The viewer is directed to see first the round form in the
lower right, because it stands out more sharply against its
background. This form sets up the comparative scale in the overall
composition by establishing its relationship to the human figures.

In Edouard Vuillard's *Woman Before a Mirror* (Pl. 13, p. 144),
the tan color of the paper is not leftover background but rather
a plane that supports the mirror. There is no precise focus;
woman, reflection, and furniture are held in one consistent plane.
The dark shape of the skirt establishes the form of the woman
as it also creates the strongest weight in the atmospheric space.
Two smaller darks relate to this dominant shape: the reflection of
the woman's hair and a small shape at the top of the skirt, also
repeated in the mirror. The color reveals a subtle play of cool and
warm; the upper part of the mirror and the surface of the
furniture are cool in a sea of allover warmth. Only in the blouse
are warm and cool tones actually mixed together. The magic
here is the artist's touch—his feeling for putting one stroke against
another to produce a glowing texture.

Student Response

The students began this assignment by drawing their own rooms after working in class on very complicated, room-filling still lifes in which the objects were placed haphazardly in all parts of the studio. They were asked not to limit themselves to one or two objects in a given spatial position, but to choose objects from the whole room and to invent relationships for them. The choice of media and tools is important, since each student must search for the medium and the tool to express an individual attitude.

The drawing in Figure 121 resembles a Dutch interior in its setting and balance. The viewer is a detached spectator, removed from the light that defines the space and its contents. The vague figure and objects in the strong light are deliberately kept at a distance. Objects balanced on either side of the door are kept in darkness, and they seem to remove us even farther from the light, for we cannot recognize them although they are relatively close. Forms are suggested, never described, so that we cannot easily become involved with particulars. Our interest is in the arrangement of the light and dark forms in a unified spatial field.

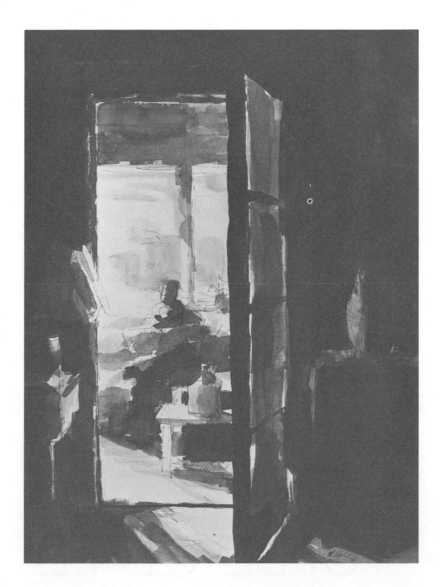

121. Vaino Kola.
Lighted Interior. 1960.
Pen and ink with wash.
Collection Yale University
Art Gallery,
New Haven, Conn.

Figure 122 gives quite the opposite effect. We are thrust directly into a space that is not fully explained, and thus we are forced to complete the environment on our own and to imagine the source of light. The artist gives us several clues to the nature of our surroundings. We know, for example, that we are directly behind a studio easel, which, although dramatically cut off at the top, clearly reveals its structure. (The holes at the bottom of the easel, which permit the artist to move it up and down, are easily distinguishable.) A low table or stool at left center is also clear. But the remaining studio furniture and the figure of the artist, whose elbow appears in the strongest light at left, are only hinted at. We are thus engulfed in a dramatically lit space with ambiguous contents. We are forced to construct a whole environment from a few clearly defined forms and the sketchy details that surround them.

In Figure 123 the exaggerated diagonal thrust of the ceiling plane, supported by heavy parallel lines describing pipes, forces us into the low-ceilinged room. Most of the objects in this interior are seen only in profile, and the pattern of darks between these profiles is concentrated in the back-center. Here the dark areas act not only to create "noise" in this silent room, but also to set up movements and countermovements. Also, and equally important, they define the plane that is farthest back in space. The naked bulb is set apart from the other elements in the room. It makes us want to lower our heads, again emphasizing the low ceiling. The light bulb adds a contrapuntal note to the rest of the composition and, to some extent, a humorous touch.

122. William Cudahy. *Ambiguous Space.* 1960. Conté crayon and white chalk. Collection Yale University Art Gallery, New Haven, Conn.

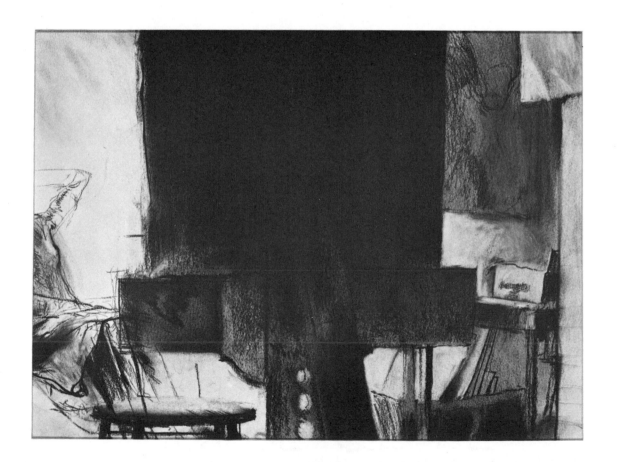

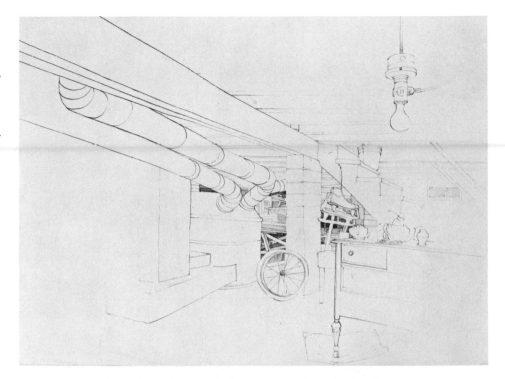

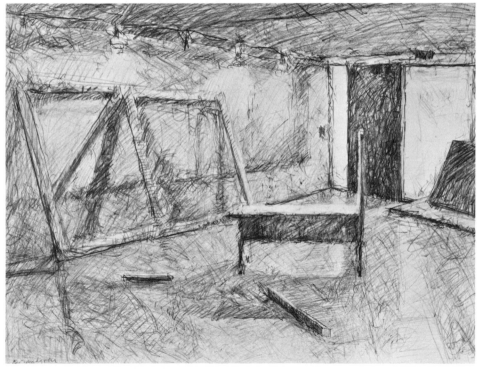

In Figure 124 studio furniture—drawing bench, canvas
stretcher, portfolios—exists eerily in the half light. It is the light
working on the objects, expressively placed at connecting
and opposing angles and set in an even-paced tempo, that creates
and controls the space. Notice how the only large pure white
is on the farthest vertical plane, and how it sets up a dialogue
with the white on top of the bench.

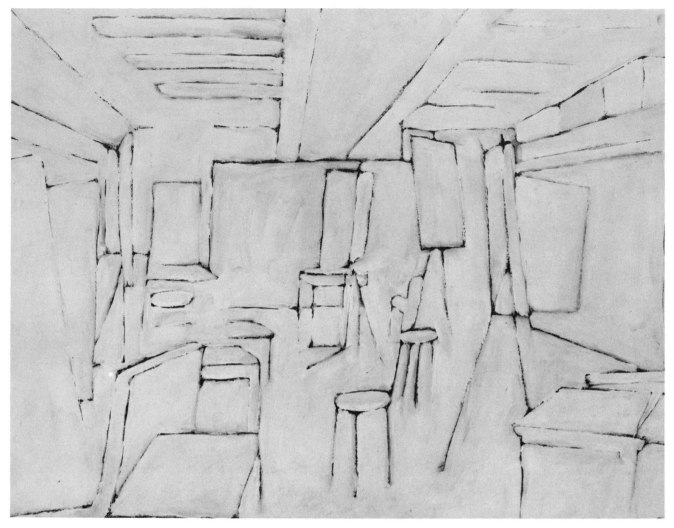

125. Frank Moore. *The Studio in White Light.* 1973.
Black and white acrylic paint.
Collection Yale University Art Gallery, New Haven, Conn.

Studio classroom furniture is also presented in Figure 125.
Thin, delicately poised broken lines are surrounded by pervasive
white light that seems to grow constantly stronger, until it
melts the weight of the objects portrayed. These tenuous lines
are produced in reverse: the paper was first coated with black
acrylic paint, then white was applied over this undercoat;
the black lines are thus the "leftovers," what the artist
left untouched.

Interiors: Indoor–Outdoor Spaces

Draftsmen and painters always have been attracted to themes
that combine simultaneously inside and outside spaces.
In a drawing by Etienne de Martellange (Fig. 126) we are outside
moving in and out of entrances and exits. We are at the same time
inside and outside, on a complicated hill of spatial choices.

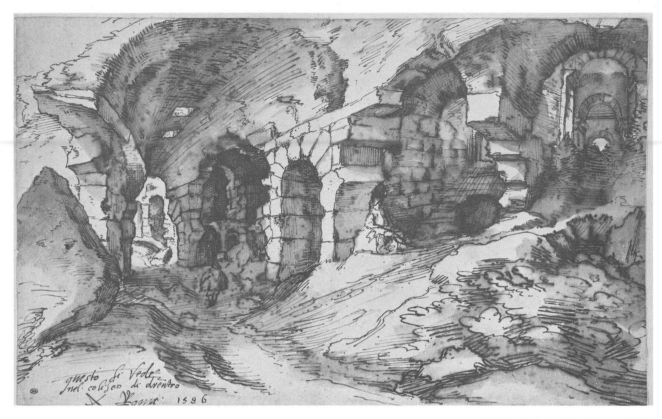

above: 126. Etienne de Martellange (1568–1641; French). *Galleria Interna del Colosseo.* 1586. Pen and brown watercolor ink with a trace of bluish watercolor, 10⅝ × 17⅛″. Louvre, Paris.

below: 127. Michael Kelley. *Elongated Wall.* 1975. Conté crayon. Collection Yale University Art Gallery, New Haven, Conn.

Student Response

In Figure 127, the aggressive, grating texture stretched across the elongated wall from entrance to exit makes us want to move quickly through the space. The nicely chosen long shape of the paper italicizes the message.

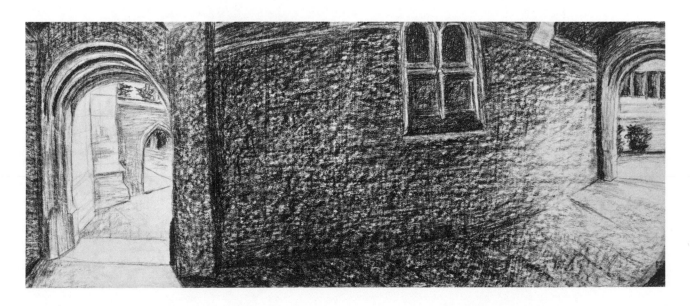

In Figure 128 we find ourselves in a mysteriously lit passage. We feel crowded by the corner of the wall moving slowly out at us, yet we want to catch a glimpse of the view from the windows. Both effects reinforce an overall tension.

Objects in the Room

A natural extension of interior space is an exploration of sections of a room or particular objects within it. In Figure 129, in conté crayon, there is a soft light on the bed supported by a corner of the room and a table. This soft light combines with the rolling rhythm of broken and soft edges of the bedding. The bedding actually serves as a stand-in for the recent occupant. Figure 130 features the same artist and theme with different materials—brush and ink. Here, the soft, rolling movement has been translated into a more aggressive statement. By speaking louder and faster and closing some of the open contours, the artist produces a totally different mood.

128. Karen Sideman. *Corner in a Passageway.* 1975. Charcoal. Collection Yale University Art Gallery, New Haven, Conn.

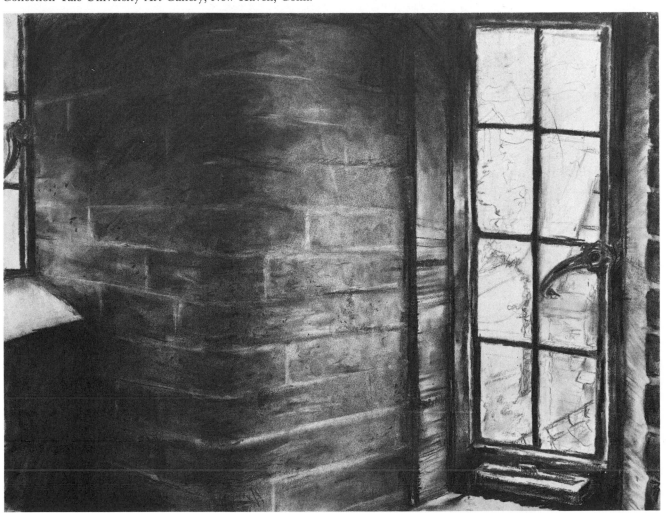

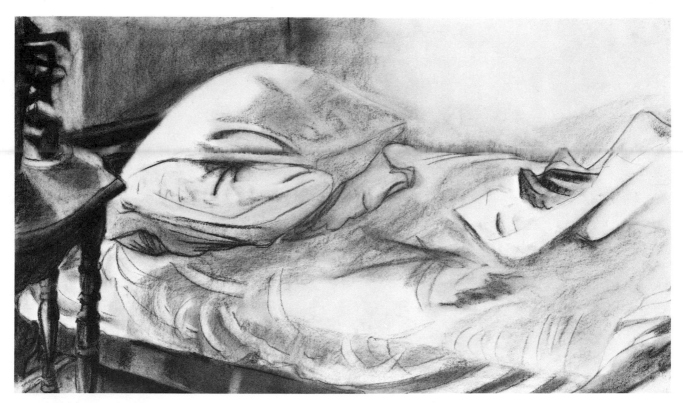

above: 129. F. Terry Arzola.
Tumbled Bed. 1975. Conté crayon.
Collection Yale University Art Gallery, New Haven, Conn.

below: 130. F. Terry Arzola.
Tumbled Bed. 1975. Brush and ink.
Collection Yale University Art Gallery, New Haven, Conn.

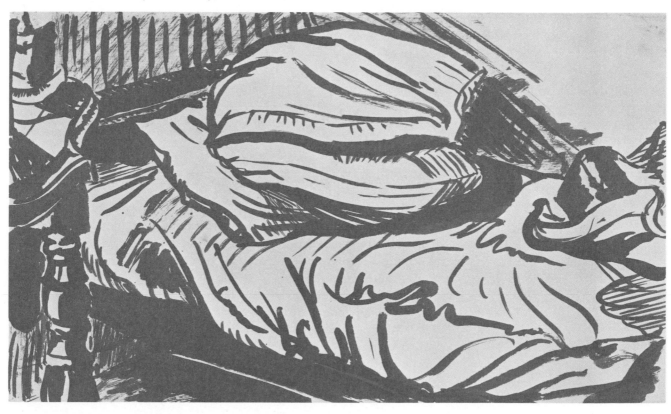

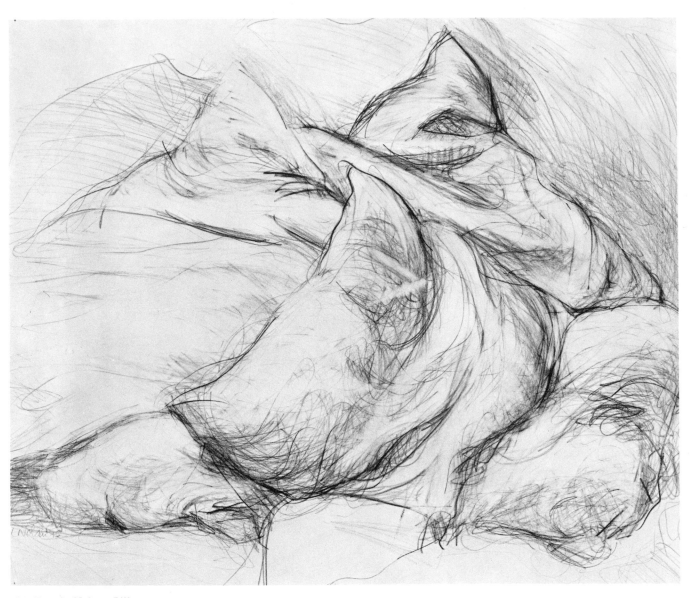

131. Laurie Nolan. *Pillows.*
1976. Graphite pencil.
Collection Yale University Art Gallery, New Haven, Conn.

The traditional method of studying drapery is to set up
materials on a wall or table and tell the students how important
it is to study the expression in these folds. The drawing
in Figure 131 reveals what may be a more natural way to get
at the same issue—to find form-life in drapery. The drapery here
also suggests figures moving and crouching; the content does not
become independent of the form.

With a minimum of pencil strokes the artist of Figure 132
builds up the delicate layers of a dress, filling the vertical span
of the picture surface. The leftover emptiness, at left, leaves room
for the dress, which seems capable of movement, to dance
into the open area.

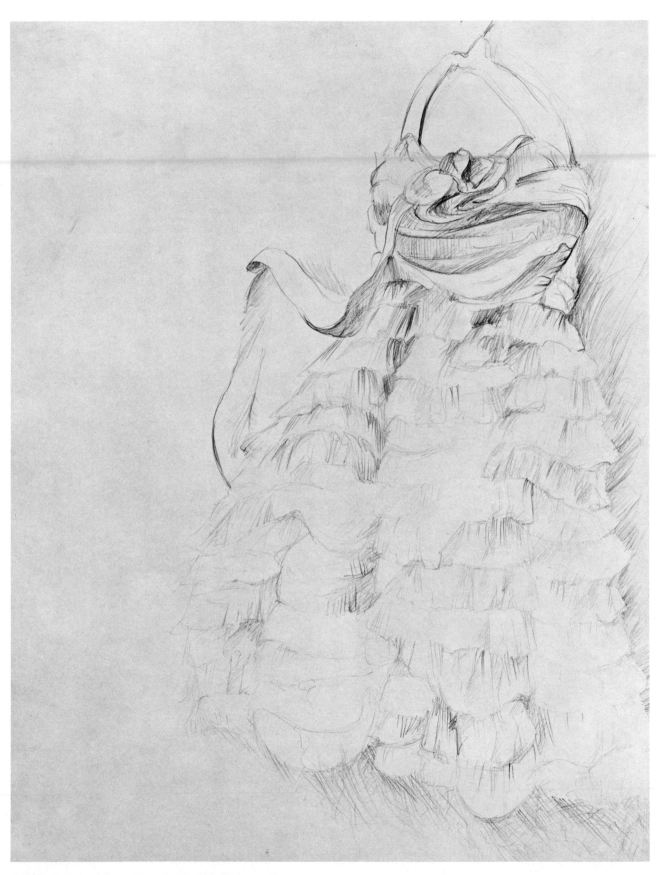

132. Julia Glass. *Prom Dress*. 1976. Graphite pencil.
Collection Yale University Art Gallery, New Haven, Conn.

Objects: Shoes and Gloves

The drawing of common objects requires more than journalistic thinking; mere description of a shoe does not probe the layers of individual perception.

In its simplest identity the shoe is a unique form mirroring its wearer. But as a subject for artistic expression its uses are much broader. Both Van Gogh and Marsden Hartley saw the shoe as a symbol of poverty and work (Figs. 133, 134).

Even when shoes are presented as portraits of their owners, we must also pay attention to the structure of the shoe itself which, after all, is designed to fit a foot with individual toes. In addition, the distinctive shapes and structure of the shoe may be exaggerated to stress its character or that of its owner. As is true with any object, these attitudes do not come from merely looking at the shoe. What we know, what we think and feel colors our reactions. The artist's experience is

133. Vincent van Gogh (1853–90; Dutch-French). *Boots with Laces.* 1886. Oil on canvas, 14⅞ × 18″. National Museum Vincent van Gogh, Amsterdam.

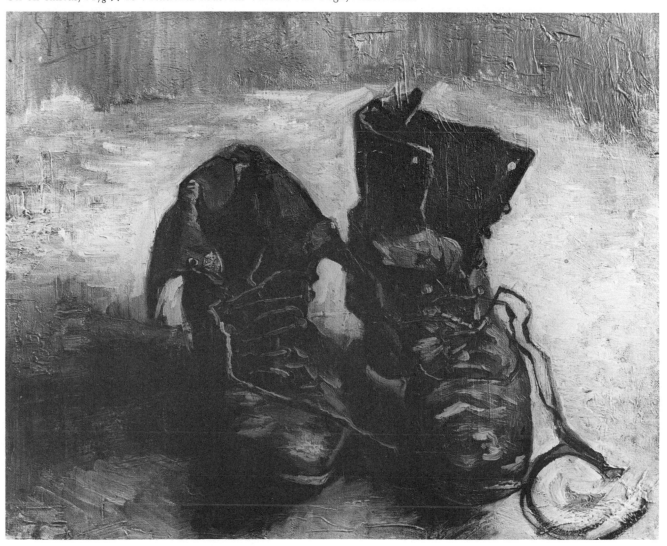

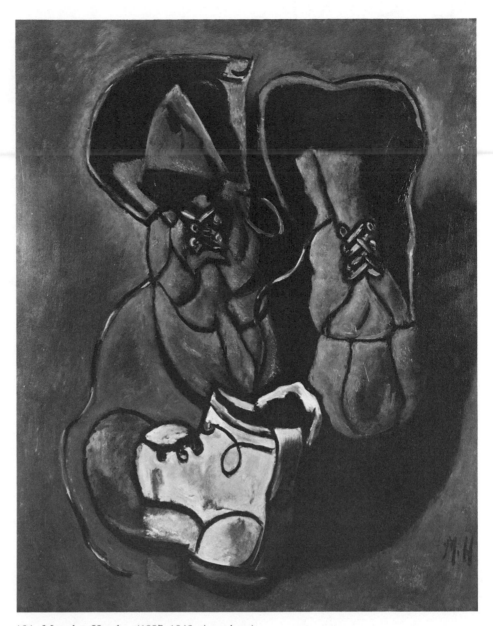

134. Marsden Hartley (1887–1943; American).
Boots. 1941. Oil on gesso on composition board, 28⅛ × 22¼".
Museum of Modern Art, New York (purchase).

more important than an effort to describe an object faithfully.
The object—in this case the shoe—should be translated
and composed in visual terms, but never in caricature.

Student Response

For this problem the students first attempted individual portraits
of shoes; later, the shoes were set up in groups on the floor,
and works emphasizing the composition of the whole picture space
were undertaken. The latter became, as it were, shoe landscapes
because of the placement of shoes on the floor below eye level.
The space is equivalent to a panoramic vista.

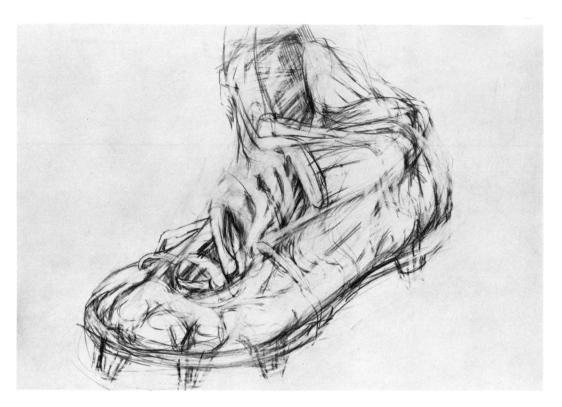

above: 135. Eugene Baguskus. *Football Shoe.* 1962. Graphite pencil.
Collection Yale University Art Gallery, New Haven, Conn.

below: 136. Arnold Bittleman. *Slouching Shoe.* 1955. Graphite pencil.
Collection Yale University Art Gallery, New Haven, Conn.

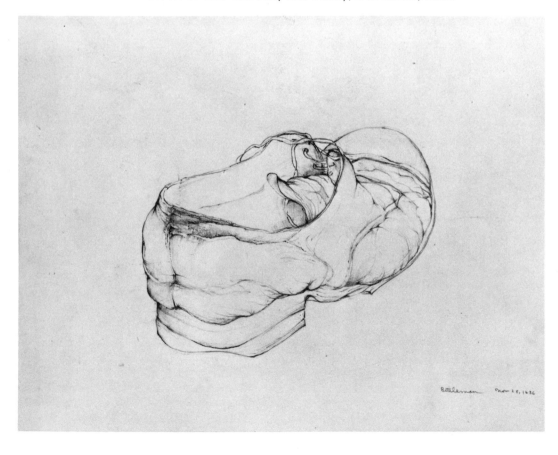

The football shoe in Figure 135 becomes a very aggressive form, filling the whole page. The instrumentation—brusque, almost crude, with many erased lines—heightens the forcefulness and underlines the artist's expression. This meeting of handwriting and scale produces a compelling portrait. Note that the toes of the football player are strongly suggested.

A quite different attitude is evident in Figure 136. The shoe is isolated in the center of the page like a specimen under a microscope, and layers of construction and destruction acting on one another are clinically examined. The tongue, the eyelets, the counter, and the stitching are carefully detailed. These details are subordinate to the slouching posture of the entire shoe, which absorbs them into its overall quality.

Both Figures 137 and 138 are good examples of the expressive use of media and the way in which a distinctive handwriting intensifies a particular attitude.

In Figure 137 the broad, rough scratching with a blunt pen point focuses on the shoelaces of the sneaker. The pen strokes thus underline the character of the model. The wide sneaker bulges toward the viewer and, with the insistent textured strokes, places the viewer face to face with the actor. The restricted space adds to its dimension.

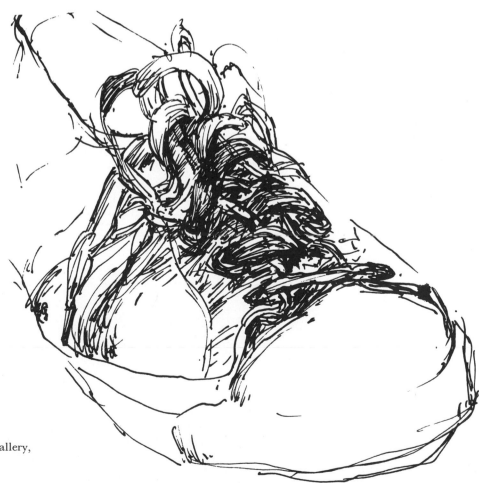

137. Student drawing.
Bulging Sneaker. Pen and ink.
Collection Yale University Art Gallery,
New Haven, Conn.

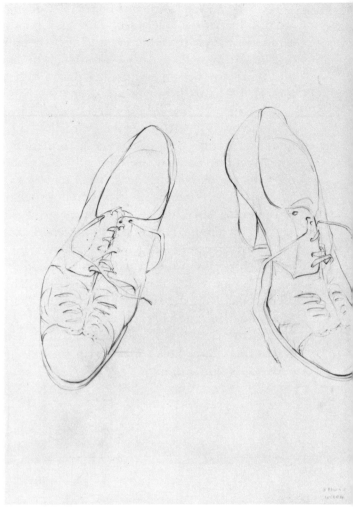

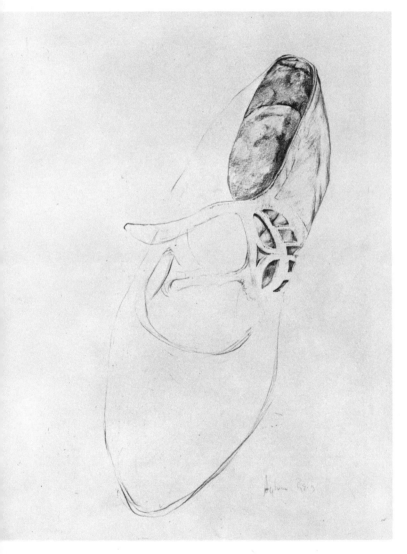

left: 138. Sylvia Reid.
Delicate Shoe. 1954. Graphite pencil.
Collection Yale University Art Gallery,
New Haven, Conn.

above: 139. William Leete.
Shoes: Expression of Character.
1953. Graphite pencil.
Collection Yale University
Art Gallery, New Haven, Conn.

Figure 138 is, by contrast, a cool whisper in keeping with the frail elegance of the model, which is placcd at an aloof distance. The nature of the instrument (pencil) and the instrumentation (pale, delicate modeling) build a portrait of individual character.

The pair of shoes in Figure 139 creates a distinct portrait. The shoes have been stretched to exaggerate their character.

Details are not clinical, as in Figure 136. More important here is
the posture of both shoes acting together in concert to make
the image. Each shoe has an individual expression, but their
gesture together is the essence of the portrait.

We do not readily recognize the sandals in Figure 140,
for the student does not let us get back far enough to focus. She
fills the whole vertical picture surface with a strong rhythmic
texture—crisscross strokes that repeat the structure of the shoes.

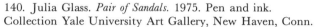

140. Julia Glass. *Pair of Sandals.* 1975. Pen and ink.
Collection Yale University Art Gallery, New Haven, Conn.

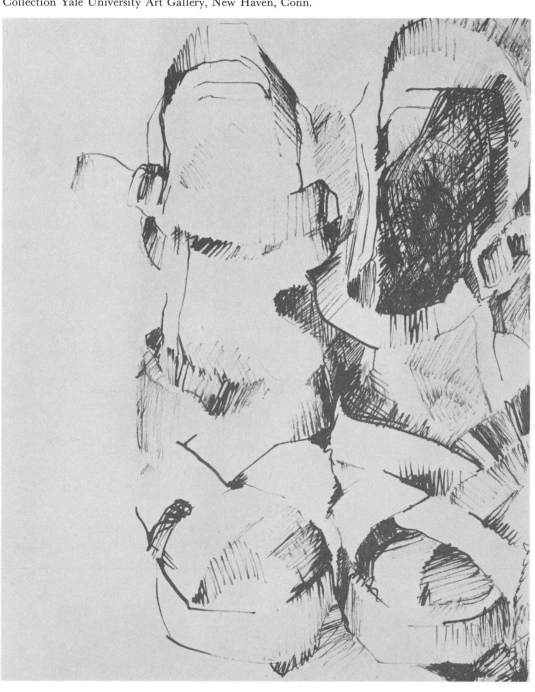

A single shoe has been moved and placed in characteristic poses to form a rhythmic quartet in Figure 141. The peculiar gestures of the army boot provided the impetus for the study, but the overriding theme is in the gestures or postures that act together. It is the total composition that makes the portrait what it is. There is reciprocal action: the shoes dance together, and these dancing rhythms reorganize the content and transform it.

One pair of shoes was the initial subject for the study in Figure 142. The artist used her own shoes, rearranged them in several combinations, and examined their shapes

141. John Cohen.
Shoe Quartet. 1954.
Charcoal pencil.
Collection Yale University
Art Gallery, New Haven, Conn.

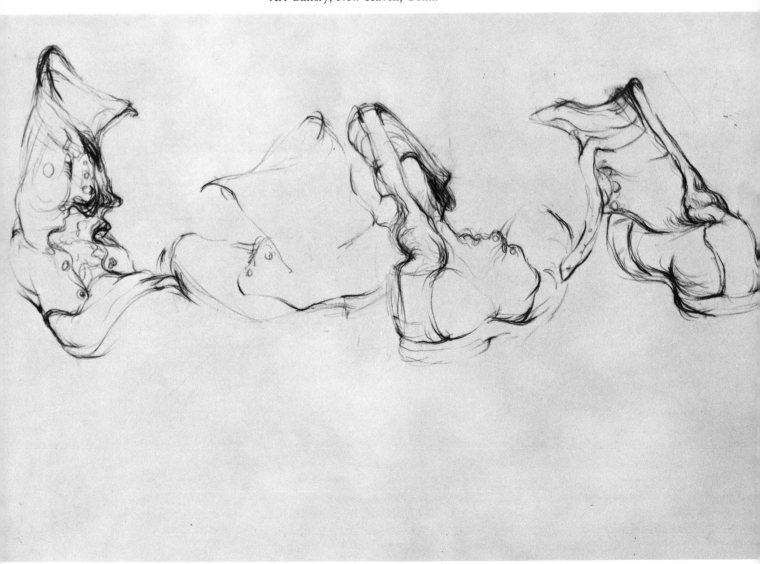

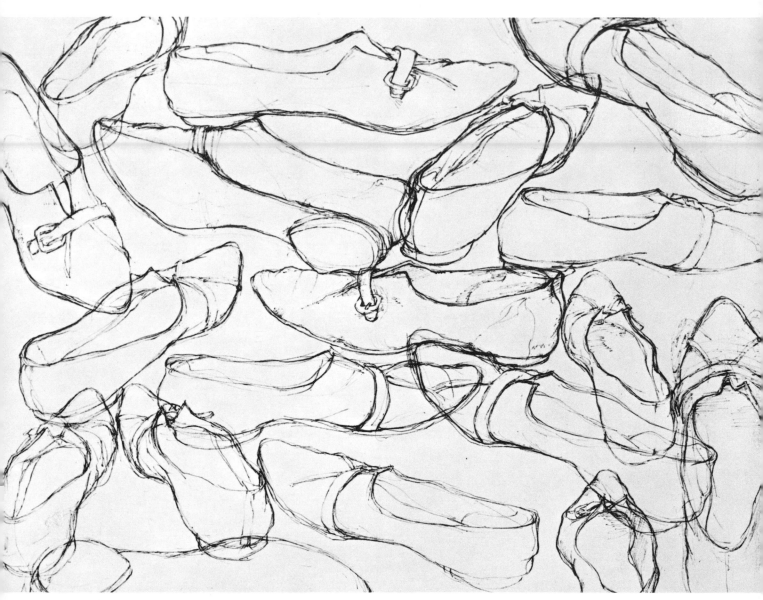

142. Sandra Whipple.
Overlapping Shoe Forms.
1961. Bamboo pen.
Collection Yale University
Art Gallery, New Haven, Conn.

from every possible angle. However, description of a
particular form is only the beginning of this study. The artist
rendered the shoes transparent and placed one shape over
another to create an allover floating arrangement. After
viewing the pattern, we may inspect each individual shape,
and these well-observed studies are interesting forms
in themselves. But the specific character of the shoe must
give way finally to the total impact of the drawing,
the expression of overlapping planes that make up the
whole composition.

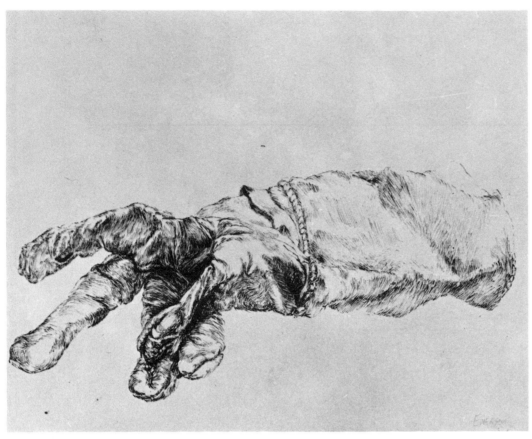

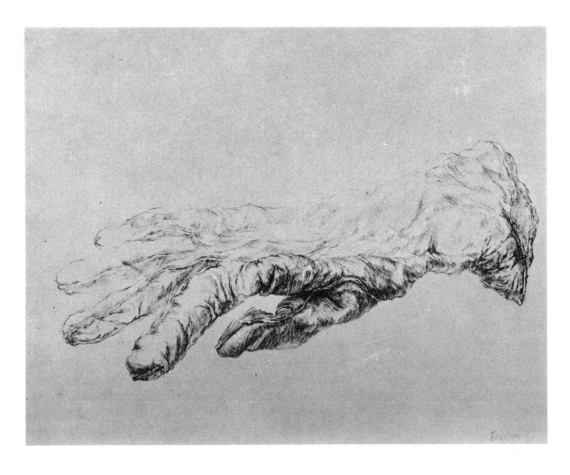

left: 143. Charles Emerson.
Menacing Glove Form. 1962.
Pen and ink.
Collection Yale University
Art Gallery,
New Haven, Conn.

below left: 144.
Charles Emerson.
Glove in Repose. 1962.
Pen and ink.
Collection Yale University
Art Gallery,
New Haven, Conn.

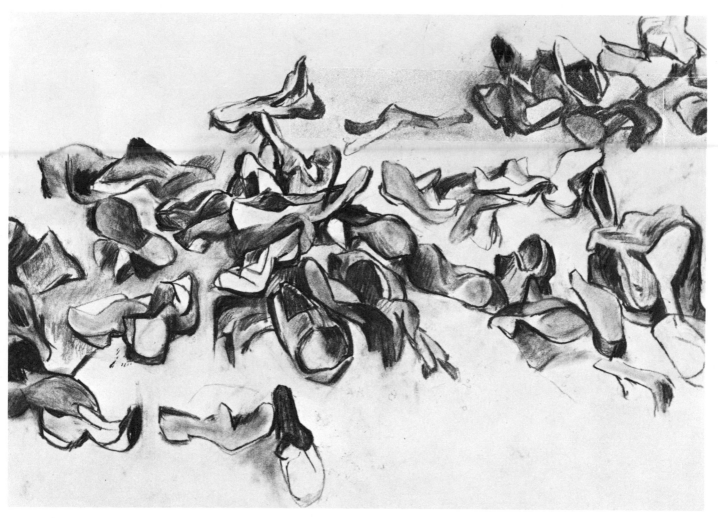

145. Student drawing.
Organic Shoe Forms. Charcoal.
Collection Yale University Art Gallery,
New Haven, Conn.

In two studies of gloves (Figs. 143, 144) the instrumentation
carries the mood. Textured lines model the leather drapery,
and these surface marks become welded to the expressive gesture
of the forms. In Figure 143 the emphasis is on the juncture
of finger and thumb. The gestures of fingers, which appear to be
frozen in the glove, are violent compared to the pose in
Figure 144, in which all the fingers are gently at rest. In the
latter case the modeling is appropriately delicate to enhance
the intended mood.

The composition of the whole page is again the overriding
consideration in Figures 145 and 146. The shoes are examined not
as individual figures but as compositional elements. In Figure
145 the forms act together organically: they crowd, move, and
rush through the composition. The broad use of the charcoal
gives weight to the forms and slows down their movement,
while the empty spaces exert pressure on the blocklike units

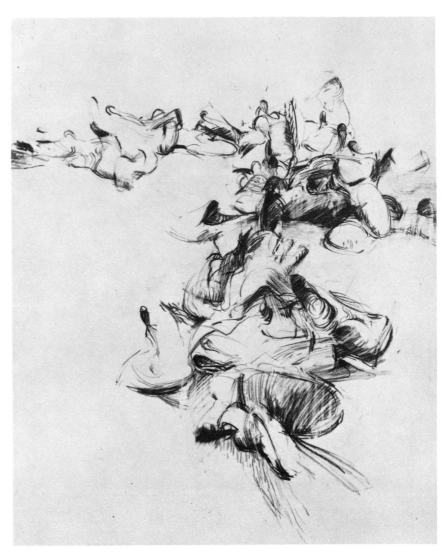

146. Michael Mazur. *Shoe Landscape.* 1960. Charcoal.
Collection Yale University Art Gallery, New Haven, Conn.

and help to define the allover space. In Figure 146 the artist
exaggerates the angle of vision. The viewer is high above the floor,
and the quick, linear charcoal strokes give us an almost
impressionistic view of the shoe landscape.

The final drawings in this section emphasize line. Figures
147 and 148 are brush drawings. Each exhibits an individual
handwriting. It is true that the medium tends toward certain
characteristics, but the individual's natural touch modifies the
effect of the tool and the material.

In Figure 147 a fine line describes each shoe, yet the
group portrait is dominant. In Figure 148 heavier brush strokes
identify clearly only the front row of shoes, yet the markings of the
brush line, from thick to thin, define overlapping shapes that
convey the essence of the shoe form without resorting to
obvious description.

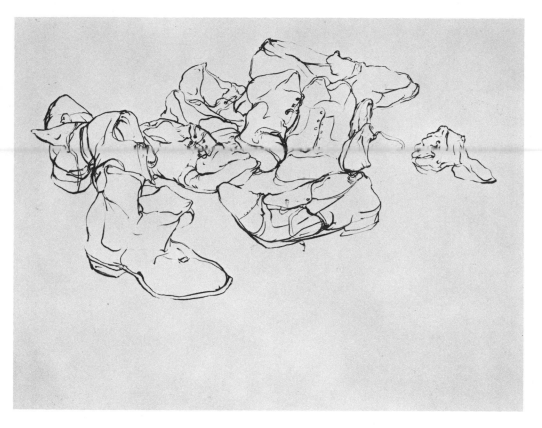

above: 147. Stephanie Kieffer.
Group Portrait of Shoes. 1957. Brush and ink.
Collection Yale University Art Gallery,
New Haven, Conn.

below: 148. Deborah Boxer.
Undefined Shoe Forms. 1959. Brush and ink.
Collection Yale University Art Gallery,
New Haven, Conn.

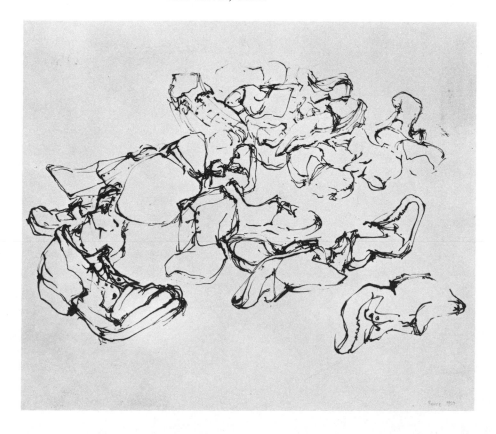

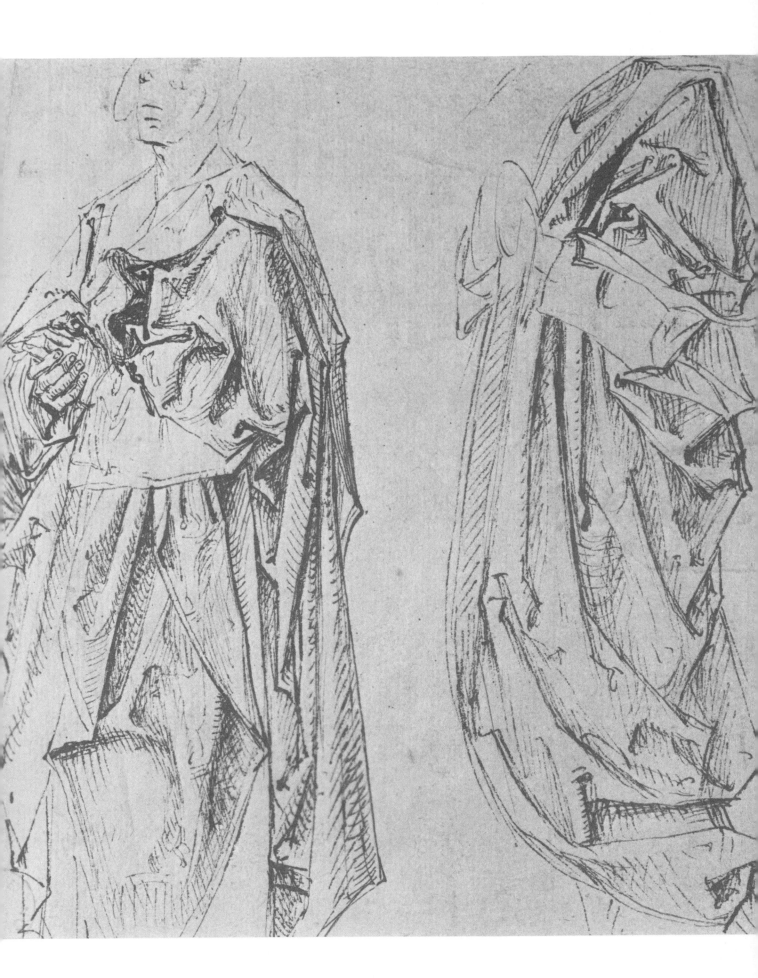

Objects: The Paper Bag

As students gain confidence and skill, the subjects presented for
study become increasingly complicated. In this problem
the varied structure of the forms precludes a single technical
approach for, with each new form, the student must search
for a new means of instrumentation and, perhaps a different
drawing instrument.

Paper bags are among the most difficult objects to
articulate because of their complicated tracery of folds. Simply
to transcribe the folds as they appear produces either bland
illustration or confusing focal points. The hierarchy of folds, major
and minor, must be perceived and articulated clearly in relation
to the overall structure of the bag and its function—to contain.

This problem suggests a study of texture and surface,
as well as concepts of drapery study. The quality of paper and the
way its wrinkles tend to spread and move over the whole
surface are important to the structure and must be carefully
interpreted in these terms. Abrupt dangling tool marks might
express the surface texture of the bag, but they tend to divorce
themselves from the architectural configuration of the folds.
In short, drawing a paper bag involves perception in the service
of concepts; what is known about the object controls
what is seen.

The problems involved in articulating the folds of a paper
bag are similar to those encountered in drapery studies.
Often, the whole character of a drawing will depend upon the
way drapery is handled. In keeping with the concepts of the time,
the drapery in a 15th-century pen-and-ink drawing (Fig. 149)
is hard and brittle, more like stone sculpture than pliant cloth.
The folds, in fact, behave like paper: each crease, minor
and major, is interlocked in a chain reaction throughout the whole
garment. This artist's forms, however, change direction,
emphasis, and focus to reveal the weight of the figure contained.

Student Response

As with the shoes, we began by studying individual bags
and then moved to group studies. Memory drawings were attempted
in this exercise as well. In the group studies students were
advised not to limit themselves to an established arrangement.
Instead they were asked to invent their own arrangements, picking
individual forms from different positions and constructing the
total composition according to their needs.

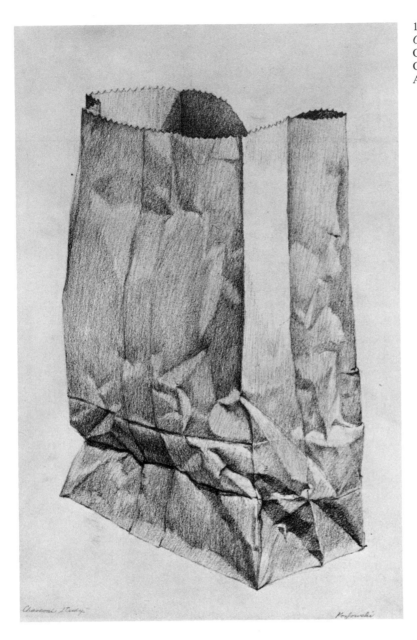

150. Edward Kozlowski.
Charcoal Study. 1954.
Charcoal pencil.
Collection Yale University
Art Gallery, New Haven, Conn.

In Figure 150, a charcoal pencil drawing, the bag is posed
in center stage and is rendered in terms of light and dark
values. When viewed from a distance the strokes of charcoal seem
to blend to produce a slick surface, but at close range each
thin stroke is evident. This surface treatment, which is difficult
to reproduce, gives a light glow to the original. The soft
and hard edges have an added life. This drawing, which seems
almost mechanical, is deliberately representational. However,
it can be criticized from another viewpoint: it leaves nothing to the
imagination of the viewer. It reminds one of the work of
portrait painters who carefully delineate every eyelash, only
to lose our interest. A more subtle approach is taken by such
masters as Rembrandt, who suggest without clearly describing, thus
demanding participation from the viewer.

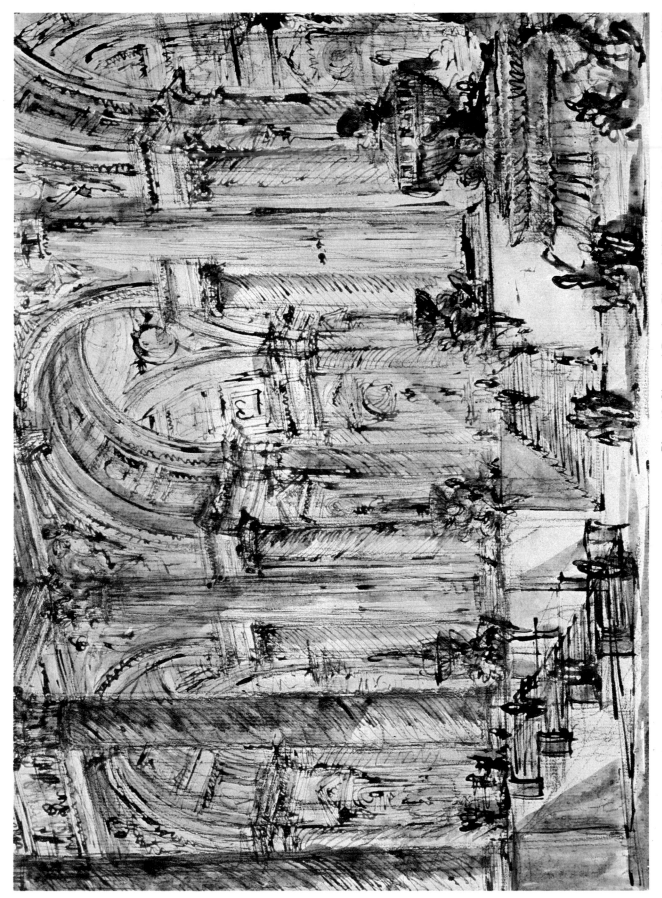

Plate 12. Giovanni Battista Piranesi (1720–78; Italian). *Architectural Fantasy.* c. 1755.
Pen and ink with brown wash over red chalk, 14⅝ × 20¼″. Ashmolean Museum, Oxford.

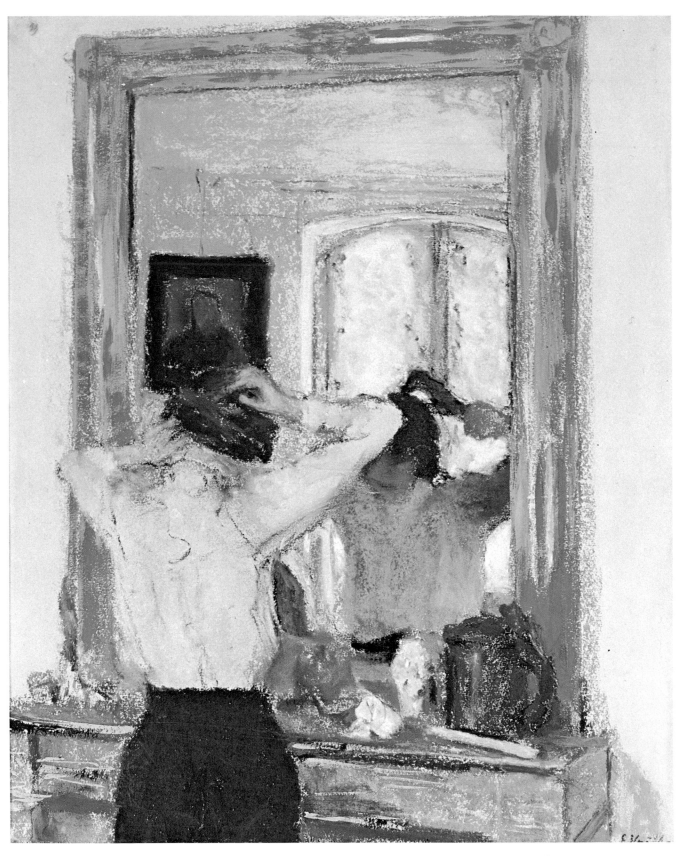

Plate 13. Edouard Vuillard (1868–1940; French). *Woman Before Mirror.*
Pastel with some touches of gouache, 22¼ × 18⅛″.
Yale University Art Gallery, New Haven, Conn. (bequest of Edith Malvina K. Wetmore).

The author of the pencil drawing in Figure 151 took
apart a paper bag and flattened it into one sheet to study its
structure. The information he acquired is obvious in this clearly
focused study of the bottom and side of a bag. He selects
this attitude and houses it in the emphasis on sharply turning planes.
This preconceived attitude expresses, too, his own visual
reactions to the form.

Similarly, in Figure 152 one corner of the mouth of the bag
is in sharp focus. The detailed modeling in this area gradually slips
from tone to line. We can see that the subject of the drawing
is not the bag itself, but the *opening* of the bag. The remainder
of the form acts solely as a support and is of secondary interest.

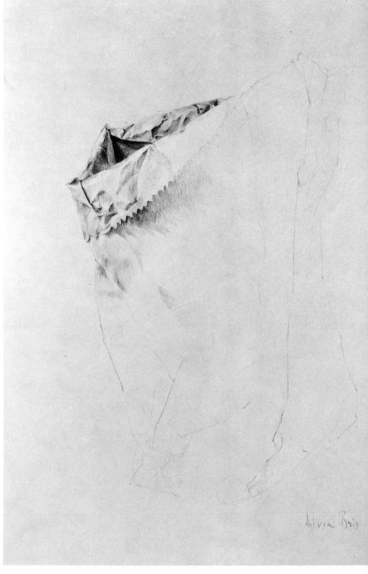

above: 152. Sylvia Reid.
The Opening of a Bag. 1954. Graphite pencil.
Collection Yale University Art Gallery,
New Haven, Conn.

below: 151. Roy Superior.
Structure of a Paper Bag.
1961. Graphite pencil.
Collection Yale University Art Gallery,
New Haven, Conn.

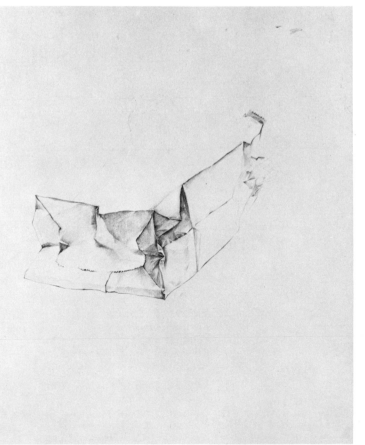

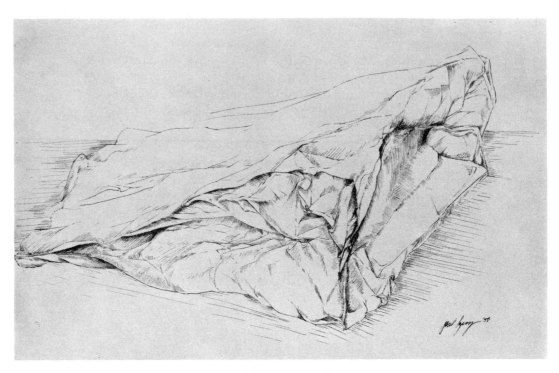

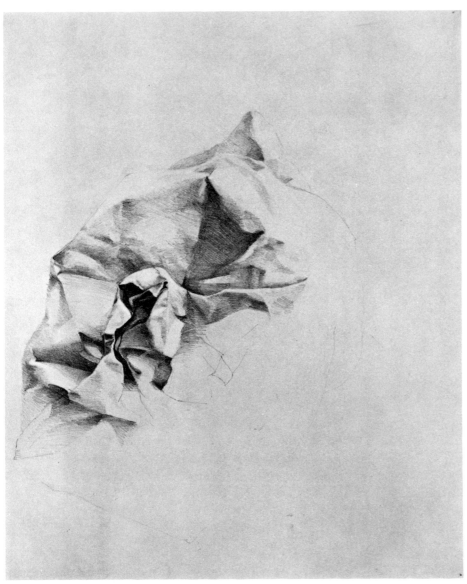

top: 153. Joel Szasz.
Flowing Surface. 1958.
Pen and ink.
Collection Yale University
Art Gallery, New Haven, Conn.

left: 154. John E. Devine.
Valley of Folds. 1966.
Graphite pencil.
Collection Yale University
Art Gallery, New Haven, Conn.

Delicate pen lines in Figure 153 encompass the entire
form of the bag. Here the interest is in the flow of the surface,
yet the underlying structural character of the container is
defined within the free-flowing lines. The corner, which is held
in focus, preserves the identity of the object.

In Figure 154 the bag is transformed into a sharply punctuated
baroque valley of folds. The drama suggested by a particular
paper bag becomes the subject of the study. The shape of the bag
itself, lost in the heightened expression, is of lesser importance.

Among the group studies the first is a pencil drawing
(Fig. 155) that achieves an architectural presence and scale.
The pattern and flow of the gently modeled and simplified block
shapes gives a monumental quality to the paper bag.

155. Vaino Kola.
Paper Bags: Architectural Form. 1960.
Graphite pencil.
Collection Yale University Art Gallery,
New Haven, Conn.

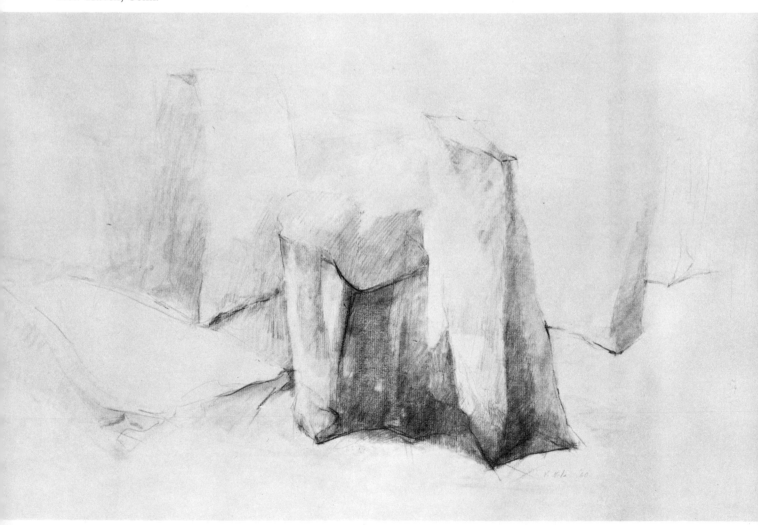

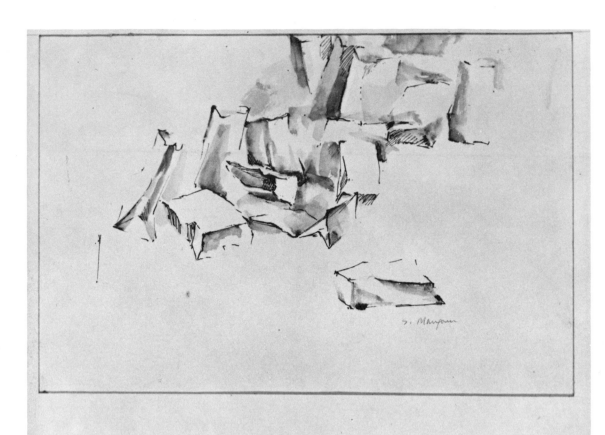

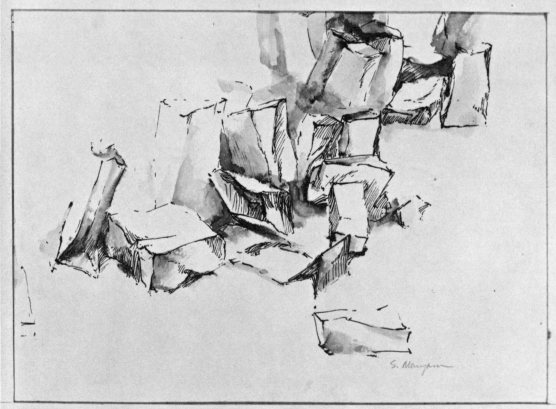

156. Susan Mangam. *Weights and Counterweights.* c. 1959.
Pen and ink with wash.
Collection Yale University Art Gallery, New Haven, Conn.

The two drawings in Figure 156 use the blocklike shapes of
bags only as the suggestion for a composition. The actual
subject of the drawings is the flow of weights and counterweights,
tipping and moving diagonally up the page. These masses
tumble and finally collapse against the back plane, and this
crowding in the background establishes gravity. A second
look shows the forms moving in reverse toward the viewer. We have
both readings, depending on where we choose to focus.

Figure 157 is a small pencil and wash drawing. The bags
are grouped and placed against a backdrop that suggests sky. They
are posed as mountains, and the whole spatial arrangement
intensifies the idea of a landscape. This small drawing with its
large-scale forms thus suggests a limitless space.

157. Donald Lent.
Bags as Mountains. 1960.
Graphite pencil with wash.
Collection Yale University Art Gallery,
New Haven, Conn.

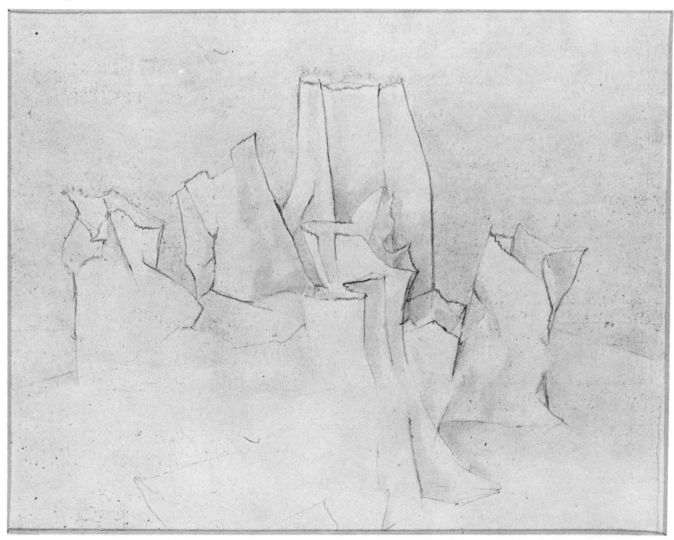

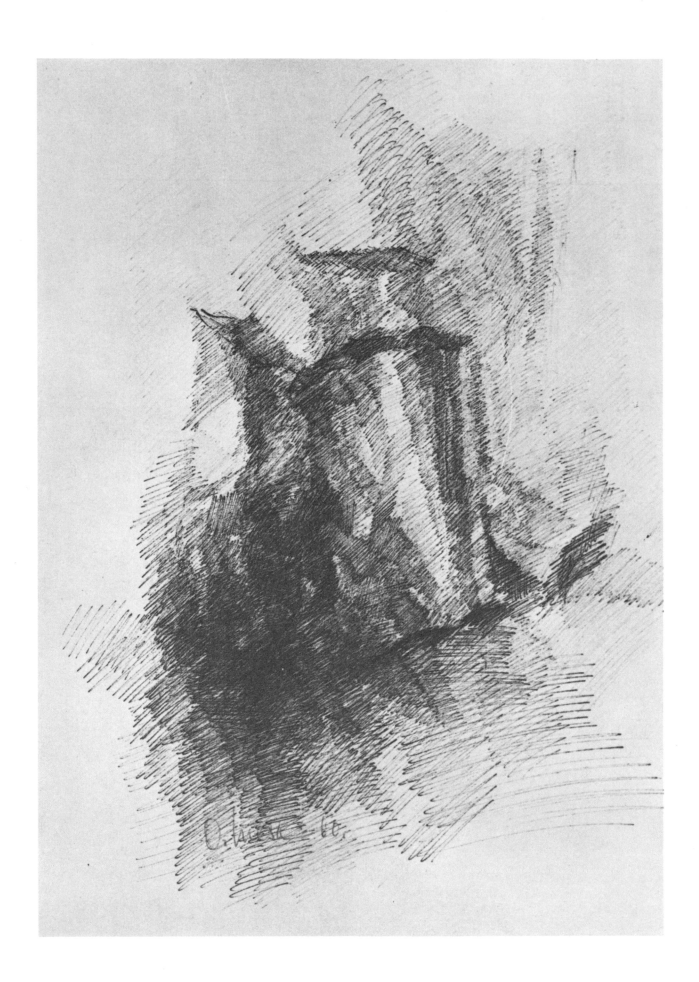

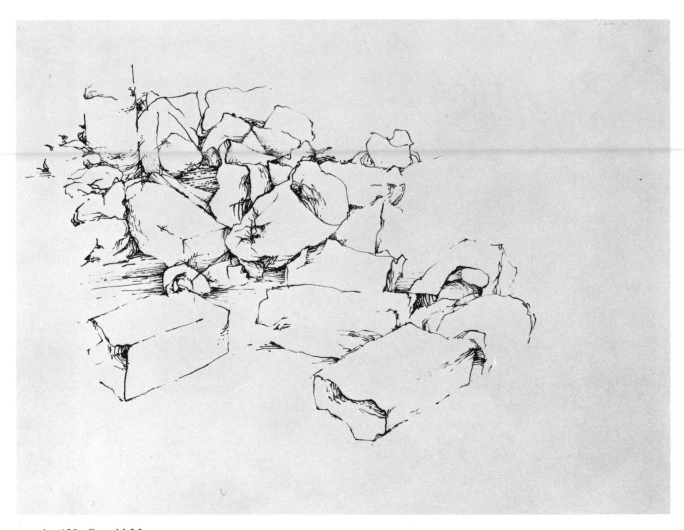

opposite: 158. Oswald Mesa.
Atmospheric Haze. 1962. Pen and ink.
Collection Yale University Art Gallery,
New Haven, Conn.

above: 159. W. R. Farrell.
Bags in Panoramic Space. c. 1958. Pen and ink.
Collection Yale University Art Gallery,
New Haven, Conn.

In Figure 158 we see the forms through an atmosphere created
by a pattern of cross-hatched pen strokes. The subject of the
drawing is this textured light. The forms emerging from the pattern
are focused in the center, and the light seems to melt them
as it spreads down the page.

Figure 159 presents the bags in a panoramic space similar
to that of the shoes in Figures 145 and 146. Individual shapes can
be seen standing, leaning on their neighbors, or lying down.
The forms overlap each other clearly and remain distinct even as
we view the whole arrangement as a coherent space. The ink
lines punctuate the points at which each form touches another.
This emphasis is clear, but it should be noted that the forms
themselves preserve the light weight of the paper bags.

8 Skulls

Having examined the environment, indoors and out, and having studied inanimate and natural forms, we next undertake a study of human and animal structure. It is a good practice to start two projects simultaneously—a study of animal skulls in the studio and experimentation with self-portraits at home. Comparative anatomy is not the goal, but certain basic structural similarities are apparent. The study of skulls is at first approached on a purely diagrammatic, informational basis. What we feel and observe must take account of this structural awareness as the key to interpretation.

Animal Skulls

The obliquely structured angle of the eye socket in animal skulls is obvious, but much more subtle in human skulls. Figure 160 is a diagram of a typical animal skull seen from the top.

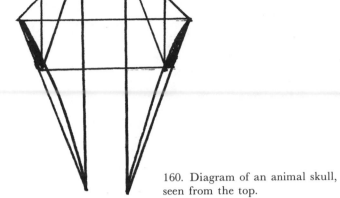

160. Diagram of an animal skull, seen from the top.

The structure housing the eyes moves back at an angle from the center so that the eye has a greater field of vision. What we know about this structure in animals is not easy to observe in a foreshortened drawing. Our personal reactions to the skull form, in terms of drawing, must presuppose this structural knowledge if we want the drawing to be more than an idle sketch. It is conceivable, of course, that the shapes themselves, as perceived by the eye, might inspire a meaningful composition. But, for the most part, awareness of the volumetric structure is the key to using the shapes organically and with authority.

Skulls obviously suggest a death image. When children draw skulls, they invariably produce Halloween symbols with black eyes and nose and outlined teeth. In a studio class of mature students the skulls are objects of horror for some and beautiful sculptured forms for others, according to the individual's frame of reference. One's own reactions to the forms may crystallize or change completely after studying the basic structure, which is stressed purposely at the expense of other values. Several weeks of merely diagraming the skull may elapse before the student is ready to react to the form or to its symbolic content in a personal way.

In this diagraming stage the studio contains the following skulls: horse, cow, dog, pig, goat, deer, rhinoceros, and hippopotamus. During this period proportional characteristics of individual skulls tend to be neglected. The fascination of fitting parts together volumetrically distracts the student's attention from the individual shape of the form to be studied. The choice of media is stressed only after the diagraming stage is completed. As with any other study, one's attitude dictates one's choice.

Student Response

Some students took a clinical attitude, experimenting with individual connections, overlapping planes, and details. Others developed expressionistic studies, and still others examined simple volumetric relationships. The drawings reproduced

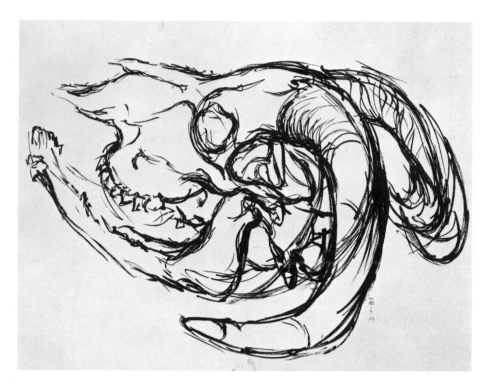

left: 161. Jacqueline Ecklund.
Goat Skull. 1954. Brush and ink.
Collection Yale University
Art Gallery, New Haven, Conn.

below left: 162. John Cohen.
Pressure Points of a Skull.
1954. Ink wash.
Collection Yale University
Art Gallery, New Haven, Conn.

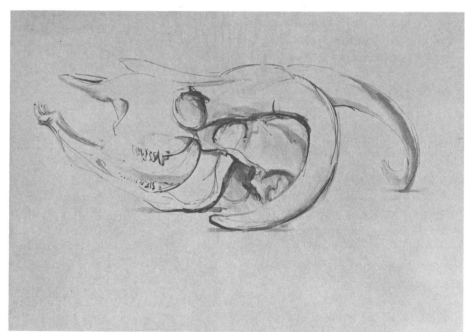

do not include the two weeks of diagraming. This stage was considered to be purely informational. The change back to the values of drawing with attention to spatial considerations and instrumentation required some readjustment.

In Figure 161, a brush-and-ink drawing of a goat skull, curving, interlocking brush strokes pick up speed and spin away into the empty spaces, so that the whole composition is in motion. The forms are carried to the edge of the page and attempt to move out of the restricted stage. The quick movements of the

brush strokes suggest the expression of the jaw, but the speed
of the instrumentation permits us only a fleeting impression.

Although Figure 162 presents almost the same view of the
goat's skull and employs the same medium, the emphasis is
quite different. The form rests in a more comfortable open space,
and the edges of the page are at a safe distance. The laughing
expression of the jaw is underplayed. Here the emphasis
is on intersecting pressure points, especially below the eye.
We work our way back through these intersecting forms that
stress changing weights and pressures.

The protruding open mouth of the skull in Figure 163
is projected at an angle toward the viewer. The emphasis is on
menacing teeth. We do not have a sense of gravity, but
rather the whole form seems to be suspended in air. The
expression of the stretching jaws is alive and threatening.

163. Michael Economos. *Menacing Skull.* 1959. Wash with black and white chalk.
Collection Yale University Art Gallery, New Haven, Conn.

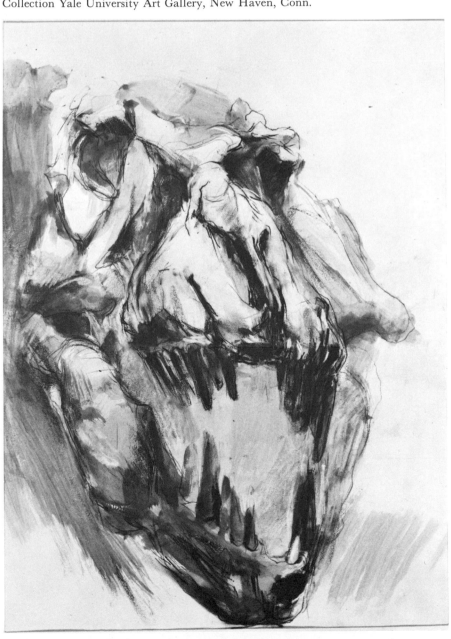

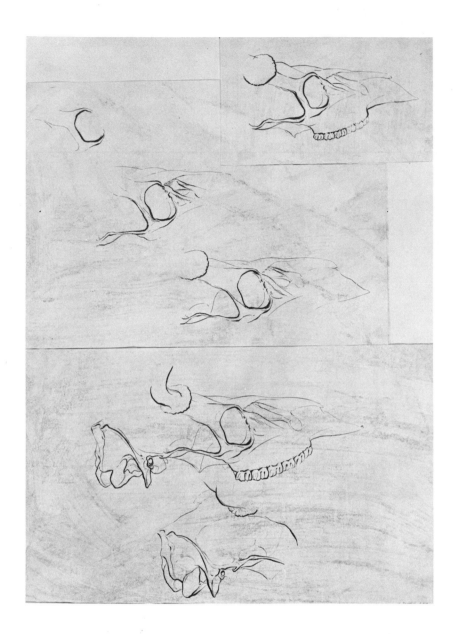

The next illustration is a clinical study—a series of
fine-line drawings of the eye structure of a deer skull (Fig. 164).
The eye socket is seen both as part of the skull and as an
individual form, with emphasis on its projected position
as a container. The beauty of this form can be isolated from
the context of the whole skull.

A back view of a hippopotamus skull is the subject of the
chalk drawing in Figure 165. The initial emphasis is on the
massive weight of the whole form. Overlapping shapes are seen
as elegantly fitted sculptural units. By contrast, the rear
view of a horse's skull (Fig. 166) focuses not on the hulking
weight or gravity of the form, but on an undulating linear
movement created by the continuous brush strokes that depict
interlocking parts. The line itself is emphasized as it moves
through space and flattens the whole form.

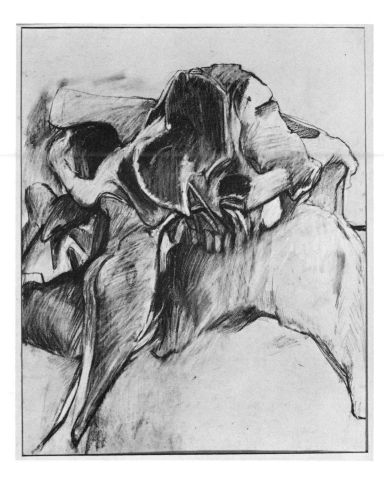

left: 165. Fred Marcellino. *Hippopotamus Skull.*
1962. Pencil with black and white chalk.
Collection Yale University Art Gallery,
New Haven, Conn.

below: 166. Sybil Wilson. *Skull of a Horse.*
1958. Brush and ink.
Collection Yale University Art Gallery,
New Haven, Conn.

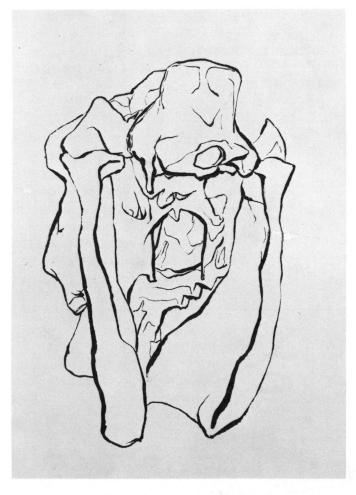

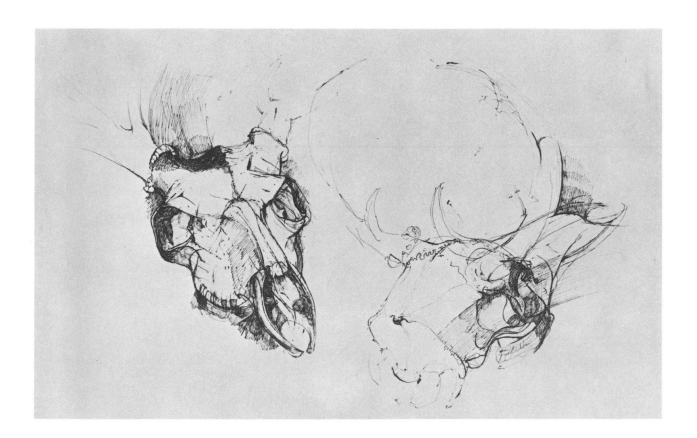

167. Arnold Bittleman.
Sculptural Essence of the Skull.
1955. Pen and ink.
Collection Yale University
Art Gallery, New Haven, Conn.

In Figure 167 the skull (at left) is reduced to its sculptural essence. The forms of the lower jaw and the forehead are not mere descriptions but are transformed into simplified masses. Stress points where one form joins another are in focus and, particularly where the nose meets the eye, are tightly forced. This attitude gives a tautness to the whole form.

The Human Skull

During the period of animal skull study, as was mentioned, the class began self-portraits on their own time. The project was started prior to the introduction of human skulls into the studio. This was done in order to test before-and-after concepts and to prove that what is known determines what is seen. The first portraits, made before study of the human skull, invariably stressed the individual features—mouth, nose, eyes, and ears—at the expense of the skull underneath. The students did not at first realize that the skull's structure is essential to the portrait's likeness.

In the early portraits the relationship of upper skull to lower mask is usually distorted and fullness of the back of the skull often reduced, thus giving an apelike appearance to the drawings. With the introduction of the skull in class, together with the study of live models, the relationships become clearer. In a woodcut by Andreas Vesalius (Fig. 168) the skull at upper left represents the "natural" head; the others are variations on the

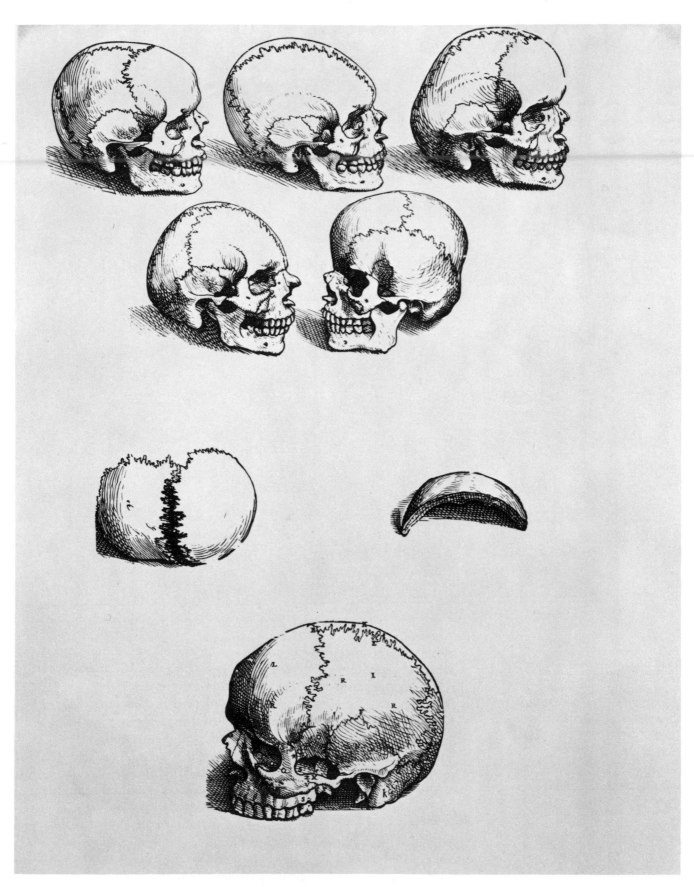

168. Andreas Vesalius (1514–64; Belgian). *Skulls*. Woodcut.

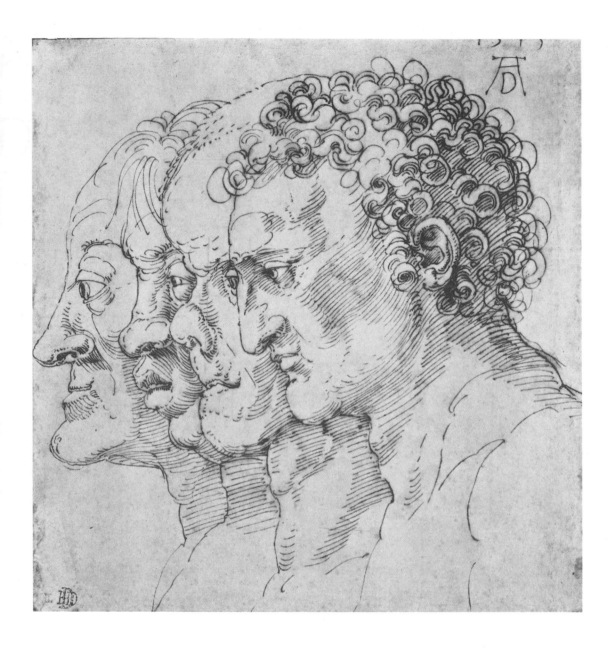

169. Albrecht Dürer
(1471–1528; German).
Four Heads. 1513–15.
Pen and sepia ink, 8¼ × 7⅞".
Nelson Gallery–Atkins Museum,
Kansas City (Nelson Fund).

model. Dürer also presents variations on the shape of the head in
a brutal caricature (Fig. 169). He concentrates on the mask—that
is, the features and their exaggerated relationships.

The structure of the skull is celebrated in Giacometti's
Self-Portrait (Fig. 170), and this structure forms the basis of the
expression. In this work the features are only suggested.
The skull is arched, and the plane from the back of the jaw
to the chin is thrust into space diagonally. The lower portion
of the drawing is empty, and this void creates a frontal plane that
pushes the whole structure back into space.

Features are clearly delineated in Dürer's head of a child
(Fig. 171), yet the structure of the skull is obvious. Eye sockets
are isolated as though a spotlight were focused upon them;
white radiating lines indicate each corner plane and its
connection with the neighboring planes.

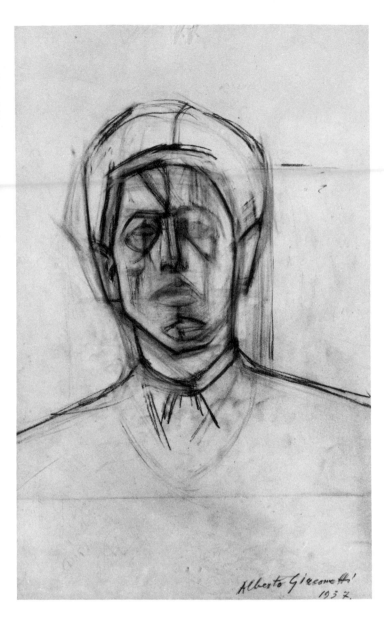

left: 170. Alberto Giacometti
(1901–66; Swiss). *Self-Portrait.* 1937.
Graphite pencil, 19¼ × 12½".
Courtesy Pierre Matisse Gallery, New York.

below: 171. Albrecht Dürer
(1471–1528; German). *Head of a Child.*
Pen and ink heightened with white ink.
Louvre, Paris.

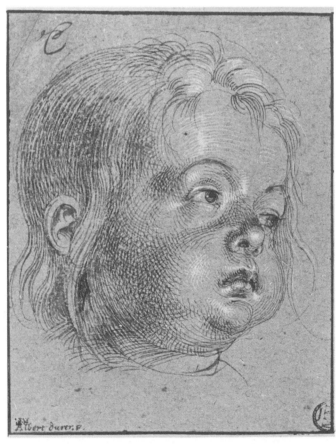

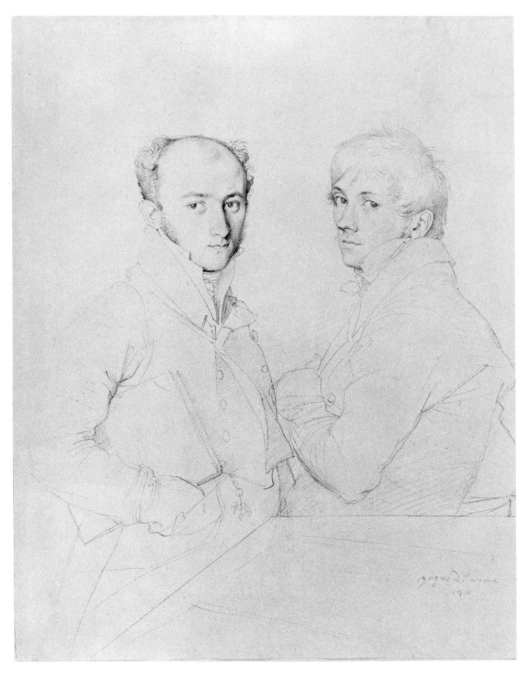

left: 172.
Jean-Auguste-Dominique Ingres
(1780–1867; French).
Portrait of Leclerc and Provost.
1812. Graphite pencil,
$12\frac{3}{8} \times 9\frac{5}{8}''$.
Smith College Museum of Art,
Northampton, Mass.

opposite: 173.
Anthony van Dyck
(1599–1641; Flemish).
Erasmus, detail. Etching.
Collection the author.

Underlying structures are subtly hidden in Ingres' *Portrait of Leclerc and Provost* (Fig. 172). Nevertheless, the simplified head mass becomes a uniquely characteristic shape. The position of the eyes is exaggerated so that they seem to move around the head. Contours of the cheekbones and the arch of the eyes on the figure at left subtly move into space. Both figures recede into the page because of the placement of the table in the foreground. Ingres directs the viewer's eye with light and dark masses: we see first the dark head and then its echo. The soft contour of the coat at far right underplays the impact of its strange shape.

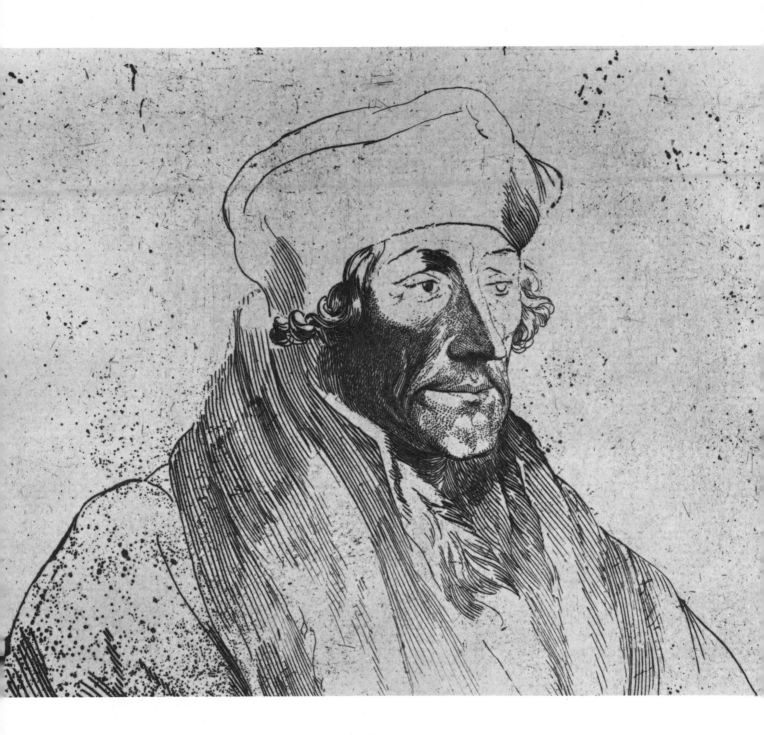

The etching by Anthony van Dyck in Figure 173 was probably
considered unfinished, yet it affords us a unique look at a
master's process of organizing linear strokes to create texture.
Skillful transitions between textures represent hat, nose, cheeks,
eyes, clothing, and hair in a flow of open and closed contours.
The etching features as well a subtle X-ray of the skull—
a virtuoso performance by the artist.

A subtle aura of silence engulfs a portrait of a woman by
Cosme Dumonstier (Pl. 14, p. 177). The mass of the head
has been reduced to a soft-edged egglike shape, which has been
coaxed gradually out of the paper by short, delicate modeling marks.

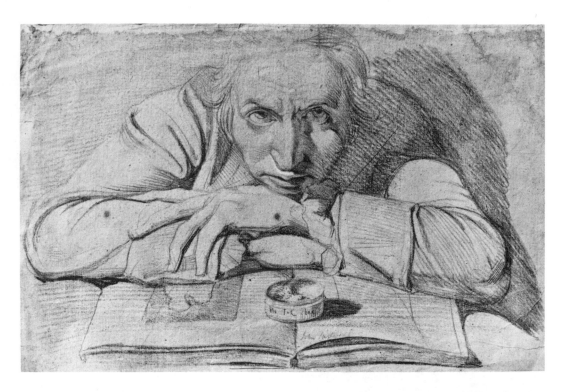

above: 174. Henry Fuseli
(1741–1825; Swiss-English).
Self-Portrait.
Pencil, 12¾ × 19¾″.
National Portrait Gallery, London.

right: 175. Giovanni Bellini(?)
(1430?–1516; Italian).
Head of a Man Looking Up.
Black chalk, 15⅛ × 10⅛″.
British Museum, London.

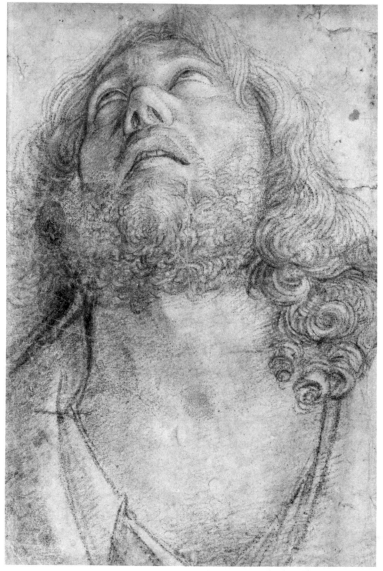

176. Henri Matisse
(1869–1954; French).
Self-Portrait. 1937.
Charcoal, 18¾ × 15⅜".
Baltimore Museum of Art
(Cone Collection).

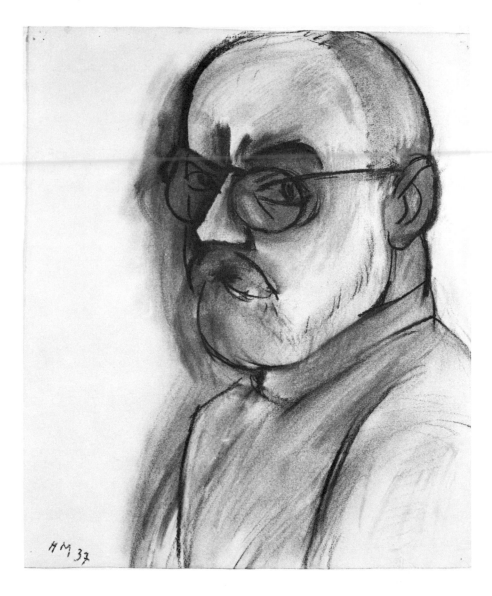

Sharp, clear movements of planes and line-edges add up
to an unusual sense of immediacy in a *Self-Portrait* by Henry Fuseli
(Fig. 174). This technical urgency joins the effect of psychological
penetration that finally dominates the work.

The overall glow of Giovanni Bellini's magificent *Head
of a Mun Looking Up,* obviously in religious ecstacy, can
be only hinted at in reproduction (Fig. 175). This drawing is more
linear, looser and more flowing in its modeling than Dumonstier's
work in Plate 14. In contrast to the Giacometti self-portrait
(Fig. 170), the process of lining up the planes to project them
spatially is hidden. Notice, too, the tiny dots on the lines,
showing that the drawing was pricked for transfer to a panel;
these dots slow down the flow of linear movement.

In a *Self-Portrait,* Matisse uses bold, simple thrusts to push
the head diagonally into space (Fig. 176). At the same time,
he crowds the viewer by bringing the whole image forward. The
apex of the rounded skull is cropped, creating anxiety, for
incomplete shapes make us feel their disconnection.

In *Head of a Woman* by Philip Grausman (Fig. 177) we see again that the artist's vision produces the manner, the technique. A sculptor who works directly in metal, Grausman pulls and stretches the linear thrust in the same way that he hammers and stretches metal. Also following a sculptor's vision, he simplifies the ear form and tucks it into the head so that the two elements become one form.

In pen and ink, Ellsworth Kelly produces a penetrating portrait (Fig. 178). Within a sharply drawn, masklike oval frame, in an asymmetrical arrangement, Kelly explores the character of each feature.

177. Philip Grausman
(b. 1935; American).
Head of a Woman. 1974.
Pencil. Courtesy the artist.

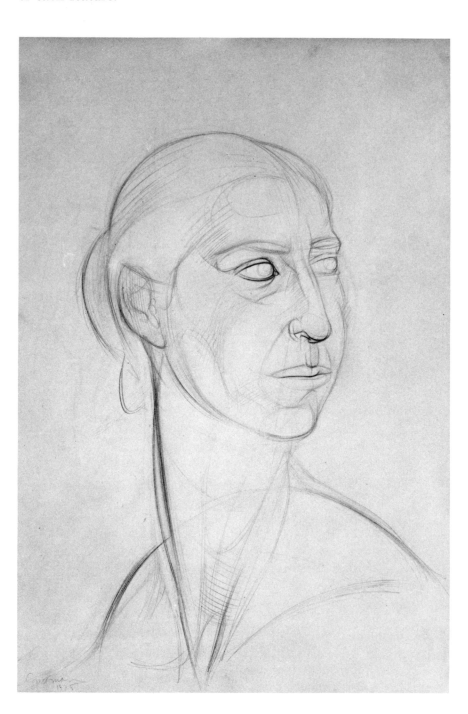

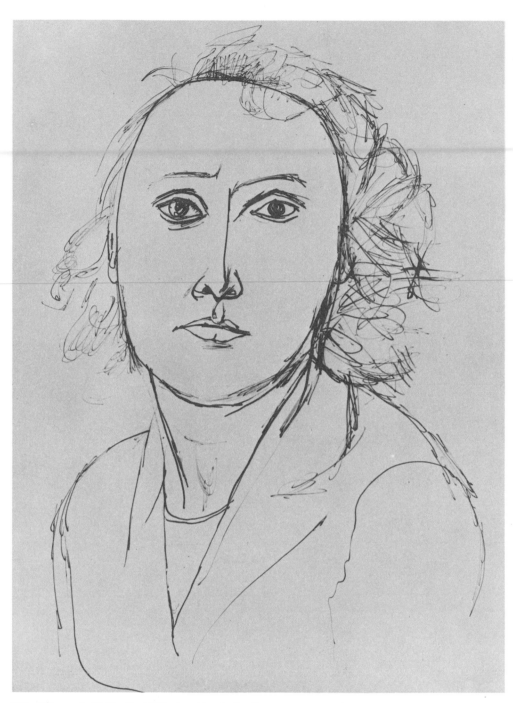

178. Ellsworth Kelly (b. 1923; American). *Pauline.* 1949.
Pen and ink, 18⅞ × 12⅛″. Collection Pierre de Croisset, New York.

Student Response

While Vesalius' exercise (Fig. 168) illustrates the basic
shapes of human skulls, our study in class emphasized the volumetric
projection of masses. The students drew skulls and immediately
invented features to fit into and over them. Reversing this
procedure, they drew from the model and projected the
skull underneath.

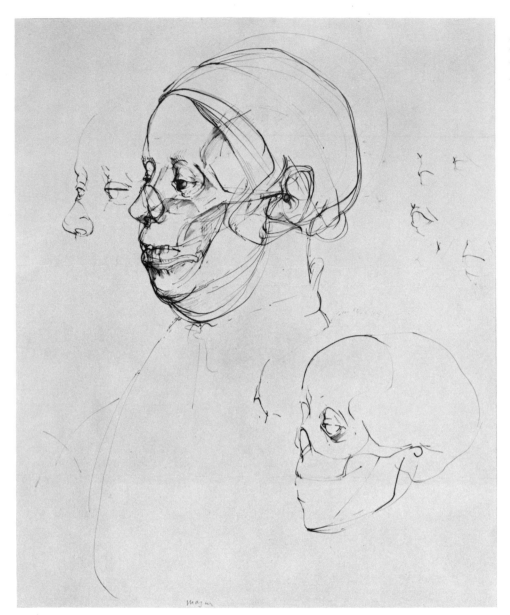

179. Michael Mazur.
Parts of the Skull. 1960.
Graphite pencil.
Collection Yale University
Art Gallery, New Haven, Conn.

Figure 179 is a page of pencil studies made directly from a model. A kind of X-ray vision is the frequent product of this type of study. In the large head the artist attempts to locate particular features in the skull simultaneously, so that we do not feel a sense of overlapping. In other studies on the page the skull and individual parts are examined separately.

Figure 180 is a self-portrait, and in this case the shape of the head is gently attenuated. From the lips down the form cuts back into an extremely foreshortened jawline. The collar of the shirt pulls forward to enhance the effect of the foreshortened chin.

A second self-portrait (Fig. 181) emphasizes the surface movement of the skin. We sense muscles rippling underneath the tightly stretched contours of the mouth. This pulling of the skin is a counterpoint to the boniness of the nose.

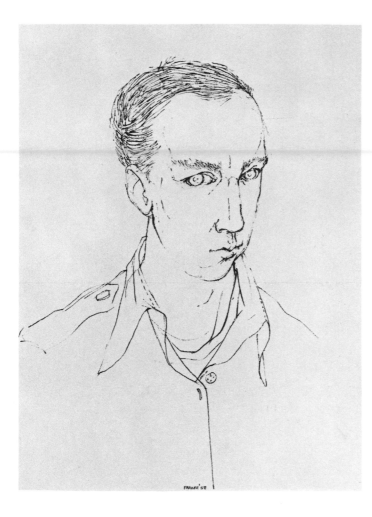

left: 180. John Frazer.
Self-Portrait. 1959. Pen and ink.
Collection Yale University Art Gallery,
New Haven, Conn.

below: 181. Stephen Barbash.
Self-Portrait. 1960. Graphite pencil.
Collection Yale University Art Gallery,
New Haven, Conn.

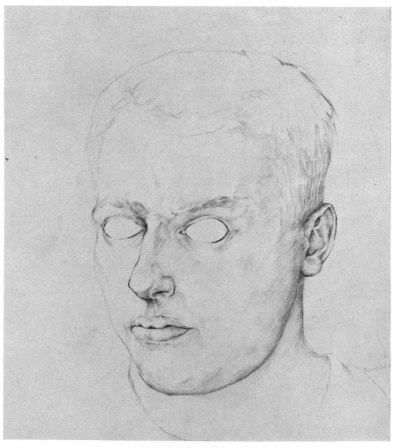

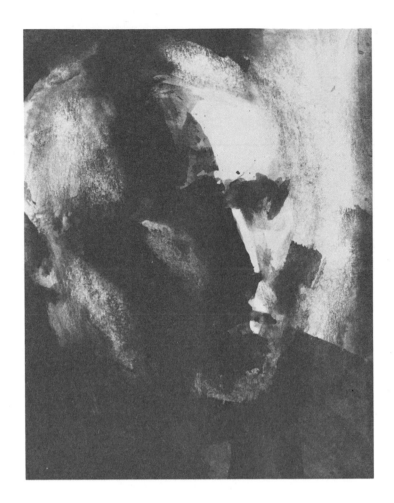

right: 182. Paul Covington.
Self-Portrait. 1961. Wash and chalk.
Collection Yale University
Art Gallery, New Haven, Conn.

below: 183. Peter Milton.
Study from a Model. 1960.
Graphite pencil.
Collection Yale University
Art Gallery, New Haven, Conn.

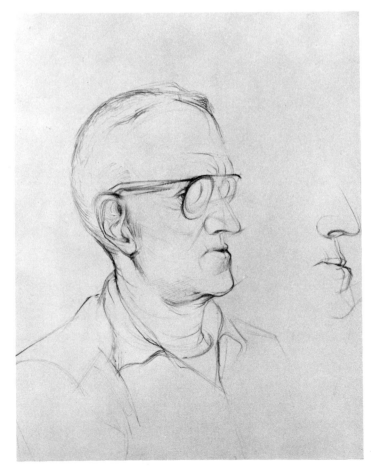

Figure 182 focuses on the planar structure of the head
in directed light. The light is sharp as it hits the major planes
at the right, but it is clearly stated as well in the soft darkness of
the nearest plane. We sense space in front of the form,
freely moving around the head and finally anchored in the soft,
dark stripe at the extreme right of the composition.

Figure 183 was drawn from a model in class. The angle of
the glasses is thrust against the protruding lower jaw and
countered by a flowing ear form. Pencil strokes that define these
opposing masses are used in a liquid manner that is beautiful
in itself.

In Figure 184 the essential compositional device is three ovals
representing (from top to bottom) the head, the slouching back
and the shoulders, and the chair. Within this linear framework,
in a broad and direct attack, the student accounts for the shifting
weights in space.

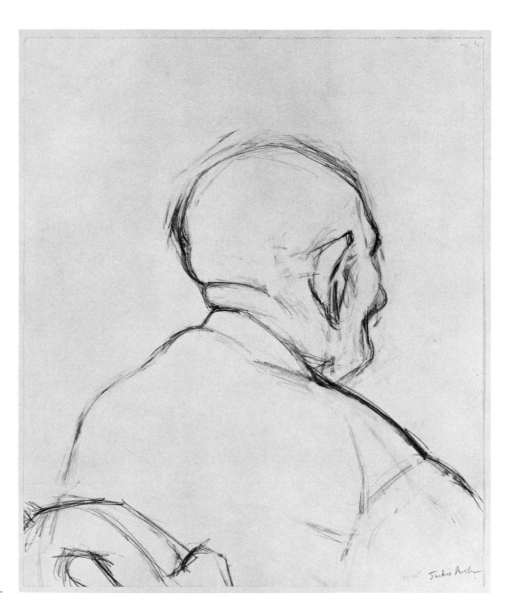

184. Jacqueline Austin.
Back View of a Seated Figure.
1975. Graphite pencil.
Collection Yale University
Art Gallery, New Haven, Conn.

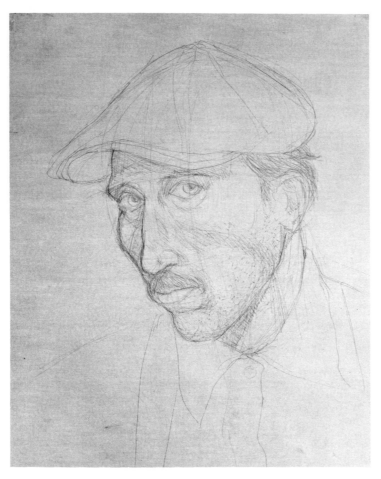

above: 185. John M. Hull.
Self-Portrait in a Hat. 1976. Silverpoint.
Collection Yale University Art Gallery,
New Haven, Conn.

right: 186. Blair Dickinson.
Head Looking Down. 1973. Graphite pencil.
Collection Yale University Art Gallery,
New Haven, Conn.

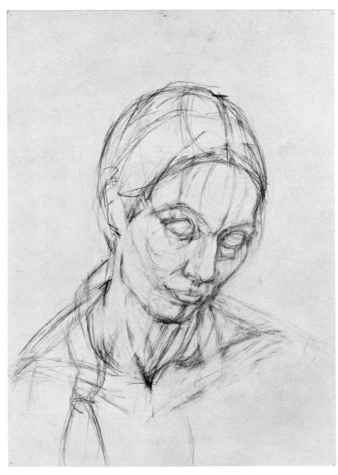

Silverpoint, as already mentioned, is a medium that does not allow for erasure. The artist must build up the forms deftly. In the self-portrait illustrated in Figure 185 the student subtly handles the foreshortening from the eye bridge to cheek and then sharply down to mouth and chin. Head and neck form a single large mass anchored by the underpinning of shirt and shoulders; the linear hat is form-fitted to the skull. Knowing that silverpoint will not permit a dark gouge, the artist has slowly built up the simplified head in light gray lines.

Following Giacometti's example, the author of the drawing in Figure 186 wants to account for all the planar movements. Not satisfied with just the major planes, she tries to trace each secondary plane within the large spherical thrust.

Figure 187 explores a difficult vantage point. With clear contours, the rising cylinder of the neck holds the searching, constructive notes of a view from below. By massing groupings of open-contoured strokes, the artist blocks out turning lips, triangularized nose, and eye sockets that bend in space within a rounded arc.

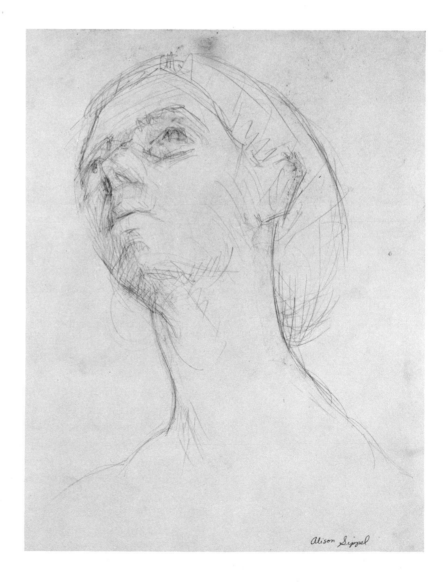

187. Alison Sippel.
Head Looking Up. 1974. Graphite pencil.
Collection Yale University Art Gallery,
New Haven, Conn.

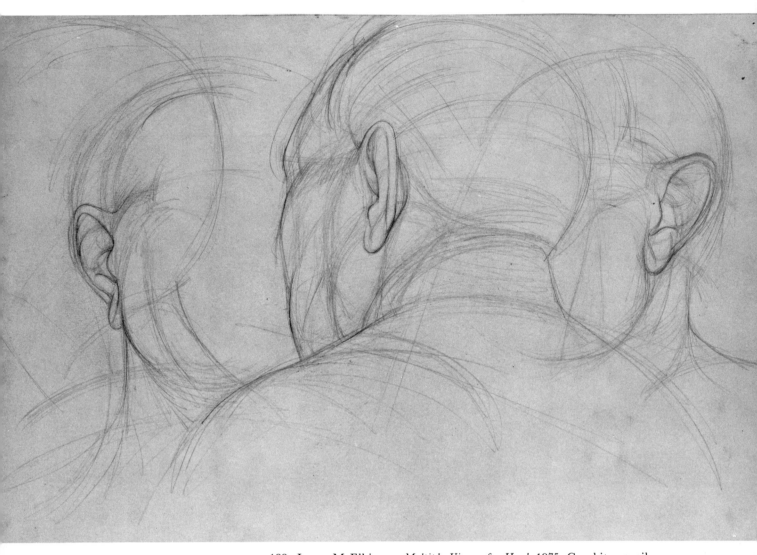

188. James McElhinney. *Multiple Views of a Head.* 1975. Graphite pencil.
Collection Yale University Art Gallery, New Haven, Conn.

Figure 188 presents multiple views of the way ears fit
onto the skull. The artist also examines the character of those
particular ears in what could be called an "ear portrait."
The format of the whole page, with its staging of interlocking
circles, becomes part of the visual experience.

At the end of our studies of individual heads, the students
worked from a clothed model for several weeks and attempted a
number of experiments. They tried to draw the whole figure
in a room without putting features on the head in order to stress
the feeling of a particular space, rather than the structure
of a form. This permits a concentration on the unique shapes of the
whole figure in a given room. In a similar experiment the students
drew only the space of the room around the figure. These
exercises are designed to develop an awareness of spatial
composition in conjunction with individual structures.

9 Animals

An exercise devoted to animals used mounted skeletons to further
the examination of bone structure as a prelude to figure study.
The class worked for several hours in a museum of natural history,
and this automatically restricted the size of the drawings
and the choice of media. However, it also made possible a
spontaneity of drawing performance.

The project emphasized locomotion and articulation, the
character of individual species, and economy of means.
Locomotion and articulation were stressed to give the feeling
that the parts of the total structure fit together and form an
interdependent mechanism that can move in a certain manner.
Character was defined as the peculiar proportions and posture of the
whole animal. It was pointed out that the goal of economy
is *essence,* rather than simplicity of presentation.

Economy is evident in Rembrandt's quill-pen drawing, *Camels*
(Fig. 189), where the structure of the head, which is almost

a caricature, is reduced to its essence. The underlying planes of the skull, projected in two views, are masked by the artist's search for particular facial expressions. This is accomplished in a direct, rather offhand and whimsical manner.

In Figure 190 Delacroix studies the profiled head of a lion with particular emphasis on the structure of the eye socket. This feature is brilliantly diagramed in a fluid penmanship.

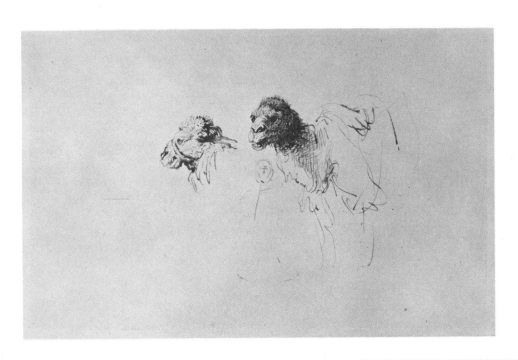

above: 189. Rembrandt
(1606–69; Dutch).
Camels. Quill pen and ink.
Kuntshalle, Bremen
(destroyed in World War II).

right: 190. Eugène Delacroix
(1798–1863; French).
Head of a Lion, Profile.
Pen and ink, $7\frac{7}{8} \times 6\frac{3}{8}''$.
Private collection.

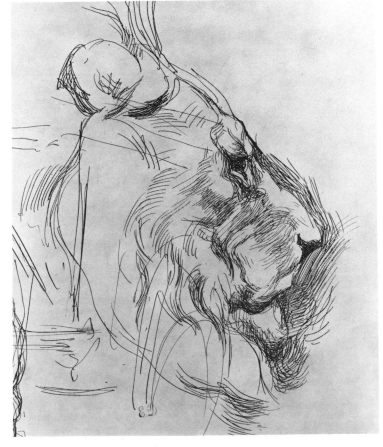

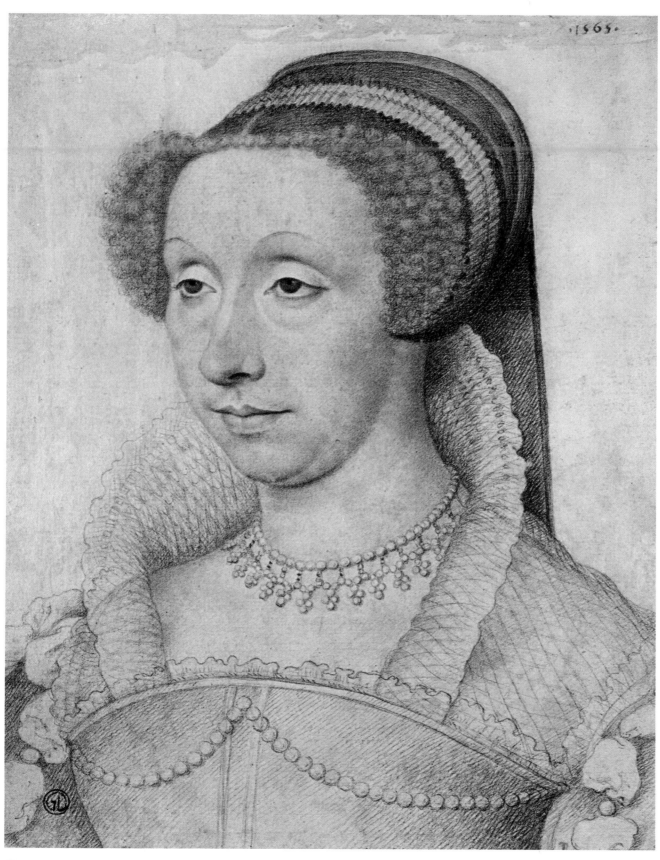

Plate 14. Cosme (?) Dumonstier (d. 1605; French). *Portrait of Françoise de Longwy.* 1565.
Black, red, and brown chalk; 10⅜ × 8″. Collection Wildenstein & Co., Inc., New York.

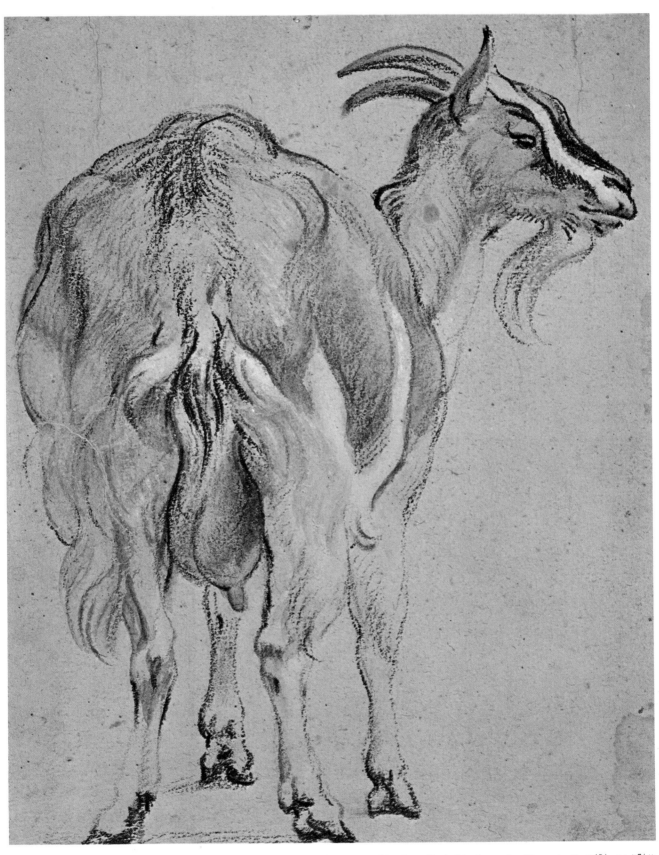

Plate 15. Jacob Jordaens (1593–1678; Flemish). *Goat.* Red, black, and yellow chalk; $9^{15}/_{16} \times 7^{7}/_{8}''$. Yale University Art Gallery, New Haven, Conn. (Everett V. Meeks Fund).

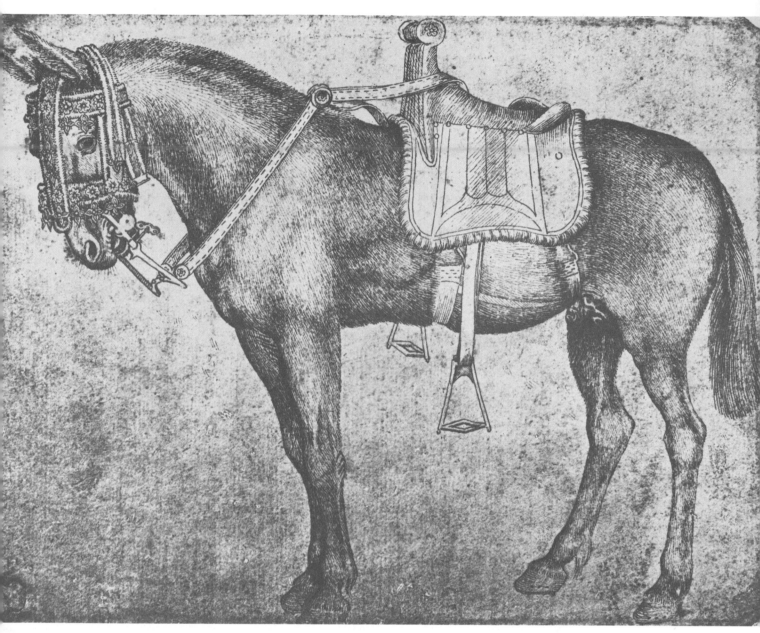

191. Antonio Pisano Pisanello
(1397–1455; Italian).
Mule. Pen and ink.
Louvre, Paris.

Articulation is illustrated in Pisanello's *Mule* (Fig.
191), where the tight, short strokes of the pen serve two
purposes. They show textured hair on the animal's hide—the way
it moves and grows on the surface; and, more important,
in describing the rippling coat they reveal the animal's bone
and muscle structure. The skin is pulled so tight that it
becomes transparent. We are made to see the inner structure
and the outer covering simultaneously.

Hokusai's didactic diagrams of projected volumes illustrate a timeless lesson in seeing geometric substructure (Fig. 192). The method could still be used today, although without Hokusai's graphic elegance.

A sense of locomotion is brilliantly portrayed in a notebook sketch by Toulouse-Lautrec (Fig. 193). The individual shapes of each part of the horse—head, neck, torso, and widespread legs—are interlocked to give us an instantaneous transcription of a unique posture.

Jacob Jordaens' *Goat* (Pl. 15, p. 178) has been drawn in chalk with touches of wash, probably accomplished by deftly wetting the chalk. The humorous rear view, the animal's stance, the articulation of the joints, and the placement of the form so that it fills most of the space all contribute to a brilliant characterization. Notice, too, the tonal range of the black chalk, from light, gentle, open-contoured strokes along the right front leg to the dark punctuations in the head and hoofs. The darks along the bottom also serve to anchor the form in the absence of a drawn ground plane.

The character of Cranach's *Wild Boar* (Fig. 194) is expressed in the menacing silhouette of a dark shape against a white background, coupled with the triumphant pose and open jaws. This creature may be seen as an invention of horror or of humor (or a combination of the two), depending on one's interpretation. The dashing white lines of the fur suggest speed, but the dominant shape of the animal suspends this action.

192. Katsushika Hokusai (1760–1849; Japanese). Drawings from *Quick Lesson in Simplified Drawing*. 1812. Brush and ink. Museum of Fine Arts, Boston (gift of William Sturgis Bigelow).

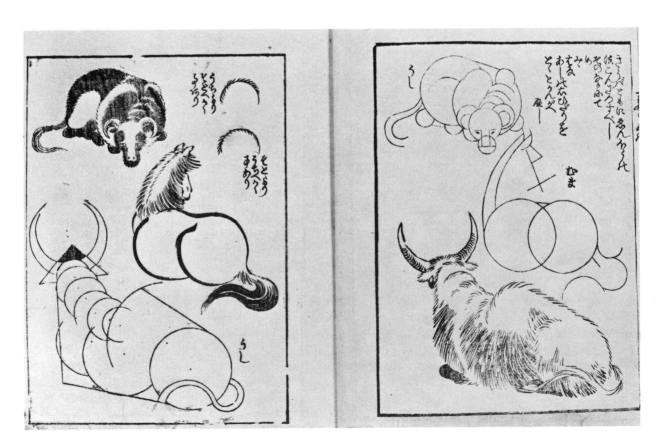

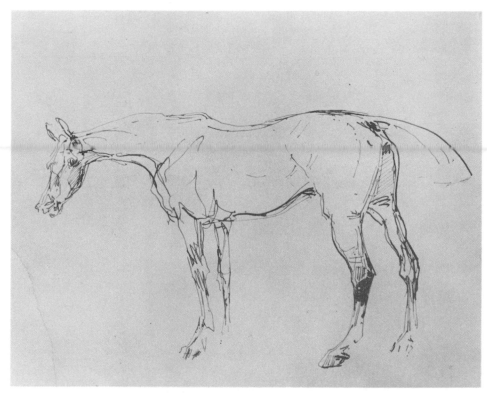

above: 193. Henri de Toulouse-Lautrec (1864–1901; French).
Standing Horse. Before 1880. Pen and ink, $4\frac{1}{8} \times 7\frac{1}{4}''$.
Print Department, Boston Public Library.

below: 194. Lucas Cranach the Elder (1472–1553; German).
Wild Boar Facing Left. Pen and ink with watercolor, $6\frac{3}{4} \times 10''$.
Kupferstichkabinett, Dresden.

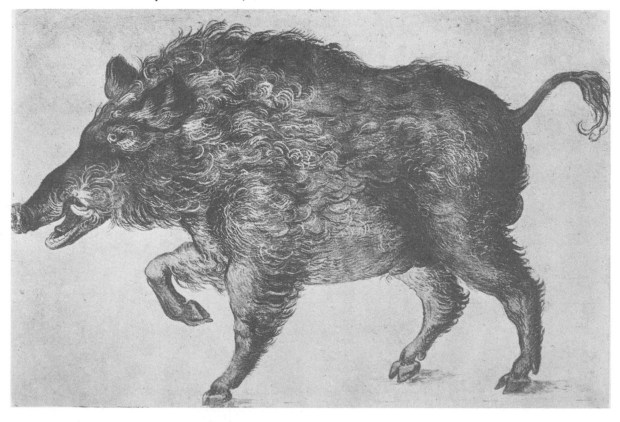

below: 195. *Elephant,* Persian drawing. Late 15th–early 16th century. Museum of Fine Arts, Boston (Golonbew Collection).

bottom: 196. Rembrandt (1606–69; Dutch). *Elephant.* c. 1637. Black chalk, 6 x 9″. British Museum, London.

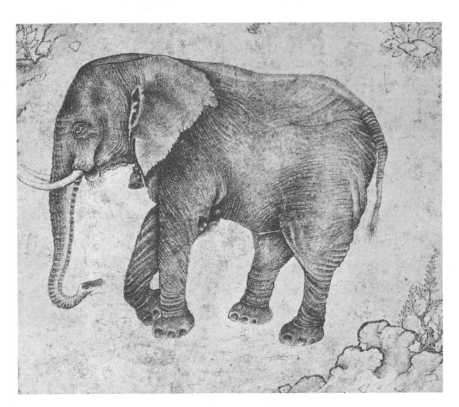

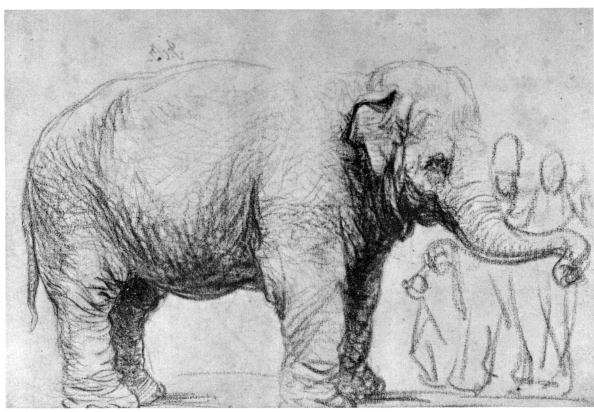

The Persian drawing in Figure 195 seems, at first glance, to be similar to Pisanello's rendering of a mule's skin (Fig. 191), but in the latter the surface suggests foreshortening, gravity, bone and muscle. The Persian drawing, on the other hand, presents the skin as a beautifully designed arabesque of drapery. This does not imply praise or criticism of either drawing. It merely points out that each culture sets its own values and its own frame of reference.

Rembrandt's *Elephant* (Fig. 196), with its comical, awkward hulk, might be mistaken for a portrait of a man in an elephant suit. The tensions and articulation of the skin are generalized to preserve the characterization, which is the point of the drawing. This attitude toward the elephant is in keeping with Rembrandt's total vision as an artist. Each work of art is produced by a form attitude, which in turn is produced by a larger artistic culture.

A master of many graphic languages, Anthony van Dyck seems to be dissecting the cows in this study sheet (Fig. 197). He peels away the outer layer of flesh, muscle, and bone, yet he still captures the stance, posture, and proportion of the cows.

197. Anthony van Dyck (1599–1641; Flemish).
A Group of Cows. Pen and brown ink, $12\frac{3}{4} \times 20\frac{5}{8}''$.
Devonshire Collection, Chatsworth
(reproduced by permission of the Duke of Devonshire and the Trustees of the Chatsworth Settlement).

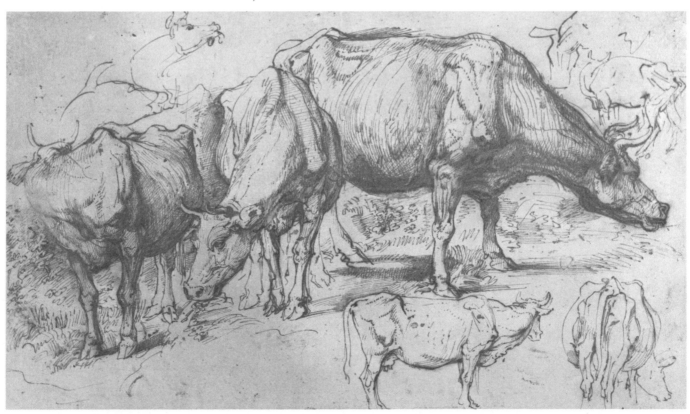

Student Response

Although articulation, locomotion, character, and economy
of means are the broadly defined goals, it is the student's
responsibility to pinpoint individual interest, for the ultimate end,
as we have constantly reiterated, is the development of a
personal attitude.

In the pencil drawing in Figure 198 the organization of
the whole page is considered, as is each animal's characteristic
posture and articulation. The animals move as a group, and
our focus is directed from one to another, yet as we pause to
examine each one, we sense its individual locomotive mechanism.

The conté drawing in Figure 199 was done at a zoo,
and it owes an obvious debt to Rembrandt's elephant studies
(Fig. 196). A student's response to the work of the masters is
at least as important as working from nature, for masterworks
permit us to see nature in a new way. In the large figure at left
the weight, gravity, and stance of the elephant is expressed
in the tension between the accented half circle, representing
the body, and the contoured volume of the front leg. This
junction is the focus of the work.

An angle of vision that places all four extremities in a tilted
projection gives added life to the drawing in Figure 200.
Without this volumetric exaggeration the detailed information and
the carefully articulated joints are merely descriptive.

198. Patricia Coughlin. *Study of Animals.* 1960. Graphite pencil.
Collection Yale University Art Gallery, New Haven, Conn.

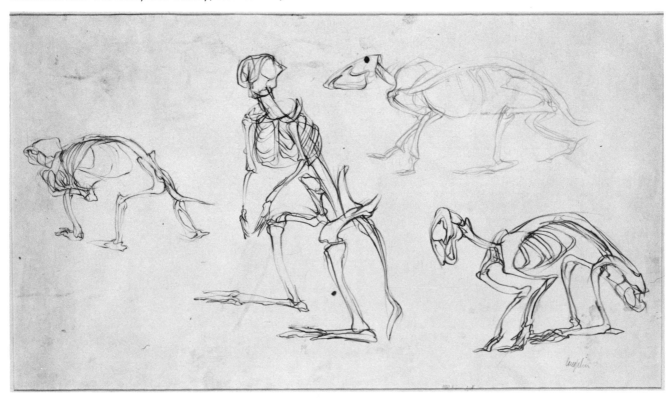

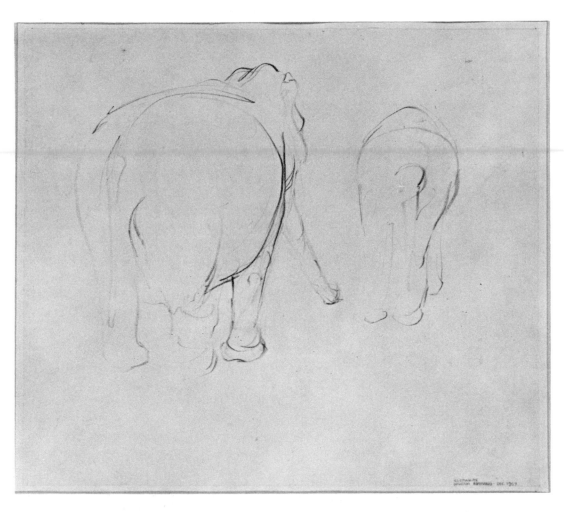

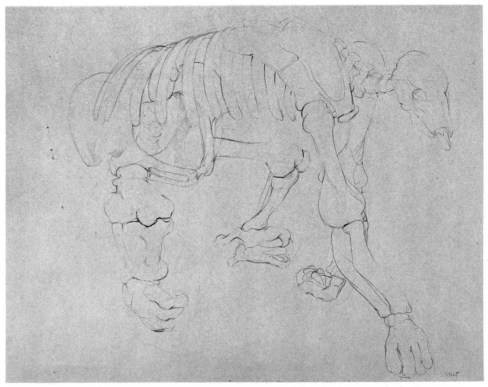

above: 199. William Reimann.
Elephants. 1957. Conté crayon.
Collection Yale University
Art Gallery,
New Haven, Conn.

left: 200. Elizabeth Matz.
Skeleton of a Ground Sloth.
1959. Conté crayon.
Collection Yale University
Art Gallery, New Haven, Conn.

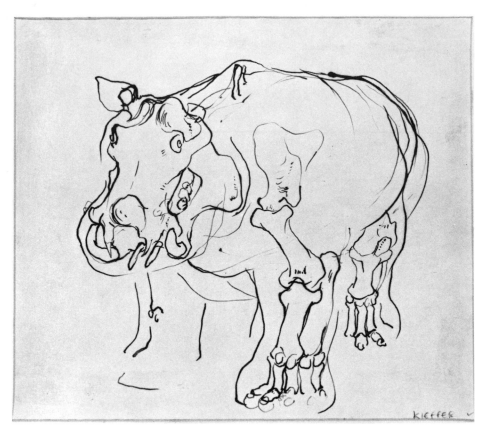

left: 201. Stephanie Kieffer.
Hippopotamus. 1957. Pen and ink.
Collection Yale University
Art Gallery, New Haven, Conn.

below: 202. Susan Draper.
Skeleton of a Dinosaur. 1956.
Felt-tipped pen.
Collection Yale University
Art Gallery, New Haven, Conn.

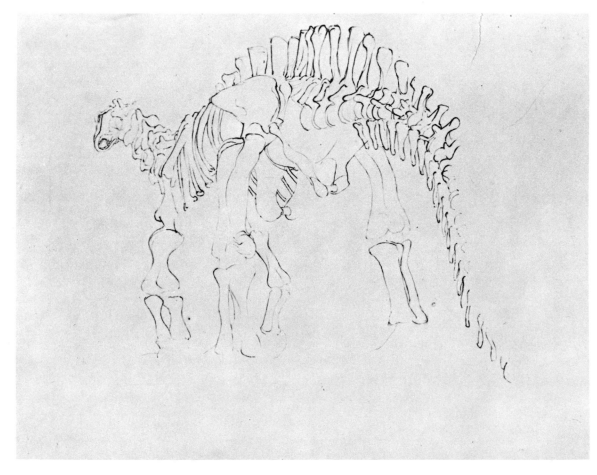

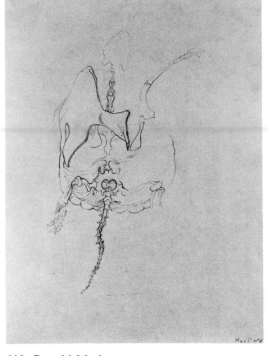

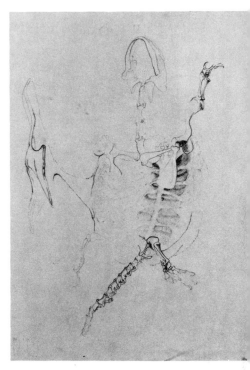

203. Ronald Markman.
Studies of a Turtle. 1956.
Graphite pencil.
Collection Yale University
Art Gallery, New Haven, Conn.

The hippopotamus in Figure 201 stands, in a fixed, dumb
trance, directly in the center of the drawing. The animal is
quickly sketched with an X-ray vision, but, nevertheless,
the shapes of the head, body, and feet are clearly represented
and readable.

In Figure 202 the skeleton of a dinosaur inspired an interest
in the rhythmic intervals of the spinal column. The line,
which in turn darkens and disappears with the alternating pressures
of the pen, carries us along as it moves between bone shapes
and interspace. This instrumentation, with its undulating
movement, directs us on our visual journey and becomes, in a
sense, more important than the subject.

Figure 203 consists of three studies of one turtle, drawn
on separate pages and matted together. Each study focuses
on a separate aspect of the form, unlike a scientific illustration
which would concentrate on a clear and equal description
of all parts from one point of view. Here the forms are composed
and stressed by choice, and they therefore take on a visual life.

The portrait head of a warthog takes up most of the space in Figure 204. The forms of the upper jaw, with its protuberant nostrils and teeth, are darkened and pulled forward in an exaggerated perspective. The instrumentation distorts and stretches these threatening forms in an elastic tension. In this respect it is similar to that in some of the studies of roots in Chapter 6. These tensely drawn forms italicize the author's attitude; they are not simply a technical device.

204. Elton Robinson. *Head of a Warthog.* 1956. Charcoal pencil. Collection Yale University Art Gallery, New Haven, Conn.

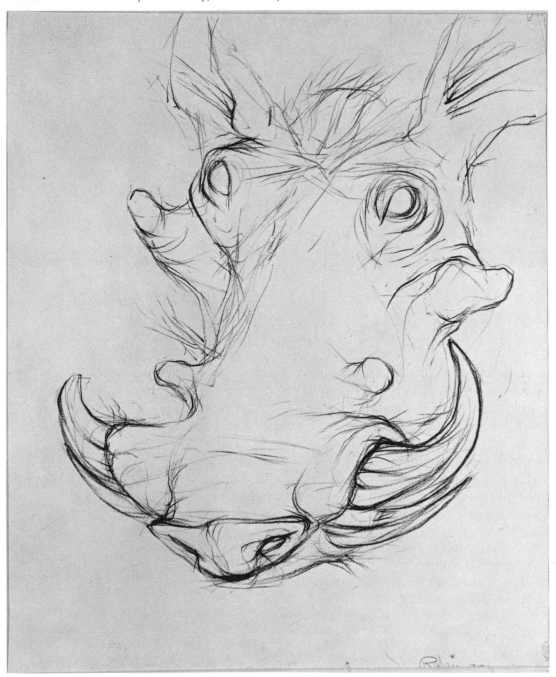

10 *Introduction to the Figure*

Although many of the celebrated painters and sculptors of the recent past and the present deal with the figure, it is no longer the focal subject of art. The academies of the past, reflecting the official artistic cultures of their time, considered the figure to be the center of interest. Each academy represented a different ideal and featured its own style of presentation.

With the proliferation of art reproductions—one of the results of the technological revolution—we have access to many cultural heritages, and we can study and make use of their special form vocabularies. We have learned, in short, to regard nature, including the human body, in a new light. Furthermore, we have learned to see our own Western tradition in terms of fresh concepts.

Western figure drawing centers on gravity—volumes and weights adjusting themselves to a solid floor plane seen in perspective. Within this framework, individual masters have re-created the human figure in a variety of ways, each according to a particular vision. It is through study of these interpretations

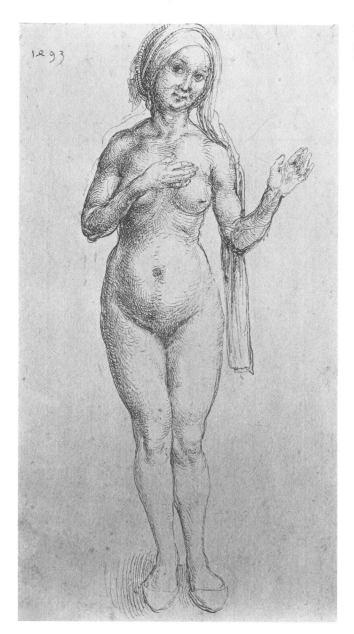

205. Albrecht Dürer (1471–1528; German).
Nude Woman. 1493. Pen and ink, $10\frac{3}{4} \times 5\frac{7}{8}''$.
Musée Bonnat, Bayonne.

that we begin to formulate our own preferences and attitudes
in seeing and, ultimately, in drawing.

In a page from a notebook by Pisanello (Pl. 16, p. 211),
a group of figural sketches has been composed into a beautifully
balanced arrangement. The two studies at lower left repeat
the investigation seen in Figure 191, this time in terms of the human
body. As in the drawing of the mule, the skin has been rendered
transparent, so that the artist may test his knowledge of what it
conceals. The figure at far right displays a different attitude:
it concentrates on the rounded, sculptural masses of the form.

Dürer's *Nude Woman* (Fig. 205) presents the figure
from a rather unusual point of view: the navel is set at eye level.
All the forms below the navel are seen in a foreshortened
downward perspective, and these foreshortened volumes are

reduced to their simplest forms. The stomach protrudes like a
sphere, while the cylindrical forms of the legs move down
and back from the frontal plane of the page. The musculature
of the legs is reduced to a minimum in order to accent further
the downward thrust. Sharp, contoured edges define the
junctures of thigh and knee, and the entire weight of the figure
is thrown on these tension-filled joints. All the forms above
the navel are seen from a low vantage point. The head in
particular looks down at us, reinforcing the logic of the fixed eye
level. Volumes are strongly modeled at the point where one
form intersects another, and the line continually changes from
contour to modeling and back again.

The foreshortening is severe in Degas' *Dancer* (Fig. 206),
for the artist pushes the head far behind the fan. This becomes
obvious when one covers the fan. The dancer's head is then seen
as sharply back from the right arm. Below the fan the arms establish
the middle space of the page. The feet, which are the most
clearly outlined forms, define the frontal plane, while setting
up a strong gravitational pull. The sense of foreshortening
is intensified by a reverse reading—from feet to arms to head—
which further illustrates how far back in space the head is placed.

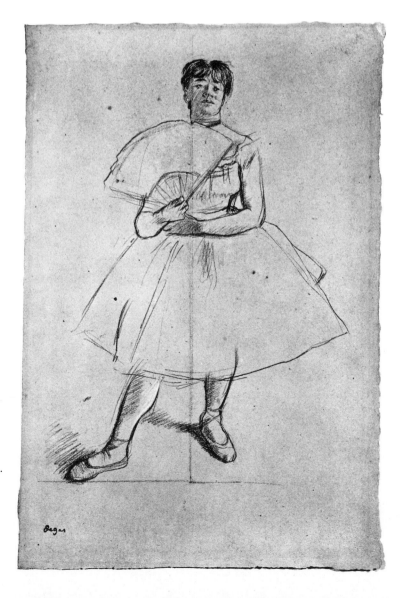

206. Edgar Degas (1834–1917; French).
Dancer. 1878–80. Chalk, 19¼ × 12⅝″.
Museum Boymans–van Beuningen,
Rotterdam.

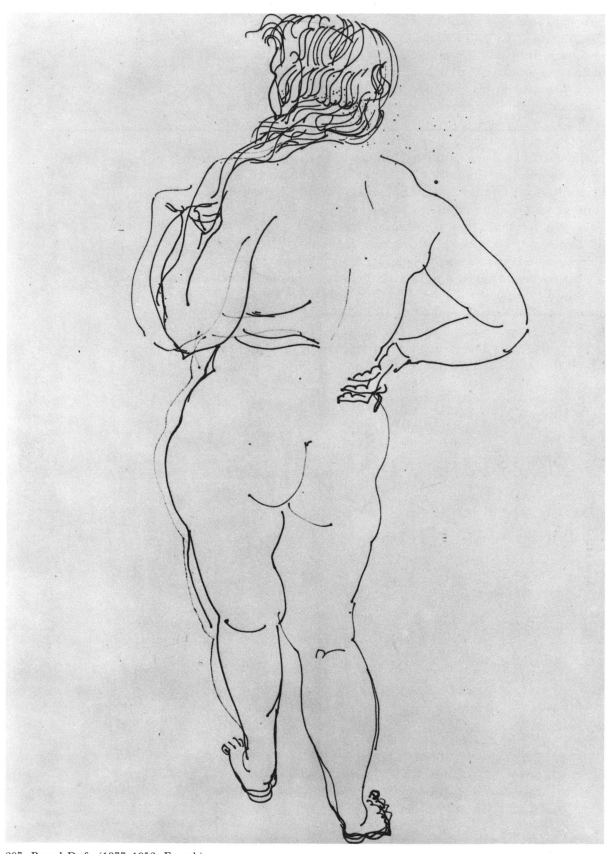

207. Raoul Dufy (1877–1953; French).
Back View of a Nude. Pen and ink.
Courtesy Galerie Louis Carré, Paris.

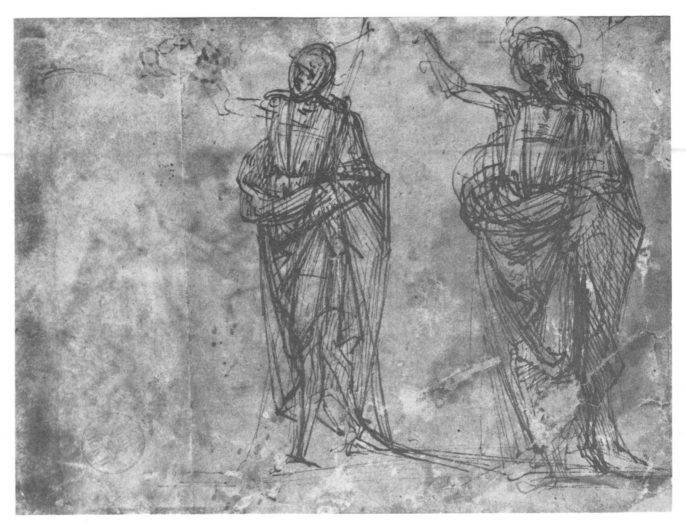

208. Fra Bartolommeo della Porta
(1475–1517; Italian).
Two Studies of John the Baptist.
Pen and ink. Kunsthalle, Hamburg.

Dufy's pen drawing, *Back View of a Nude* (Fig. 207),
is a virtuoso performance in the use of line, which is employed here
to contain dramatic shifts of weight. The posture of the figure
is more exaggerated than in Dürer's nude. Dufy persuades us that
line can express weight without modeling, or more precisely,
that line may be another kind of modeling. He makes rapid
corrections in contour in this swiftly executed but convincing study.

Fra Bartolommeo's *Two Studies of John the Baptist* (Fig. 208)
is, like the previous illustration, basically a line drawing.
In this work, however, the line is not continuous but dissolves in
mid-air to become a faint thread or a point in the suggested
interaction of figure and space. The lines representing drapery
encircle the forms and, at the same time, imply space around the
figures. Especially noteworthy are the postures of the two figures.
In the study at the right the swing from hip to floor suggests
weight, even as the line all but disappears.

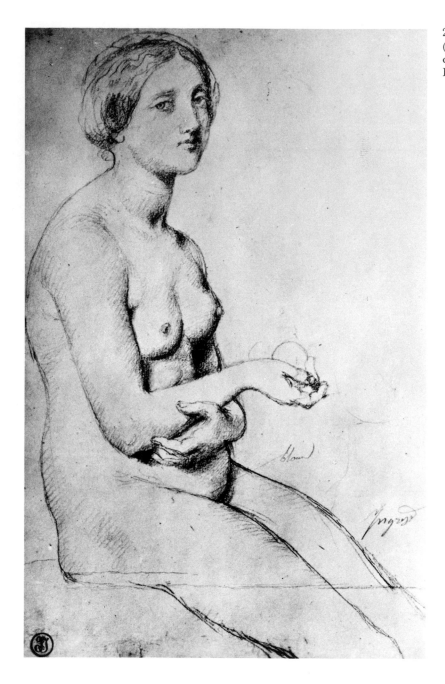

209. Jean-Auguste-Dominique Ingres (1780–1867; French). *Seated Female Nude.* c. 1841–67. Graphite pencil, $12\frac{7}{16} \times 8''$. Baltimore Museum of Art (Cone Collection).

In Ingres' *Seated Female Nude* (Fig. 209) the volume of the model's back is described by a soft, contoured pencil line. The back, full and gently arching, is countered by the thrust of the protuberant stomach. Subtle shading emphasizes the curve of the abdomen, thus providing a shift of weight from the line of the back. Other dark areas separate the arms from the torso; the shading against the back arm defines the contour, hidden by the arms, that joins the line of the abdomen. The pressure caused by the weight of the whole figure is centered in the buttocks, which rest on a surface that is implied but not actually visible, and a delicate line across the legs further describes this unseen resting place.

In Baccio Bandinelli's *Two Male Nudes* (Fig. 210) we are concerned, as in all the drawings here, with the exaggerated posture of the figure. This drawing, however, does not stress simplified sculptural volume. Instead, the emphasis is on a surface arabesque of muscles as they intertwine and overlap. These surface rhythms, balanced and counterbalanced, take on a life of their own beyond muscular description.

Exaggeration is carried even further in a drawing of *The Three Graces* by Jacopo Pontormo (Pl. 17, p. 212). In this drawing Pontormo, influenced by Dürer, takes a satirical view

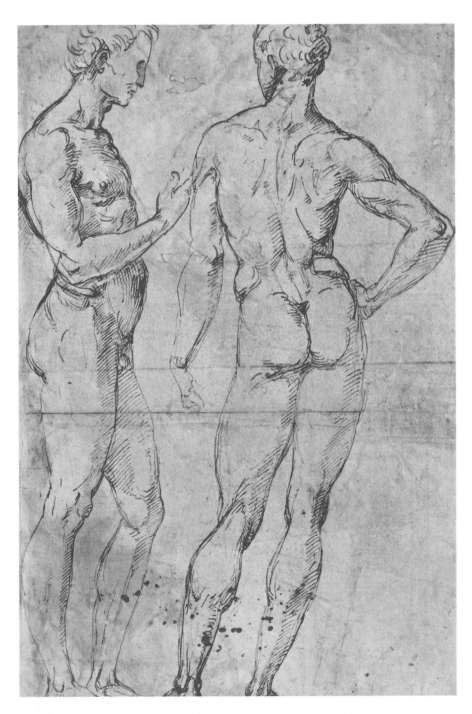

210. Baccio Bandinelli (1493–1560; Italian). *Two Male Nudes.* c. 1560. Pen and ink. Albertina, Vienna.

of a classical theme, which in traditional art implied a symmetrical harmony of smoothly poised forms. Where the pose was graceful, Pontormo makes his version awkward; where articulation of limbs was even and predictable, he renders the joints heavy; where rhythms should be smooth, he disrupts the surface. Proportion, harmony, and symmetry are dictated not by conventions, but by personal vision.

In Degas' charcoal sketch (Fig. 211) the figure is beautifully enclosed in the space of the page, or, to put it another way, the page itself seems to hold the figure rather than remaining a neutral backdrop. The background space is a partner. The main shapes of the figure are boldly set, with contours varying from dark and heavy to soft and open. The fusion of form and surrounding space also houses another event: a slowly constructed

211. Edgar Degas (1834–1917; French).
Woman Drying Her Hair. c. 1890. Charcoal, $23\frac{1}{2} \times 26\frac{3}{4}''$.
Courtesy Paul Rosenberg & Co., New York.

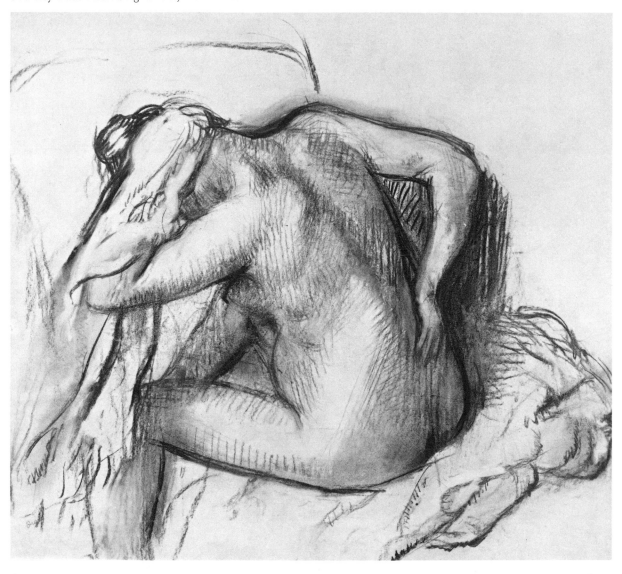

212. Ivan Le Lorraine Albright
(b. 1897; American). *Three Love Birds.*
1931. Charcoal on canvas, 7′ × 3′8″.
Courtesy the artist.

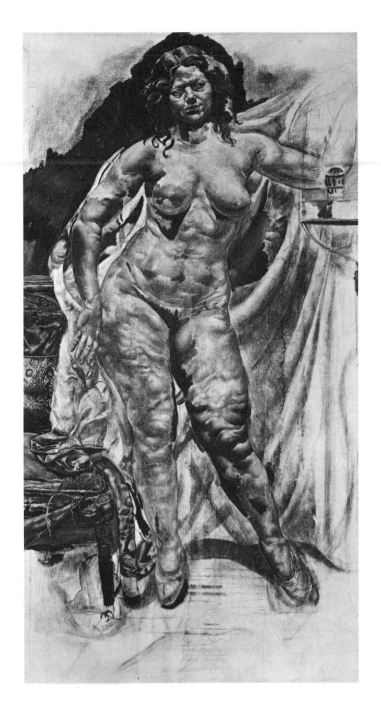

search for the gently pulling forms of the back. We are gradually
directed to see the back forms being coaxed out of the housing.

A distinct contrast in the attitude toward body surface appears
in the following two examples. In Ivan Albright's *Three Love Birds*
(Fig. 212) the subject, decidedly, is flesh. The skeletal
frame is barely suggested. Here the supple, modulated form of
Ingres' nude (Fig. 209) has vanished. Instead, Albright wraps
his figure in three-dimensional knots of rippling, ropelike
forms, accented with ornamental flesh patterns. This treatment
is invented to underline the artist's portrayal of flesh as a
symbol of decay.

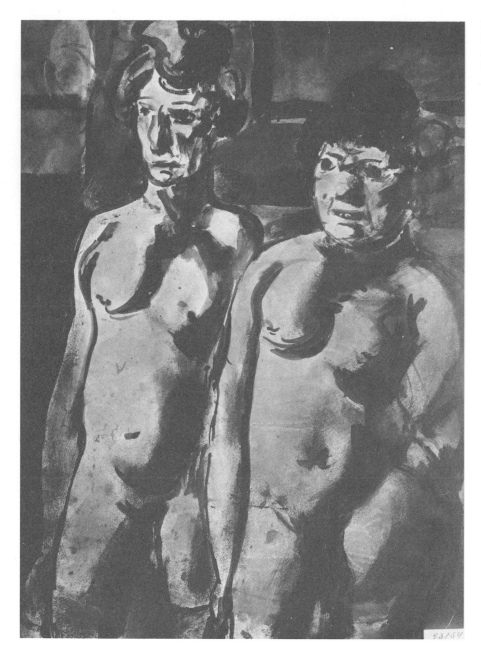

213. Georges Rouault
(1871–1958; French).
Filles. c. 1906. Watercolor.
Courtesy Galerie Bernheim-Jeune, Paris.

In Georges Rouault's *Filles* (Fig. 213) flesh takes the form
of simplified sculptural masses that shift dramatically from
hip to torso to breast to shoulder. The dominant impression
in this drawing is, of course, the strong message implicit in the
subject, and this message is dramatized by the artist's structuring
of the forms and of the whole composition. The figures dominate
the space; they are compressed and stand in a frontal plane
with light savagely raked across them. All of these devices
intensify the form and give visual life to the message.

Villon's nude (Fig. 214) reminds one of a sculptor's armature
with bundles of wire mapping out the tensions between masses.
Each mass seems to stretch independently, yet all move in
complementary shifts of weight.

The total environment is the subject of Giacometti's *Nude in a Room* (Fig. 215). The space of the room is investigated both around and through the figure. We are led into the room by lines along the bottom, and these lines turn sharply to make a ruglike floor plane below the feet, which acts as a pedestal for the figure. The room is dissected by transparent objects and interspaces, and the figure, the clearest object in the composition, interacts with the objects and the space. All elements are woven together and rotate constantly, yet their relationships are maintained by the seemingly casual sketched lines.

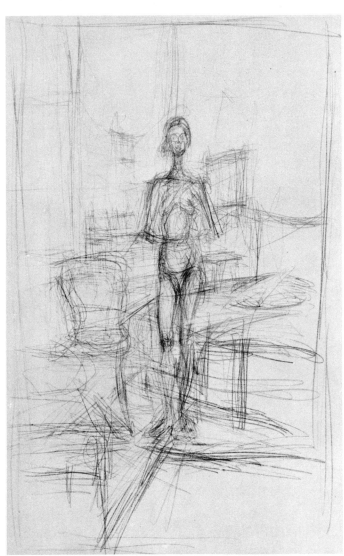

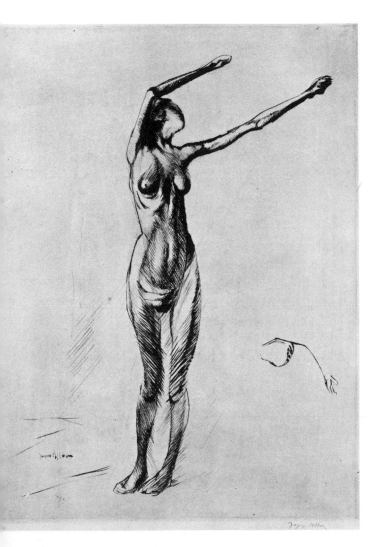

left: 214. Jacques Villon
(1875–1963; French).
Standing Nude with Arms in the Air. 1909.
Drypoint, $21\frac{5}{8} \times 16\frac{11}{16}''$.
Museum of Fine Arts, Boston
(Lee M. Friedman Fund).

above: 215. Alberto Giacometti (1901–66; Swiss).
Nude in a Room. Pencil.
Courtesy Galerie Maeght, Paris.

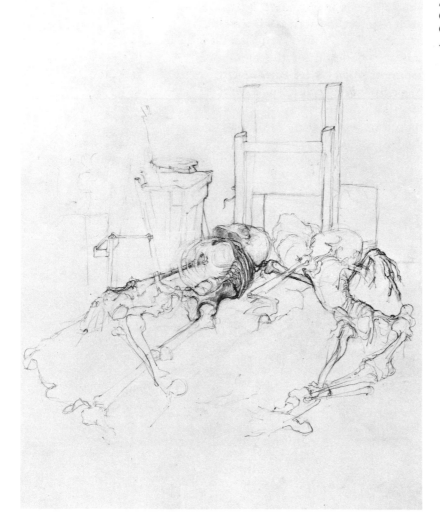

216. Richard Kinscherf.
Study of Skeletons. 1967.
Graphite pencil.
Collection Yale University
Art Gallery, New Haven, Conn.

Student Response

It was stressed in Chapter 8 that basic structural facts must be
taken for granted during the period when personal attitudes
toward form are developing. In the academies of the past this
anatomical awareness was taught through drawings of sculptural
casts and the study of charts and diagrams, but in recent years both
practices have increasingly been seen as of limited value.

  This exercise was begun with studies from the human skeleton,
both alone and in combination with a model. The skeleton was
arranged in simple sitting and reclining poses, while the
model assumed the same poses, and the students were asked to
draw the two simultaneously. Some drew them side by side,
as in Figure 216; others combined their perception of both in one
figure. The choice was left to the individual student. The goal
here was not simply a diagram showing the outer skin with the
skeleton neatly placed inside. Instead, students were asked to
assume the responsibility for studying the articulations they
personally did not understand. Two ideas were stressed:

the foreshortened simplification of volumes and the fixed-eye-level
viewpoint as in Dürer's nude (Fig. 205). This requires that all
diagraming and note-taking be performed within a three-dimensional
approach; all bone and muscular connections must be conceived
in terms of volumes moving in space.

To follow this exercise, a difficult test is worth trying.
Each student was asked to select a painting or piece of sculpture
and create a skeleton to fit the figure either by drawing the
skeleton into the drawn copy or superimposing it on a piece of
tracing paper. One student, with a sense of humor, picked
a painting by Renoir containing soft, fleshy figures with few
hints of muscular or skeletal structure (Fig. 217) and then translated
these figures into skeletal forms (Fig. 218). For the study in

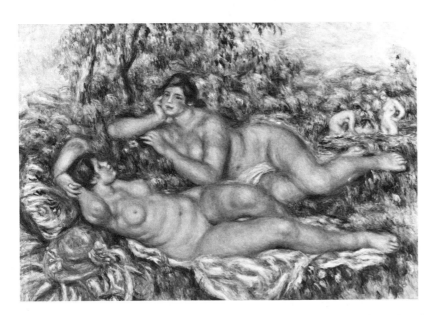

left: 217. Pierre Auguste Renoir
(1841–1919; French). *Bathers.* 1918.
Oil on canvas, 3′7¼″ × 5′3″.
Jeu de Paume, Paris.

below: 218. Jean Farquhar.
Study after Renoir's Bathers. 1973. Pencil.
Collection Yale University Art Gallery,
New Haven, Conn.

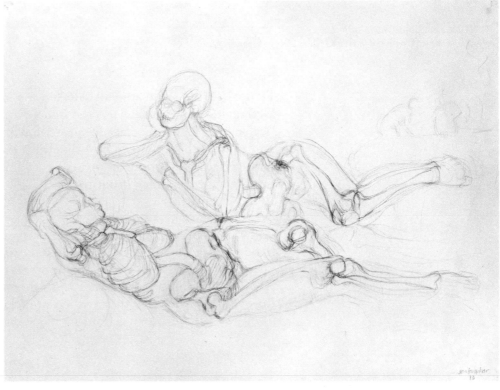

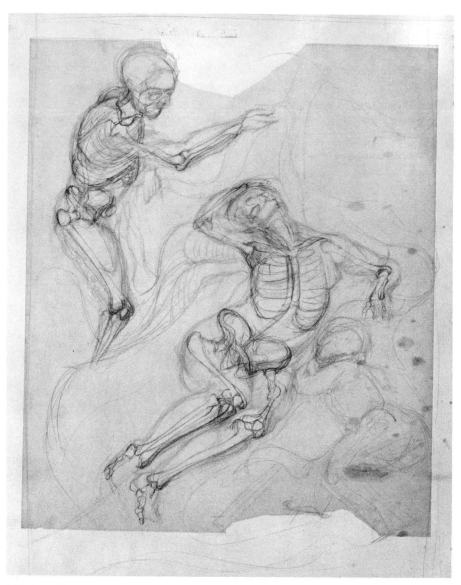

219. Jean Farquhar. *Study after Correggio.* 1973. Pencil.
Collection Yale University Art Gallery, New Haven, Conn.

Figure 219 the same student selected a very difficult painting by
Correggio—difficult because the figures are posed in exaggerated
perspective. Both these studies test what the examination of bone
and muscle charts and frontal diagrams cannot teach: the knowledge
required to foreshorten the structure of the figure. The ability
to do this, particularly from memory, is a fundamental necessity
to figure drawing.

In the same study of the model several exercises were
undertaken. The same pose was seen from four angles, the model
making a quarter turn on the pedestal after each twenty-minute
pose. All four poses were to be composed on one sheet (Fig. 220).
Another problem required that the students study the model without
drawing for as long as they wished and then leave the room
to do the actual drawing from memory.

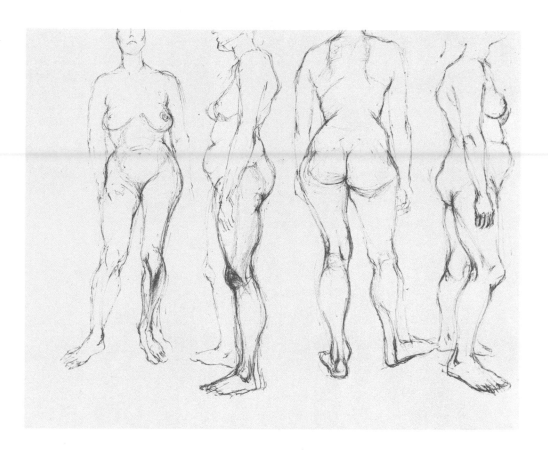

In still another exercise the model was asked to pose spontaneously in five different places in a prearranged space within a two-hour period. Here, too, all the poses were to be drawn on the same sheet of paper, with emphasis on the composition of the total page. Fitting each pose to the others is the obvious problem (Fig. 221). Similarly, for the study in

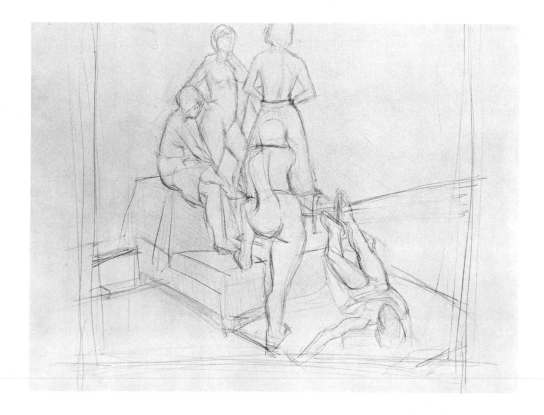

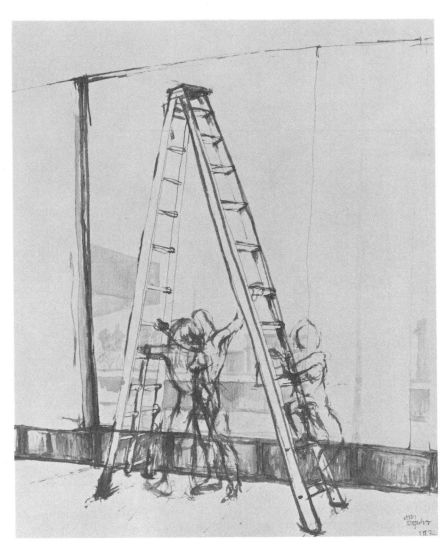

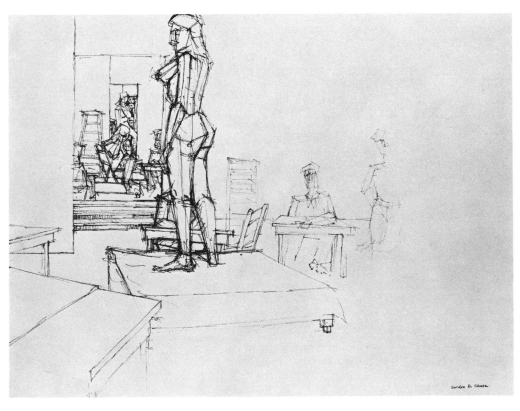

left: 222. Jean Farquhar.
Figures with Ladder. 1972. Brush and ink.
Collection Yale University Art Gallery,
New Haven, Conn.

below: 223. Gordon Chase.
Nude in an Environment. 1967.
Bamboo pen and ink.
Collection Yale University Art Gallery,
New Haven, Conn.

Figure 222 the model posed around a ladder in three places. Finally, the students drew the whole room with the figure considered as only one objcct in thc spacc (Fig. 223). These last three exercises again stress the dual approach to form studies in the volume—both the structural and the compositional attitude.

In Figure 224 the transition from one connective joint to another is presented as a series of gliding masses that strongly suggest locomotion. The student examines connections between masses with a focus on the joints. Flesh is seen as tightly pulled over the bones and muscles, yet both of these structural elements are visible. The outer contours appear and disappear in the tracery of fine lines.

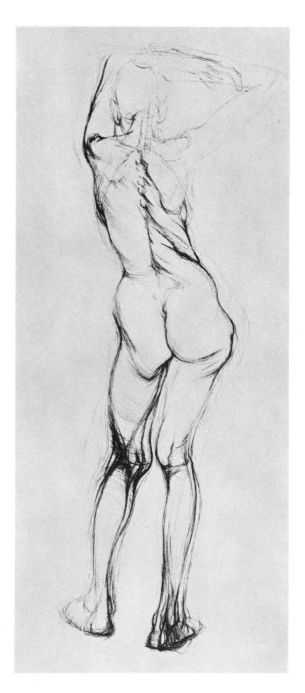

224. William Cudahy.
Masses and Joints. 1960. Pen and ink.
Collection Yale University Art Gallery,
New Haven, Conn.

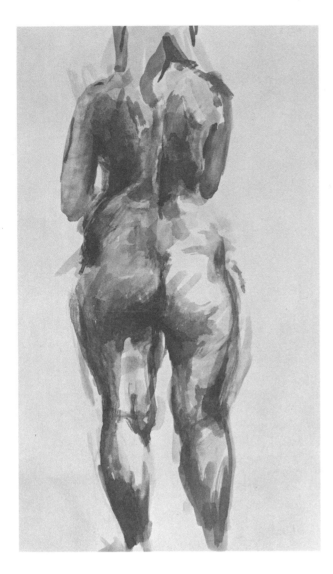

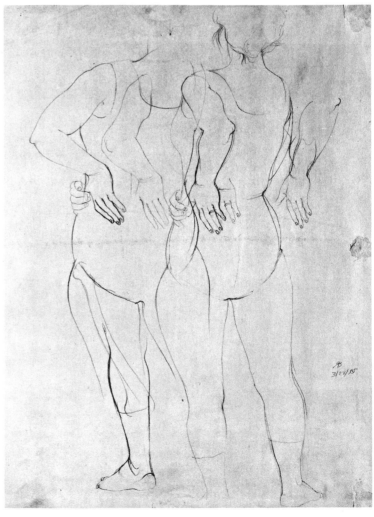

left: 225. Paul Moscatt.
Masses and Contours. 1960.
Wash and white pastel.
Collection Yale University
Art Gallery, New Haven, Conn.

below: 226. Robert Birmelin.
Overlapping Forms. 1955. Graphite pencil.
Collection Yale University Art Gallery,
New Haven, Conn.

In Figure 225 the contours of the form are a by-product of its masses; that is, the edges of the masses create the contours. The edges themselves are blurred, but the masses, conceived from the center toward the outer contour, distribute their weights in space.

A motion-picture effect is created by the drawing in Figure 226, in which the hand on the hip is repeatedly drawn across the page, sometimes clearly stated, sometimes as a ghost. The artist had a double interest—the composition of the whole drawing and the study of individual parts—and these two ideas combine to produce shapes that echo across the page.

The emphasis in Figure 227 is on the angularity of the pose. Intersecting and opposing planes are presented in a directed sequence: We see first that the movement of planes where the knees cross is pushed forward, representing the most frontal plane; the hand, head, and right shoulder come to our attention next, in one unit, as they push back into space; the left hip is pulled farther to the right in an attempt to locate it in space. This set of spatial tensions, which we are made to see in a particular order, is not intended to be a faithful description of details, but rather it is the visual theme of the drawing.

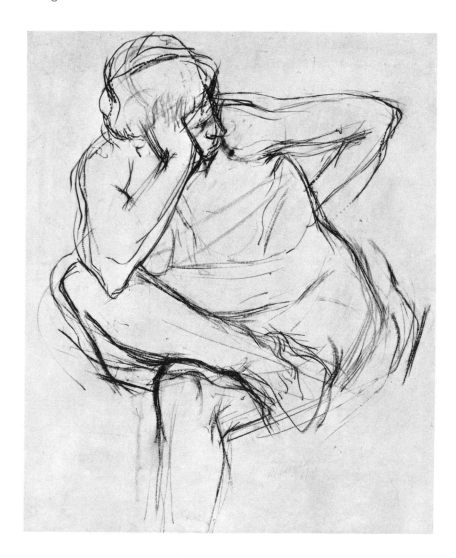

227. Michael Economos.
Seated Nude. 1959. Conté crayon.
Collection Yale University Art Gallery,
New Haven, Conn.

In Figure 228 the concept of weight through contour
is explored. The weight of the line is sensitive to its function as
an edge of foreshortened, bulging volumes. This very pale drawing
is obviously meant to be seen at close range, whereas bold, dark
drawings are conceived of and should be viewed from a distance
(although artists often choose to examine them at close range to
study their instrumentation). Each drawing sets up its own viewing
distance, as directed by the artist's intention.

Although in Figure 229 the weighty legs are constructed to
respond to the gravitational pull of the floor plane, the visual focus
is held by the turning arms of the disrobing model. This focus
suspends the weight of the figure by visually emphasizing the
content: the act of removing the dress.

In Figure 230 both the weight and the projection of forms into
space are achieved by a line that turns from sharp to soft and
alternately pulls and breaks. There are no lazy contours here.

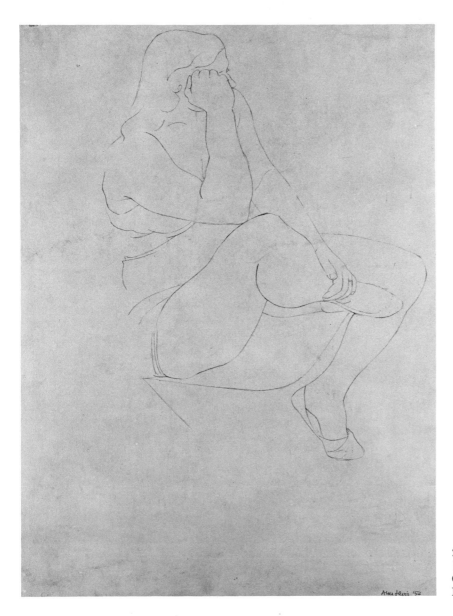

228. Arne Lewis.
Weight and Contour. 1953. Graphite pencil.
Collection Yale University Art Gallery,
New Haven, Conn.

right: 229. Langdon Quin.
Model Undressing. 1976. Charcoal.
Collection Yale University Art Gallery,
New Haven, Conn.

below: 230. Anne Parker.
Reclining Nude. 1972. Pencil.
Collection Yale University Art Gallery,
New Haven, Conn.

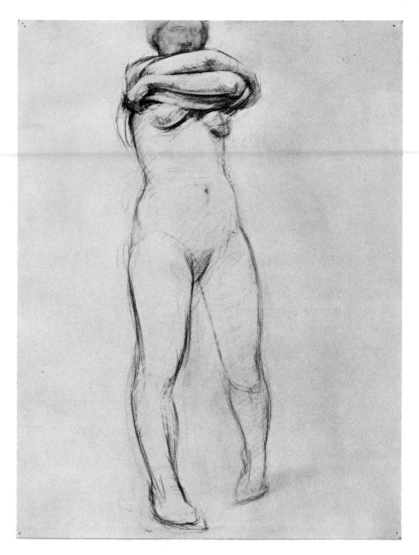

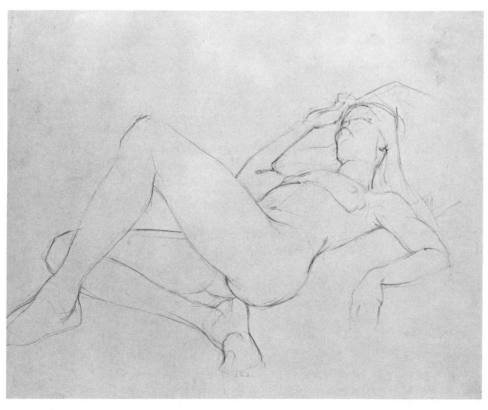

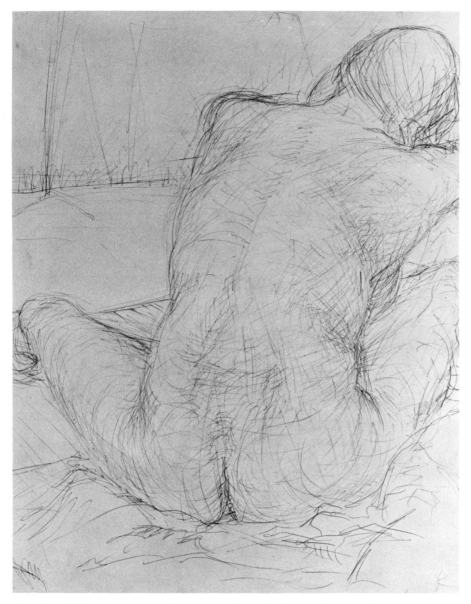

231. Sam W. Dunlop. *Seated Nude from the Back.* 1976. Graphite pencil.
Collection Yale University Art Gallery, New Haven, Conn.

The motif of Figure 231 is the total space, as well as the
figure it contains and controls. The gentle turning of the head is
maneuvered into a continuous flowing relationship with the
stretching shoulders and firmly anchored hips—all fixed in the
limited space by subtle horizontal space divisions.

One's initial response to the drawings in this chapter might be:
"These do not look like real people." This may be true, but
it is important to remember that figure drawing concerns
itself with the search for visual structures, real or invented.
When the search is successful we may see bodies in real life in a
new way. In drawing, as in art generally, great inventions
make us look at nature with fresh insight.

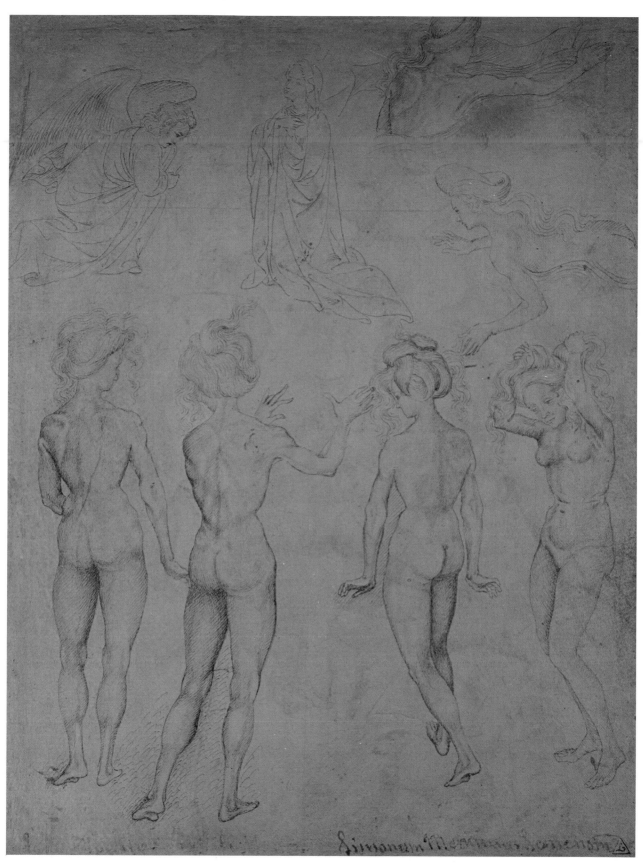

Plate 16. Antonio Pisano Pisanello (1397–1455; Italian). *Four Female Nudes.* c. 1423–27.
Brown ink on parchment, 8⅝ × 6½″. Museum Boymans–van Beuningen, Rotterdam.

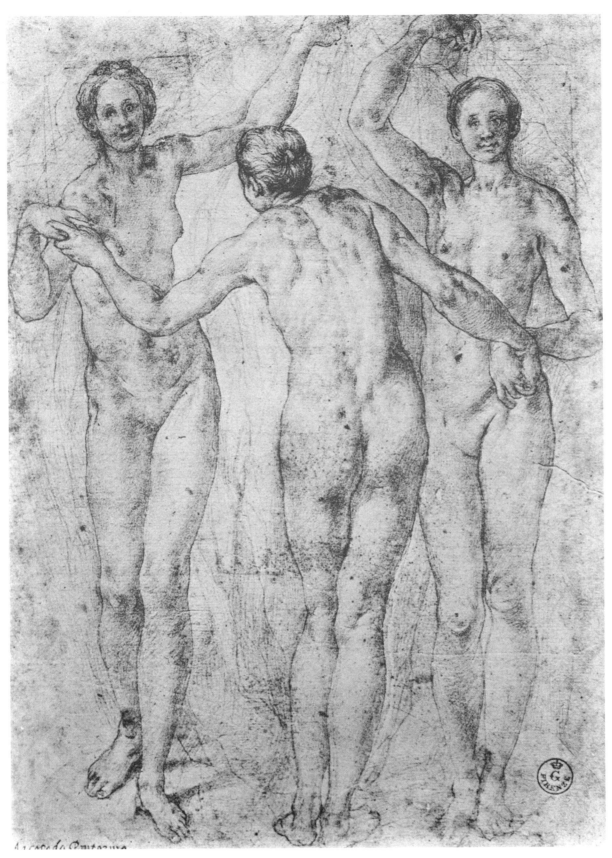

Plate 17. Jacopo Pontormo (1494–1556; Italian). *The Three Graces.* c. 1535–36. Red chalk, 11½ × 8¼". Uffizi, Florence.

212

11 Individual Projects

Each of the preceding chapters in this section explored a specific, dictated problem in terms of the studio class. We discussed the experience of master artists and presented the student response. This type of directed learning experience is valid and necessary for the beginning artist, but there is a point beyond which it produces diminishing returns. In large studio classes the potential for dialogue between teacher and student is reduced, as is the opportunity for group interaction—the individual criticism and group discussion that can create a true environment for learning. The purpose of this chapter, then, will be to record the experiences of nine students in advanced individual projects, outside the formal classroom setting.

For these projects each student chose a particular theme that was to be explored in depth for a full year or for one semester. The course was structured as a tutorial seminar: Each student met with the instructor alone once a week, and

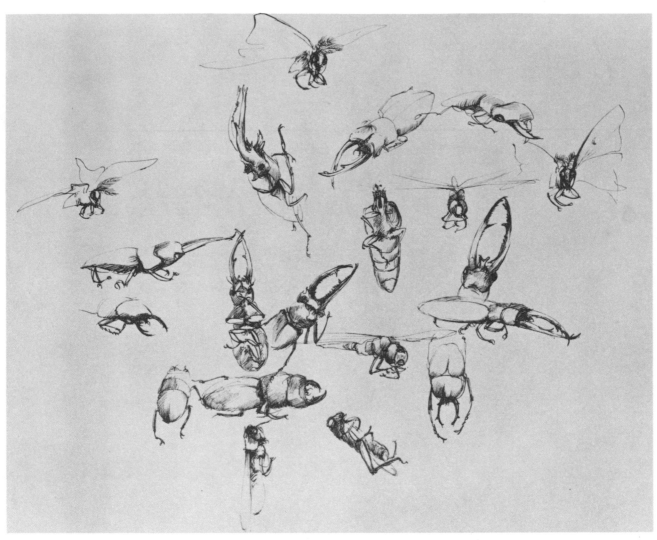

232. Mark Fennessey. *Insects I.* 1965–66. Pen and ink.
Collection Yale University Art Gallery, New Haven, Conn.

members of the group criticized each other's work several times during the year. All the students were college undergraduates majoring in studio art. Aesthetics and technical problems were not discussed beforehand, but were dealt with as they arose during the development of each project.

Such a course permits a close association between teacher and student. In this presentation of the projects the attempt will be made to illustrate the dialogue the seminar created and to explain the way in which free but serious interaction can affect the development of an idea.

Project I—Insects

In this project, which lasted for a full year, the student produced nearly a hundred drawings. Those that have been chosen for reproduction represent pivotal points or changes in direction in the student's progress.

The study of insects began with casual anatomical note-taking through a microscope. In a sense it was an almost playful investigation. The artist produced many small group drawings, such as the one illustrated in Figure 232.

Next, the student used the information obtained through the microscope to create a series of works in pen and wash (Fig. 233). The insect forms became anthropomorphic, yet they appeared as mounted specimens in a glass case, seen from the top, against a shallow, dark backdrop.

233. Mark Fennessey. *Insects II.* 1965–66. Pen and ink with wash. Collection Yale University Art Gallery, New Haven, Conn.

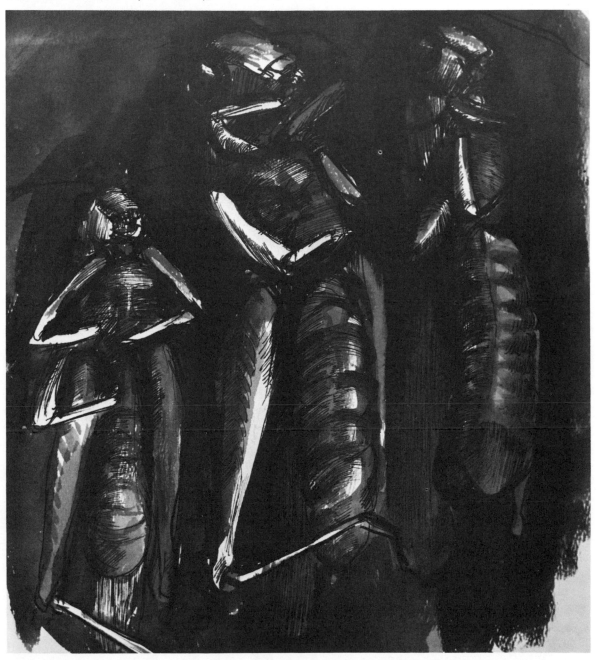

Still working from the initial notes, the student produced some single figures in charcoal, which explored the psychological possibilities. The insects, severely cropped at the edges of the page, dominate the space to produce a nightmare image (Fig. 234). Both the artist and the instructor felt that the psychological emphasis was a little forced.

The student returned to note-taking under the microscope to make himself still more familiar with the insects' forms. At this point he decided to change his instrument to brush, which he employed almost exclusively during the remainder of the project. Individual insect figures looming as large as 30 inches were set against the glare of absorbent white paper

234. Mark Fennessey.
Insects III. 1965–66. Charcoal.
Collection Yale University Art Gallery,
New Haven, Conn.

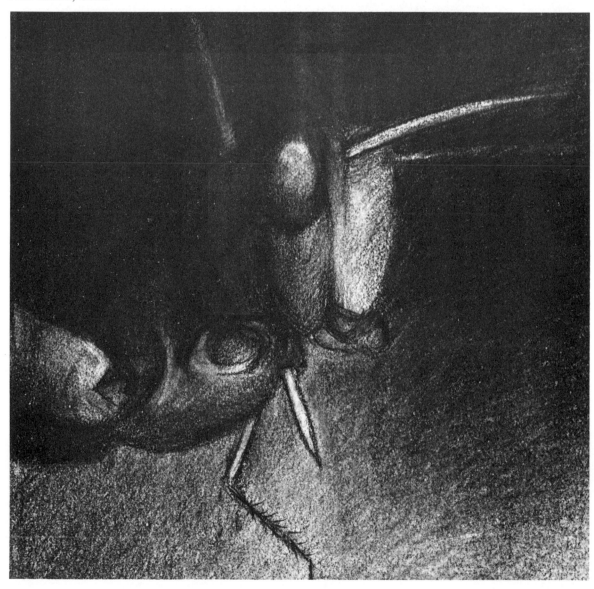

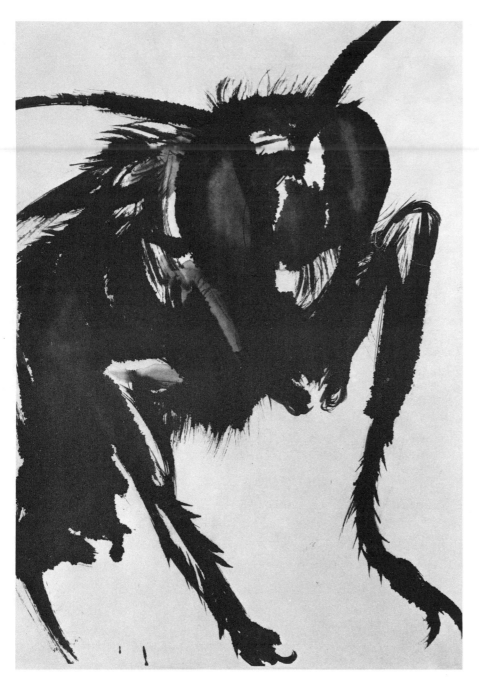

235. Mark Fennessey.
Insects IV. 1965–66. Wash.
Collection Yale University Art Gallery,
New Haven, Conn.

in direct brush strokes (Fig. 235). The criticism of this group of
works was that the placement of the figures was a bit self-conscious,
drawing attention primarily to the forms themselves at the
expense of the composition. It was suggested that the scale of the
drawings be reduced, so that the swift brushwork would be
less forced and more directly related to the interaction
of forms on the page.

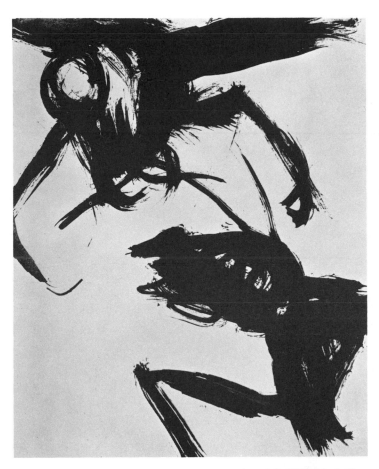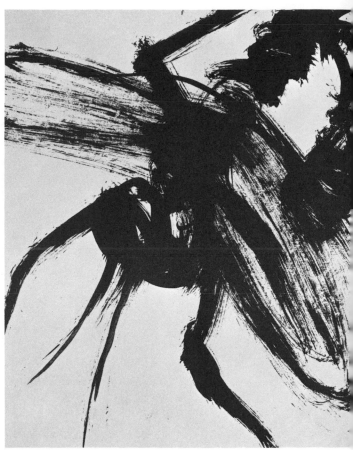

above left: 236. Mark Fennessey.
Insects V. 1965–66. Brush and ink.
Collection Yale University Art Gallery,
New Haven, Conn.

above right: 237. Mark Fennessey.
Insects VI. 1965–66. Brush and ink.
Collection Yale University Art Gallery,
New Haven, Conn.

opposite above: 238. Mark Fennessey.
Insects VII. 1965–66. Brush and ink.
Collection Yale University Art Gallery,
New Haven, Conn.

In response to the criticism, the student produced a series
of small drawings, three of which are reproduced (Figs. 236–238).
Here the life of the page, the brushwork, and the symbolic
content were in a more balanced relationship.

Figure 239, a brush-and-wash drawing on a hard, resistant
paper, initiated a change in spatial concepts. The basic
idea—crowds in a panoramic space—was sparked by studying
the works of James Ensor, Jacques Callot, and, especially
in this drawing, Goya's landscapes with figures. By this time
the student, with his acquired experience, was able to compose
more naturally.

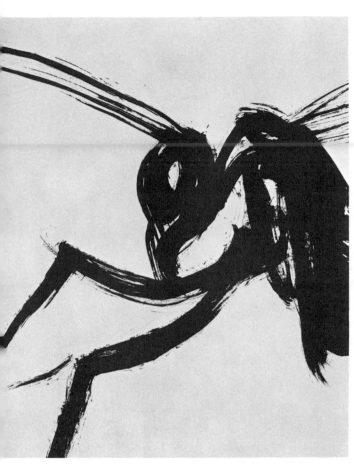

239. Mark Fennessey.
Insects VIII. 1965–66. Wash.
Collection Yale University Art Gallery,
New Haven, Conn.

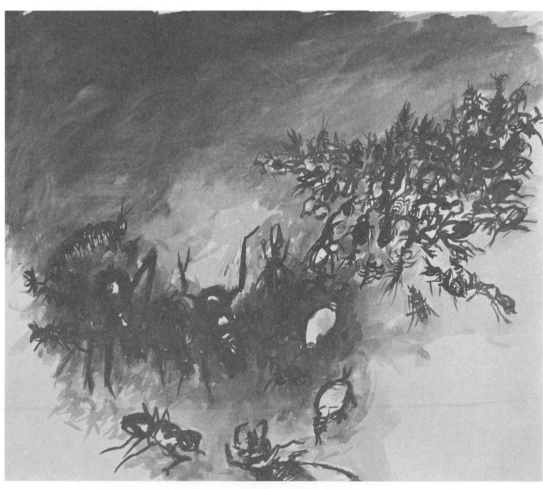

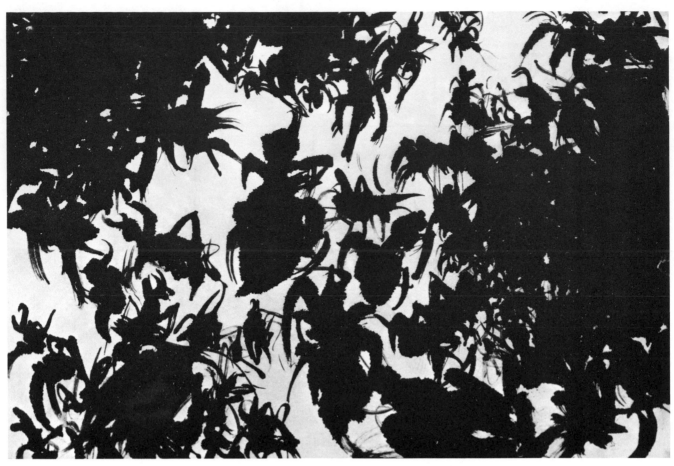

240. Mark Fennessey.
Insects IX. 1965–66. Brush and ink.
Collection Yale University Art Gallery,
New Haven, Conn.

The final group of drawings, done on rice paper, translated
the insect-in-landscape theme into very dark brush groups
in a less obviously propped-up space (Fig. 240). There is no
discernible foreground, middleground, and background.
The forms are closer to the viewer, yet, as they move across
the page, they seem to be leaving the arena of the composition.
The insect forms themselves are more wedded to the brush strokes.
Thus, the entire effect is less descriptive and more suggestive
and, therefore, seems more real as a visual experience.
The handling of the medium is more direct, and the menacing
symbolic content is stronger.

Project II—One Tree

The curving posture of one particular tree was the attraction
for the student in this single-semester theme. He employed charcoal
in Figure 241, as throughout the series, to pull together the
whole arched form of the tree in an arrangement of broken planes.
At first the rhythmical interruptions were too obviously

balanced, which tended to make the sections cancel out one
another and produced a relatively tensionless space.

In Figure 242 the entire structure of the tree becomes
one rounded, spreading volume. The darks, which were used
to create drama, were not quite in harmony with the forms and the
space around them. Some dark sections, in fact, look as though
dust has been sprayed on top. It was emphasized that the
darks must act in and with the forms that are being presented.

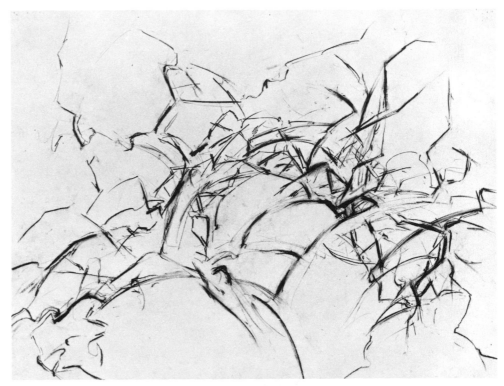

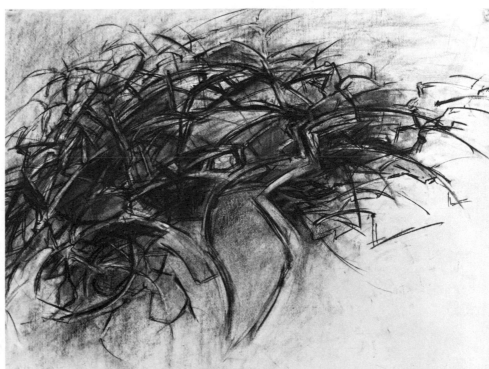

above right: 241.
H. Turner Brooks.
Tree I. 1965. Charcoal.
Collection Yale University
Art Gallery,
New Haven, Conn.

right: 242. H. Turner Brooks.
Tree II. 1965. Charcoal.
Collection Yale University
Art Gallery,
New Haven, Conn.

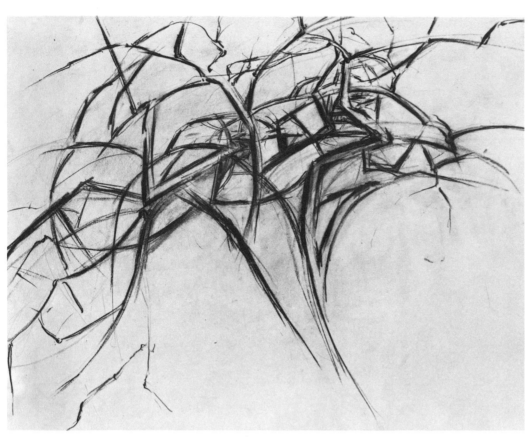

above: 243. H. Turner Brooks. *Tree III*. 1965. Charcoal.
Collection Yale University Art Gallery, New Haven, Conn.

below: 244. H. Turner Brooks. *Tree IV*. 1965. Charcoal.
Collection Yale University Art Gallery, New Haven, Conn.

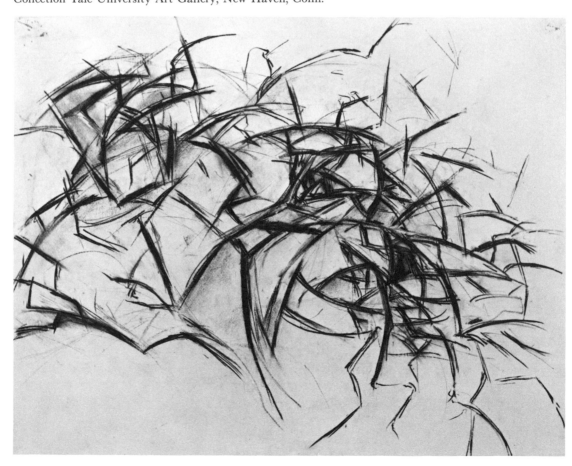

The student was prompted by the criticism to present the same
form arrangement with more reliance on linear elements.
In Figure 243 the manner is not so highly stylized, forms arc more
clearly stated, and the white interspaces between and around
the lines function to support these lines in a less obviously
designed attitude.

In Figure 244 the broken-plane idea returned, this time
with a sweeping rhythm that again suggested a single sculptured
volume. Here the student was very self-critical. He felt
that the "style" produced an almost stained-glass effect, and that
the flowing movement was too obvious. Discussion centered
around the idea that transparent planes suggesting Synthetic
Cubism—wherein all the facets of each plane are visible
simultaneously to produce an allover surface tension—must not
appear to be tacked on top of an image. Instead, the "system"
should carry the image.

Figure 245, the final drawing in the series, is an invention
based on the actual experience of the tree. The tension-filled
traffic points in the center gradually expand to hold a plane very
close to the viewer. This frontal plane is represented by
the largest dark strokes circling the edges of the composition.
Here the technique and the constructed space are made to merge.

In this project the student was obviously influenced
by Mondrian's studies of trees (see Fig. 6). Nevertheless, he has
faced issues of design versus structure—that is, the structure
of the form to be presented should dictate the design, rather than
being forced to fit the limitations of preconceived design concepts.

245. H. Turner Brooks.
Tree V. 1965. Charcoal.
Collection Yale University
Art Gallery, New Haven, Conn.

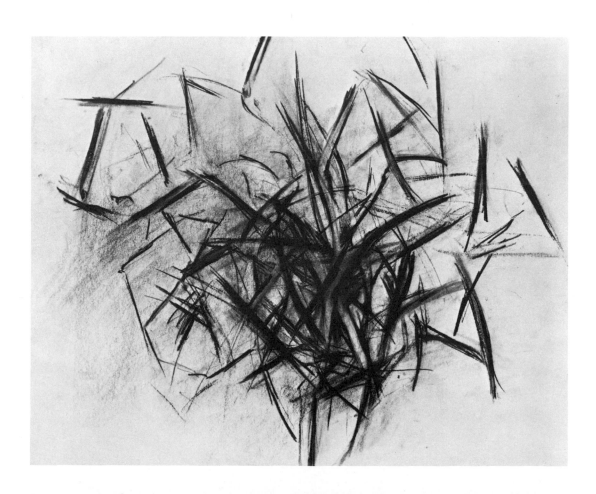

Project III—One Landscape

In this project the student restricted himself to one place, one tool (brush), and one medium (tempera—in this case one of the new commercially prepared plastic acrylic temperas). He drew directly from the landscape, and, over the course of the year, passed through three distinct stages. In stage one he elected to stretch the limits of the amount of dark or light in any one composition. He produced many very dark, almost black pictures, and some very light ones.

Figure 246 is one of the relatively dark drawings, though it does not approach the limits of darkness. The effect of light playing across the page is housed in a clearly readable space. The heavy trees in the foreground recede gradually through size diminution to the background wall of foliage. However, beyond this obvious spatial plane, the life of the drawing lies in the action of strokes grouping together and opening to the light from the back plane. The white interspaces do not act

246. Robert Ferris. *Landscape I.* 1965.
Brush and wash (acrylic tempera).
Collection Yale University Art Gallery,
New Haven, Conn.

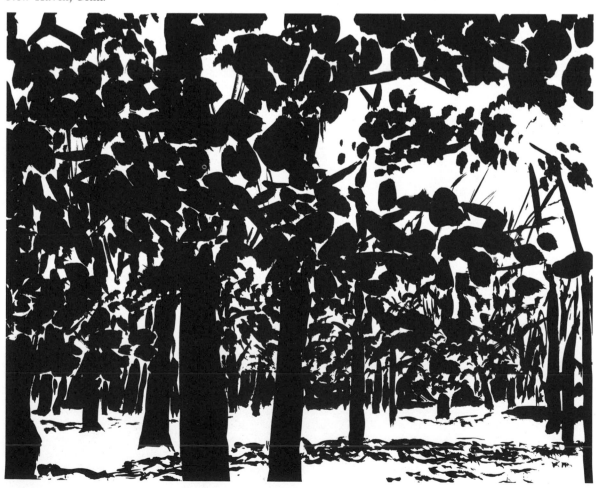

as a flat background; instead, the white opens to suggest light in
upper right and acts as a plane of gravity in the lower portion.
The white further serves to set off the foliage.

This drawing was one of the best efforts of several months' work.
Conversation during this period dealt with amounts of light
and the use of white interspace as line, light, and plane. Beyond
this, discussion focused on the limitations of the physical space to be
portrayed: How much? How far back? How close to the viewer?

The second phase was concerned with a restricted, close-up
space for foliage-inspired brush strokes (Fig. 247). It was
during this period that the student explored Japanese and Chinese
landscapes from the point of view of controlling the directed
sequence of events on a page (see Fig. 86). While studying this
concept of controlled sequential reading, the artist was faced with
the problem of imitating a master's brush strokes. To copy another's
handwriting actually prevents one from developing one's own
natural style. Yet it is the masters we admire who direct our growth
in one direction or another.

247. Robert Ferris. *Landscape II.* 1965.
Brush and wash (acrylic tempera).
Collection Yale University Art Gallery,
New Haven, Conn.

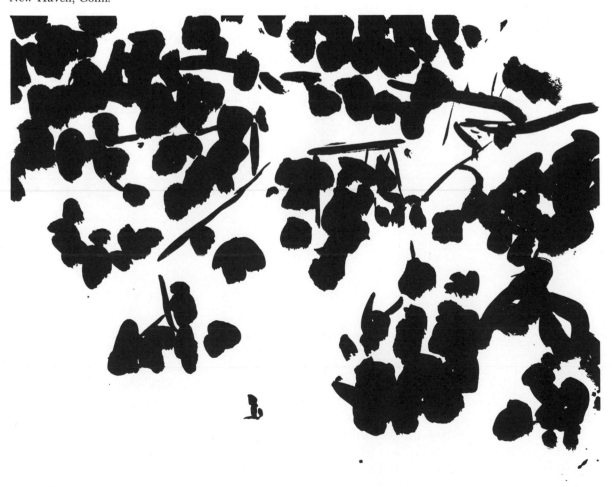

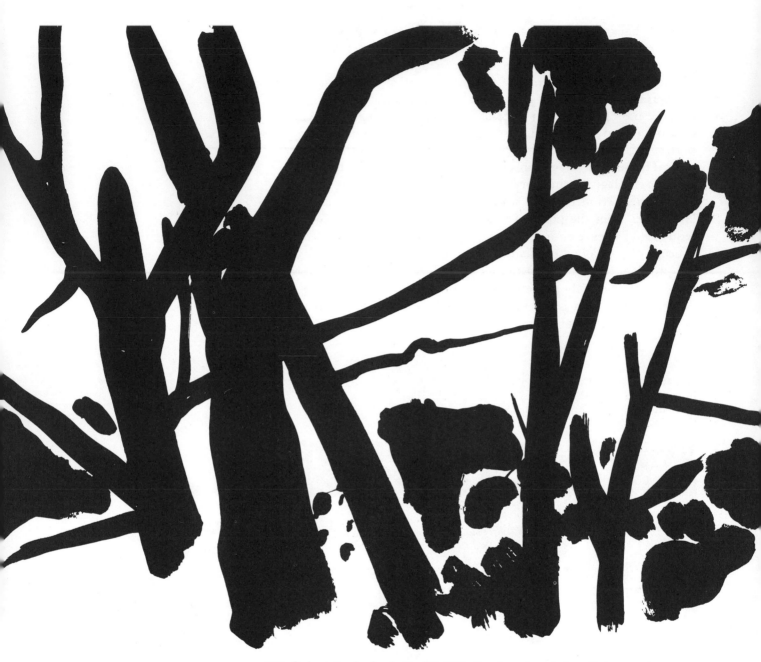

248. Robert Ferris. *Landscape III*. 1965. Brush and wash (acrylic tempera). Collection Yale University Art Gallery, New Haven, Conn.

In stage three the emphasis was on one aspect of Western spatial concepts—the idea of bisecting and intersecting planes that set up tensions (Fig. 248). We are conditioned to this kind of construction from studying some of Cézanne's work, and, more recently, the work of Max Beckmann, John Marin (Pl. 5, p. 42), and Franz Kline. The heavy tree forms in Figure 248 shift the weight of the drawing to the left, yet balance is maintained by the broken, amorphous shapes at lower and upper right.

Project IV—Train Station

The train station is the diary of a trip, our only project with
a story line. This feature does add human interest to the sequence
of drawings, but they are reproduced here because of their
invention—the invention of a scale and atmosphere that evoke
the feeling of places experienced visually. In Figure 249 we are
inside the station sitting at an empty counter. The long
curved counter and the row of stools give clues to the length
of the elongated hollow space. This space has been created with
a relaxed, sketchy line (in ball-point pen), which not
only moves rapidly around the contours of individual objects but
gradually changes its texture to become an atmospheric wall
on the back plane. Notice, too, the subtle transition of line from
edge in the front to *mass* at the back.

249. Peter Richmond.
Train Station I. 1973. Ball-point pen.
Collection Yale University Art Gallery,
New Haven, Conn.

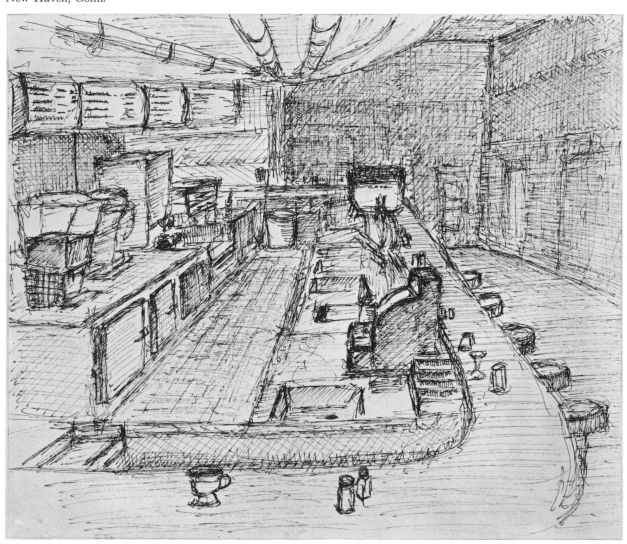

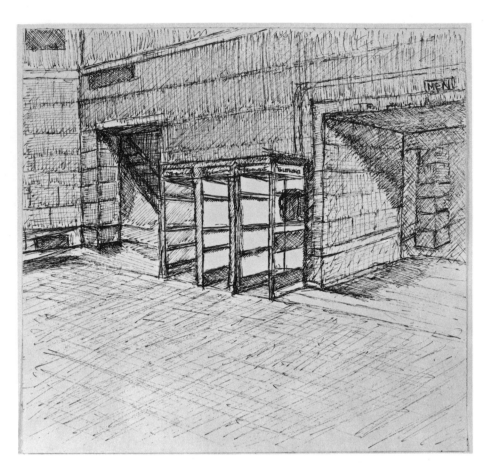

above: 250. Peter Richmond. *Train Station II*. 1973. Ball-point pen.
Collection Yale University Art Gallery, New Haven, Conn.

below: 251. Peter Richmond. *Train Station III*. 1973. Ball-point pen.
Collection Yale University Art Gallery, New Haven, Conn.

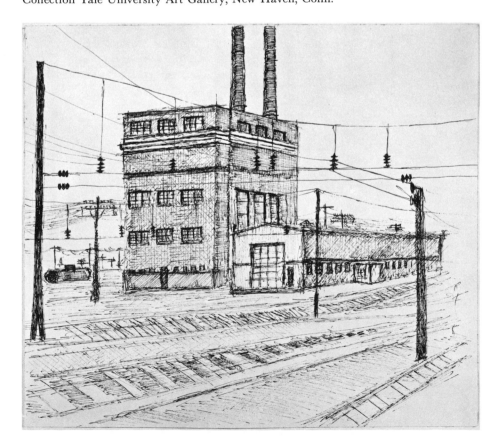

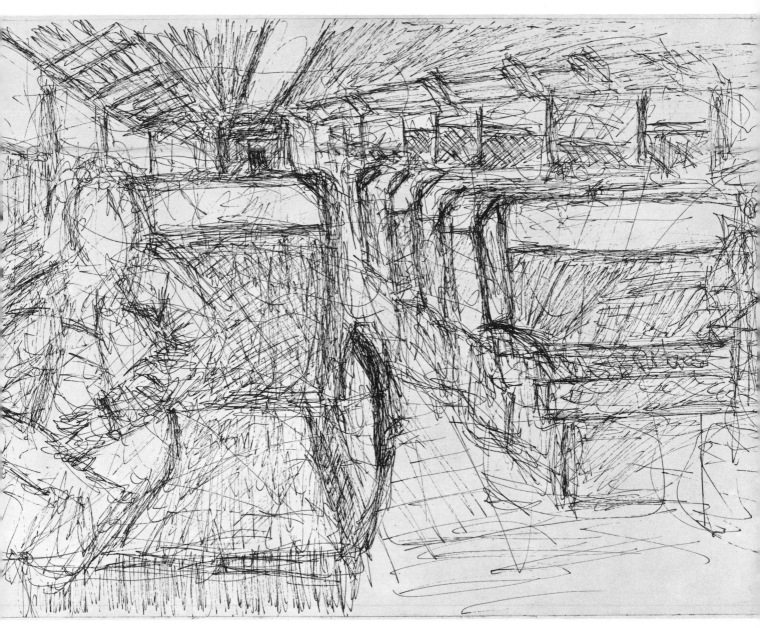

252. Peter Richmond. *Train Station IV.* 1973. Ball-point pen.
Collection Yale University Art Gallery, New Haven, Conn.

Figure 250, employing the same graphic means, shows us
another section of the station. The wall with a bank of telephones
starts almost halfway up the page. This meaningful placement
emphasizes the vastness of the whole space and carries the message
of the scale.

In Figure 251 we are out on the platform waiting for the train.
We see the station from a distance. Here too the effect depends
on expressive placement: the two chimney stacks are repeated
by the poles, left, right, and toward the building, and these
verticals are countered by the horizontal tracks and wires.

The interior atmosphere of the train in Figure 252 completes
the project, in the loosest open-edged flow.

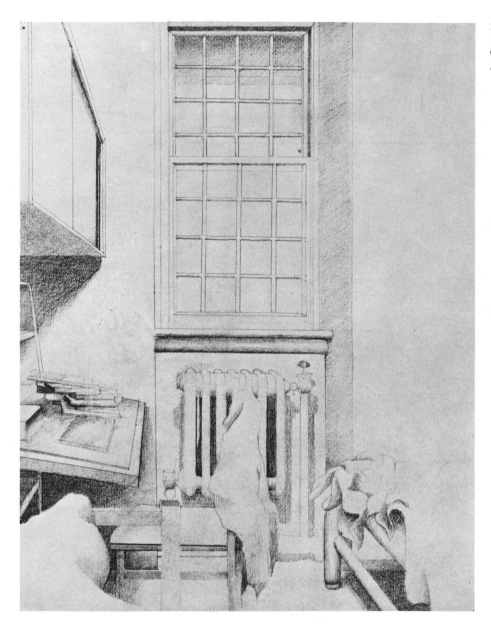

253. Howard Kielley.
Window I. 1974. Graphite pencil.
Collection Yale University
Art Gallery, New Haven, Conn.

Project V—The Window

Figure 253 sets the stage for this series. We see one wall housing
a window, a desk, a hanging cabinet, a radiator, a corner
of a bed, and some clothing. Sections of these objects appear
and then become blurred by the light. Changing light is the visual
theme of the whole series, but in this first drawing the light
is evenly distributed. We are allowed to catch a glimpse of all
the objects that will be transformed in future examples. In Figure
254 we see a smaller section of the room in a silent, dusky
atmosphere. Light is gently leaving from the window, which also
serves as the farthest plane in the composition. In Figure 255
a strong artificial light has been switched on. In the window we see
the reflection of the light fixture and the opposite side of the
room. Dark shadows pull us gently into the room.

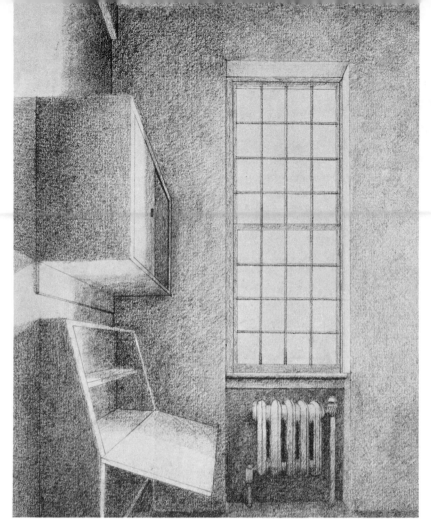

254. Howard Kielley.
Window II. 1974. Graphite pencil.
Collection Yale University Art Gallery,
New Haven, Conn.

255. Howard Kielley.
Window III. 1974. Graphite pencil.
Collection Yale University Art Gallery,
New Haven, Conn.

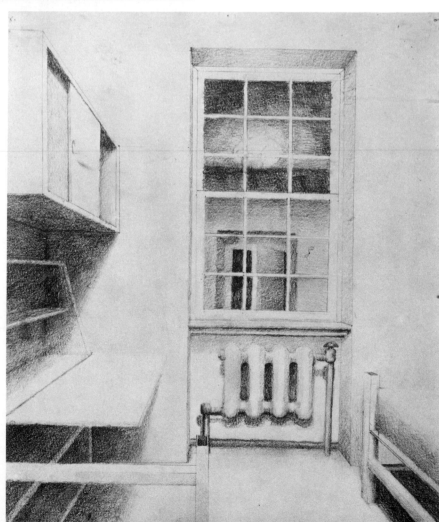

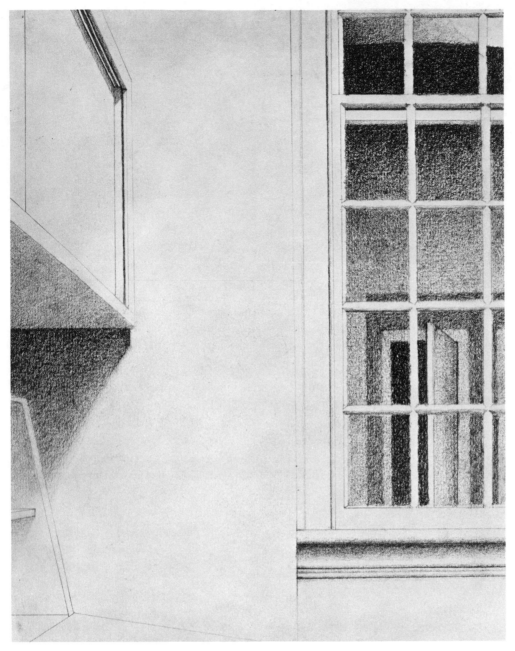

256. Howard Kielley.
Window IV. 1974. Graphite pencil.
Collection Yale University Art Gallery,
New Haven, Conn.

The preceding drawing suggested to the student the possibility
of creating a page from the details. In Figure 256 the grid of
the window panes with the reflected wall and open door play against
the triangular shadow at left. The whole creates a nicely
related geometric orchestration. The use of the pencil in this
project, as it gently and gradually fills in the medium-rough tooth
of the paper, matches the conception: the interplay of proportion,
scale, and, above all, light.

Project VI—Objects in a Room

In this cluttered room the artist makes us work hard to move through his space. In Figure 257 objects slow down our movement into the room, even trip us up as we try to get through the narrow passages. The clearly constructed and richly textured masses have a wide tonal range. This is accomplished here and in the two examples that follow with black, gray, and white pastel on a black ground. The strokes that build these forms and spaces show their marks, and this tactile effect makes us experience the process of construction.

257. Tim Schiffer. *Objects in a Room I.* 1974. Pastel.
Collection Yale University Art Gallery, New Haven, Conn.

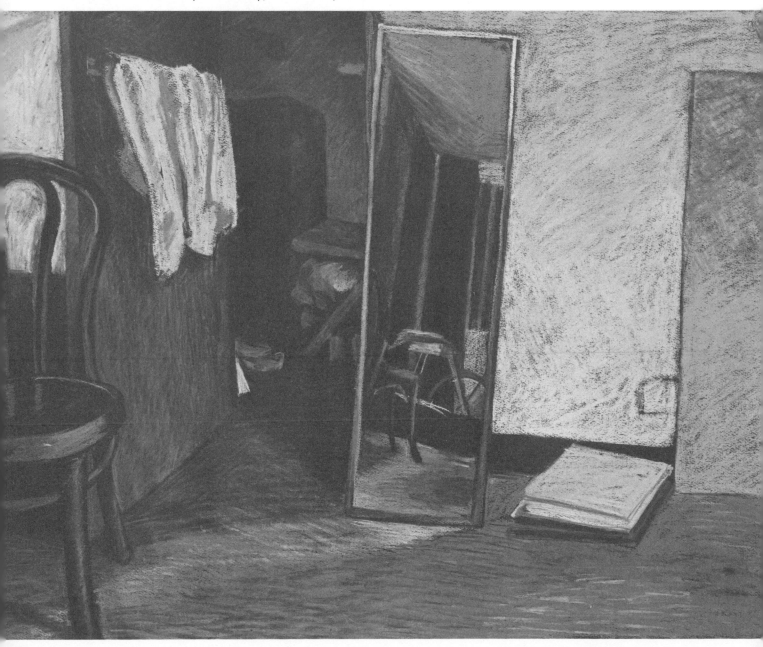

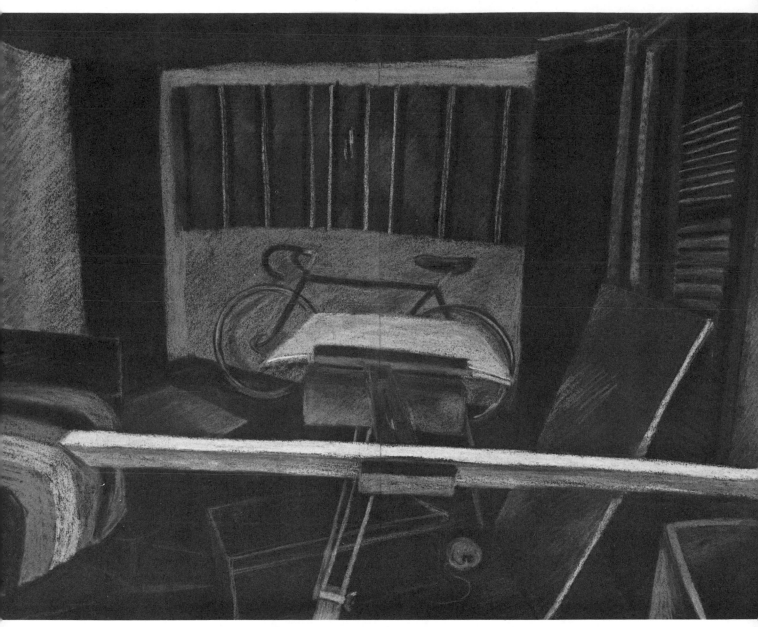

258. Tim Schiffer.
Objects in a Room II. 1974. Pastel.
Collection Yale University Art Gallery,
New Haven, Conn.

In Figure 258 the stretching form of part of the artist's portable easel cuts horizontally through the space, creating a frontal plane that bars us from walking through. Stopped against this sharp white barrier, we can gradually make out objects in the room beyond our reach.

Figure 259 shows another view of the easel, which this time gesticulates obliquely into the surrounding space. All the forms play variations on this angularity.

259. Tim Schiffer.
Objects in a Room III. 1974. Pastel.
Collection Yale University Art Gallery,
New Haven, Conn.

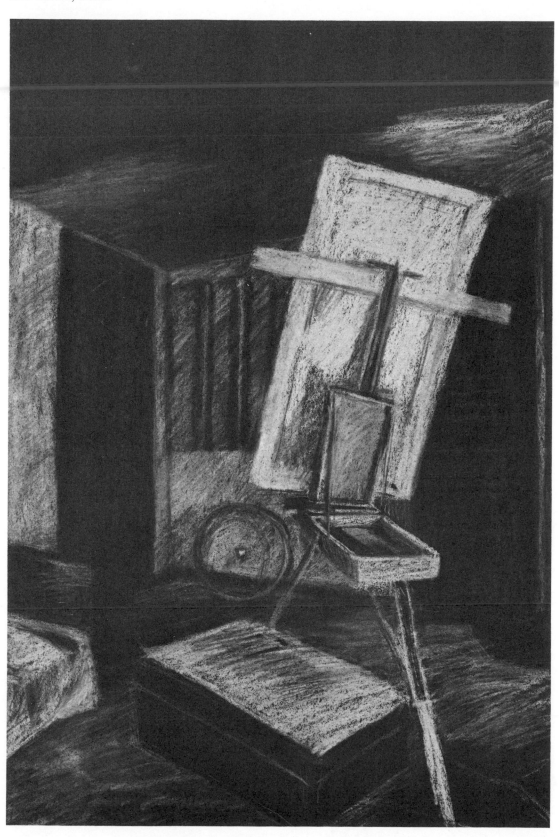

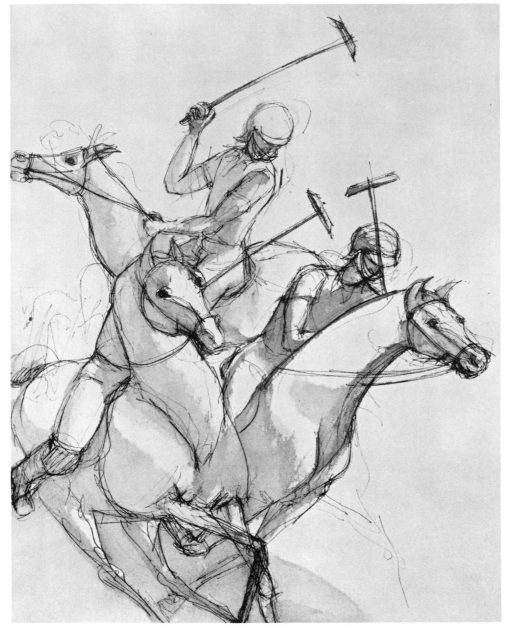

260. Lisa Gelfand.
Polo I. 1974. Pen and ink with wash.
Collection Yale University Art Gallery,
New Haven, Conn.

Project VII—Polo

The four ink-and-wash drawings reproduced here represent
a small part of more than thirty drawings on the theme of polo
produced in this project. First, the student had to work out her own
system of transcribing the action. She found she could not make
finished or even half-finished drawings in this arena of swift
movements. She gradually developed gestural, fragmented
sketches of movement, which were such personal scrawls that only

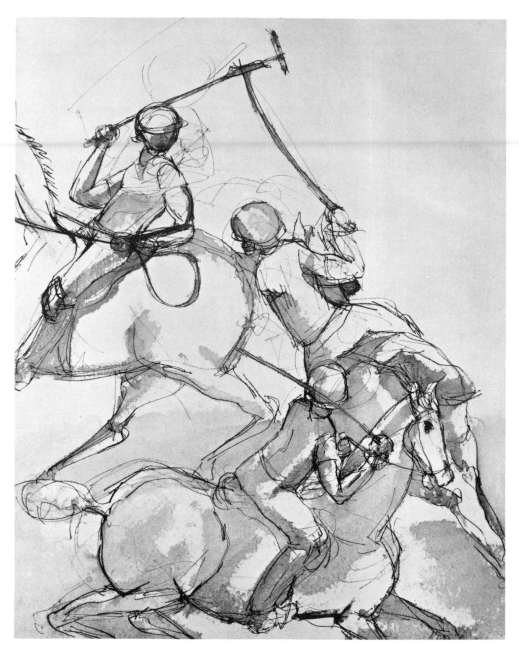

261. Lisa Gelfand.
Polo II. 1974. Pen and ink with wash.
Collection Yale University Art Gallery,
New Haven, Conn.

she could decipher them. After each of these note-taking
sessions, she began to reconstruct the visual events that stimulated
her, inventing configurations based on her sketches and her
newly learned skill of memorizing actions.

In Figure 260 horses, players, and mallets spin clockwise
and counterclockwise around a central core—an invented
construction. Figure 261 shows the three horses moving in different
directions. The focal point that holds together all the movements
is at the top, where the two mallets touch. The central player

in Figure 262 twists to the right, countering the main thrust of the horse shooting up and out to the left. The second horse and player continue a circular movement with the first player. Finally, Figure 263 consists of a row of repeated circular and semicircular forms representing players and horses moving in a narrow elliptical space. The angular linear thrust of the mallets plays a separate but interlocking game with the circular motion.

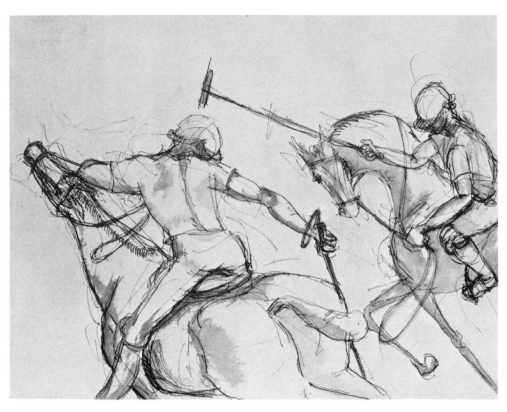

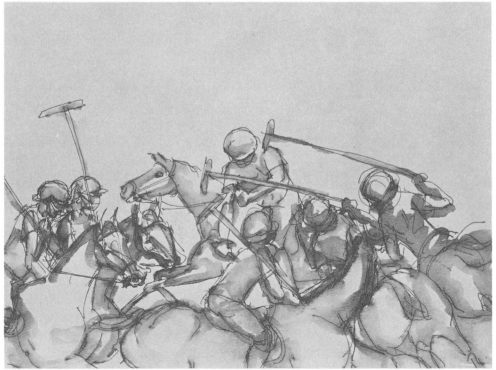

above left: 262. Lisa Gelfand.
Polo III. 1974.
Pen and ink with wash.
Collection Yale University
Art Gallery, New Haven, Conn.

left: 263. Lisa Gelfand.
Polo IV. 1974.
Pen and ink with wash.
Collection Yale University
Art Gallery, New Haven, Conn.

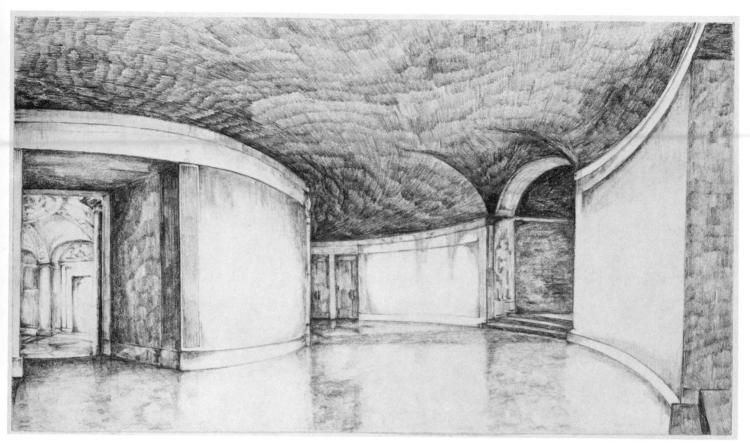

264. Konrad Marchaj.
Concert Theater I. 1976.
Conté crayon.
Collection Yale University Art Gallery,
New Haven, Conn.

Project VIII—Concert Theater

To construct a personal portrait of a large space is an ambitious
project. The student in this project became involved in this theme
after being frustrated by his inability to find a satisfactory
motif in his own room.

The problem he had at first was technical and took place
before the successful examples reproduced here. The initial drawings
in red conté crayon, a medium used throughout the series,
were too heavy, too generous in their use of plastered darks that
seemed to balance and cancel each other. His strokes, applied
with the side of the crayon, gave out little energy. They
were merely filled in.

Reacting in Figure 264 to the above criticism, the artist went
out of his way to control the darks and, by means of constructive
markings, to show the flow of the curving ceiling and the
outer wall of the theater. This technical decision—this method
of controlling and building up the strokes—is completely
in harmony, indeed integral to the theme of moving around
this curvilinear space.

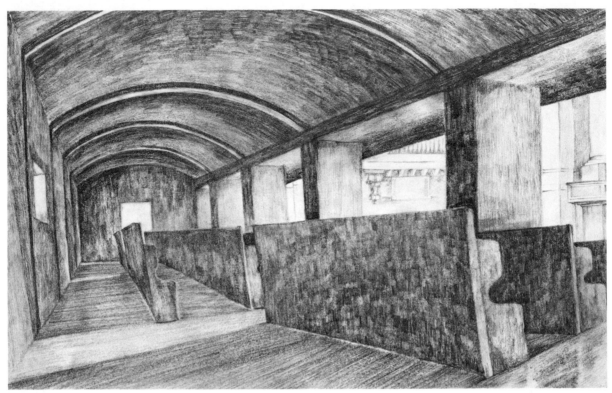

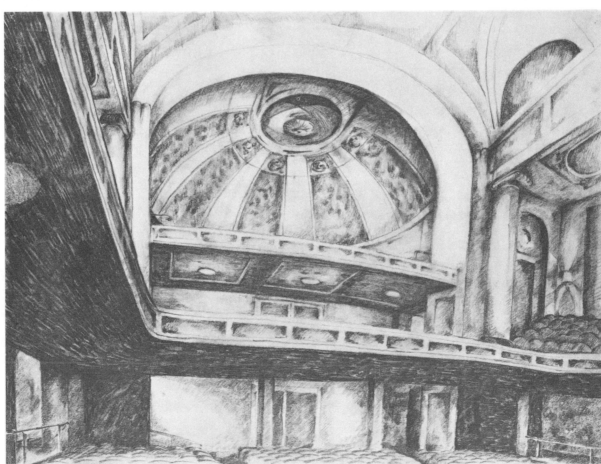

In the next drawing, a view of the rear of the theater (Fig. 265), the artist, more relaxed and at peace with the criticism, worked out a greater tonal range with various textures acting in concert.

Figure 266 places the artist and viewer in the middle of the theater. He takes us first to the top, where a strong light moves down to the balcony. Next we move down to the main force, the dark underside of the balcony constructed with strokes that direct us into and around the space. This energy is controlled in its sharp L-shaped movement, so that it does not drop out of the picture plane. Finally, the artist directs us to the bottom, with its quiet, soft chair forms. He is able to take us on a journey from light at the top, through dark strong movement, to bottom whispers. This wide tonal range is held in full control.

In the last of the series (Fig. 267) he makes us turn our heads upward to see the ceiling pattern, contained by the dark angles at top and bottom right.

267. Konrad Marchaj.
Concert Theater IV. 1976.
Conté crayon.
Collection Yale University
Art Gallery, New Haven, Conn.

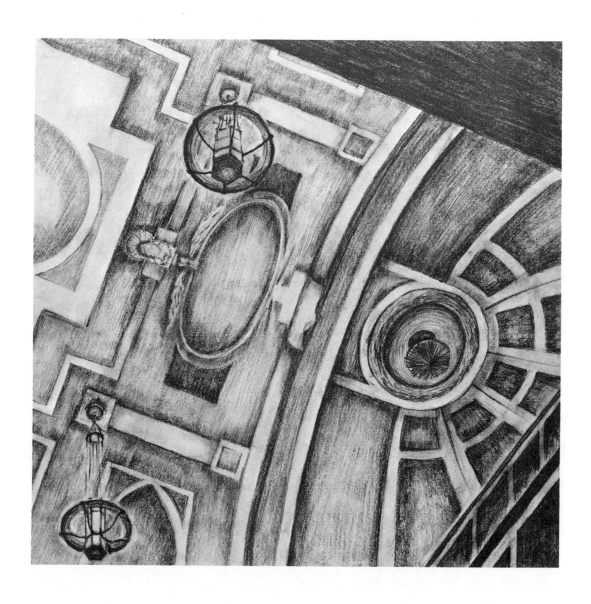

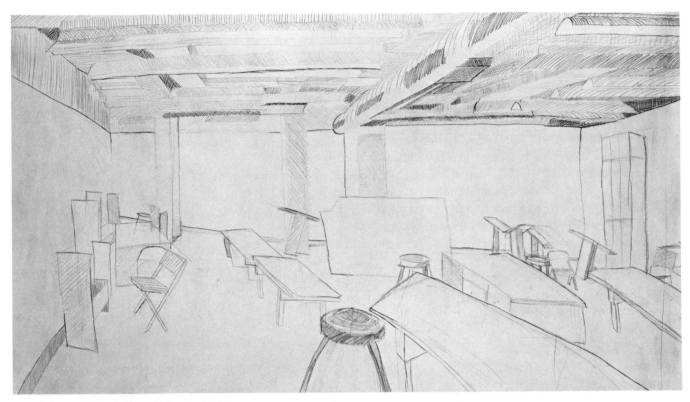

above: 268. John Kaliski. *Basement Studio I*. 1976. Graphite pencil.
Collection Yale University Art Gallery, New Haven, Conn.

below: 269. John Kaliski. *Basement Studio II*. 1976. Pen and ink.
Collection Yale University Art Gallery, New Haven, Conn.

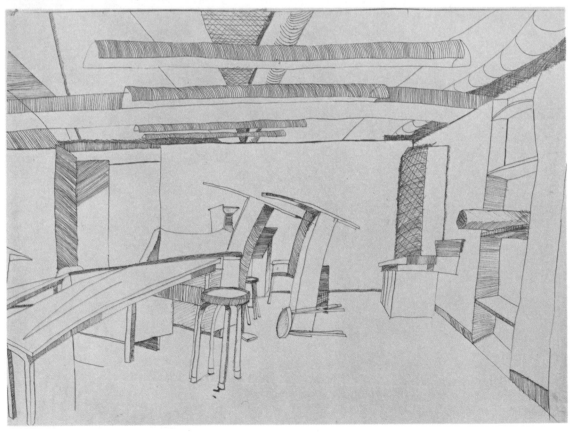

Project IX—Basement Studio

A basement studio room with a low ceiling, where the artist worked
most of the time, triggered ideas of pressure, weight, and
horizontal expanse. The first drawing, in graphite pencil (Fig. 268),
simply probes the space. The draftsman takes notes before
figuring out the particular direction in which he wants to work.
The student came up with a reaction that he did not continue
afterwards; he arranged the studio furniture to interact playfully
against the exposed ducts, light fixtures, columns, and partitions
of the room. It is this whimsical play of angles that gives
Figure 269 a form life.

In Figure 270, also in pen and ink, the ceiling takes half
the vertical space of the page, emphasizing the feeling of
tremendous downward weight against the exaggeration of lowered,
spreading walls. This threatening activity of heavy forms on the
ceiling produces anxiety, as does the purposeful shrinking of
the size of the furniture.

270. John Kaliski. *Basement Studio III*. 1976. Pen and ink.
Collection Yale University Art Gallery, New Haven, Conn.

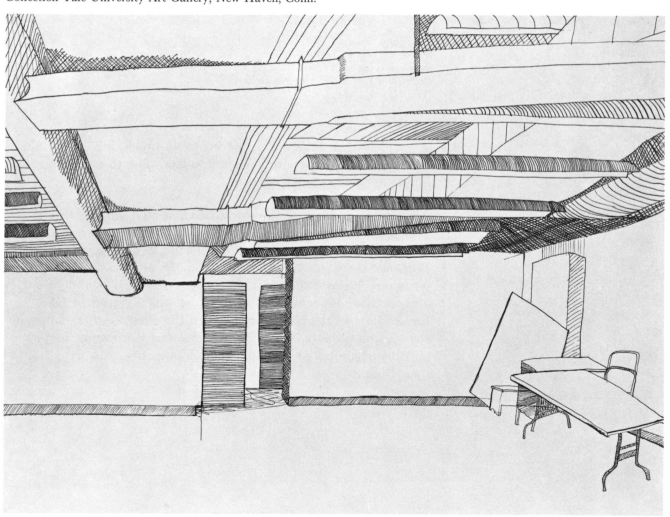

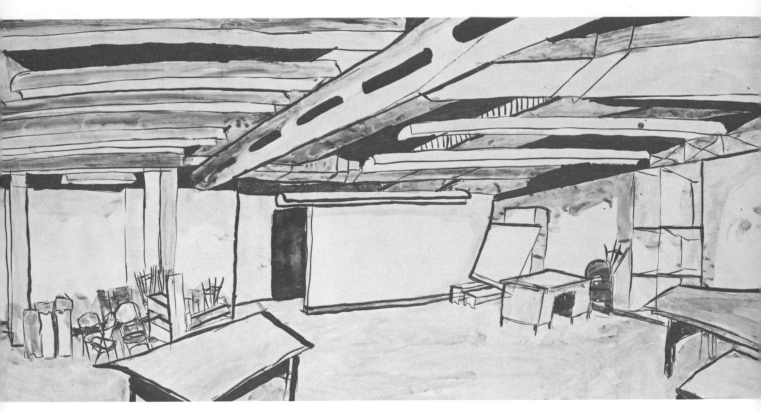

271. John Kaliski.
Basement Studio IV. 1976.
Brush and ink with wash.
Collection Yale University Art Gallery,
New Haven, Conn.

Finally, in Figure 271, a drawing in brush, ink, and wash, the artist makes an enormous work, 6 feet long, to emphasize the horizontal pull of the space.

These nine students, working to find their own answers to their own problems, produced more than twice the work possible in an ordinary classroom situation. Their personal search deepened their own attitudes, and they found it easier to learn what they did not know, for they discovered their own deficiencies and tried to master them. The point at which a student takes the lead marks the transition between the need for dictated problems (which unavoidably reflect the personal tastes of the instructor) and the beginning of individual development.

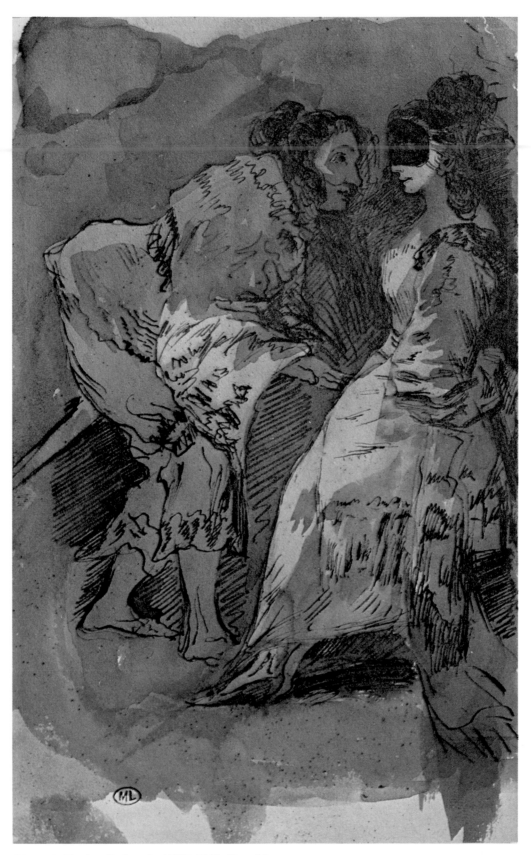

Plate 18. Eugène Delacroix (1798–1863; French).
Masquerade (after Francisco Goya, *Nadie se Conoce,* No. 6, *Los Caprichos*). c. 1830–40.
Pen and ink with wash, 8½ × 5½″. Louvre, Paris.

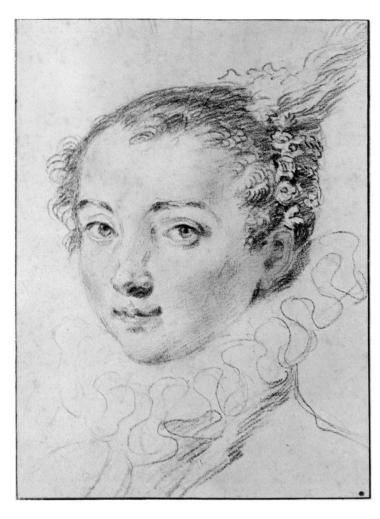

left: Plate 19. Jean-Antoine Watteau
(1684–1721; French).
Head of a Woman (after Peter Paul Rubens).
Black and red chalk, 12 × 8⅞″.
Museum Boymans–van Beuningen, Rotterdam.

below: Plate 20. Hans Holbein the Younger
(1497/98–1543; German).
Portrait of Anna Meyer. 1525–26.
Colored chalks, 13⅞ × 10⅝″.
Kupferstichkabinett, Kunstmuseum, Basel.

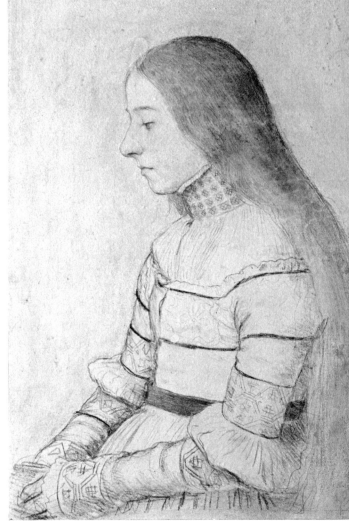

III Drawing: The Vision of the Masters

12 Instrumentation and Copying

Instrumentation

Buying a brush or a new pen can be an exciting event for an artist. One gets the "feel" of the instrument through making idle surface marks and learns how to play the instrument. This random sketching is often a sensuous experience in itself, and, ultimately, an image is born that accommodates the experience. Although a concept may dictate a certain tool, the artist must always imagine future work within the context of familiar tools and materials. Instrumentation—the way in which we make particular marks with a tool—is shaped by the demands of both the desired image and our natural handwriting. The dialogue between the instrument and instrumentation is, for some artists, a broad one (see Figs. 75, 77), but for others the choice is narrow. Obviously, it is not the range of virtuosity that measures the value of a drawing or of a particular artist.

If "technique" is seen as the interaction between instrument and instrumentation, then, in the finest sense, technique works in the service of a concept and does not act as a detached or added element. On the other hand, technique, in its worst sense, is the search for a surface treatment that becomes the main interest of the artist and of the viewer. Tools and their marks, if they are not to become the subject of the drawing, must remain always subservient to the artist's vision, for if we see how a drawing is made before we perceive the life of its forms, we are seeing only technique.

Many of Rembrandt's drawings exhibit the most spectacular free-flowing surface marks, yet one does not at first see how he made the drawing, for the strokes always function primarily as carriers of form and composition. In this chapter we shall study a series of master drawings and explore the ways in which a particular instrument or the artist's instrumentation was used to serve a vision.

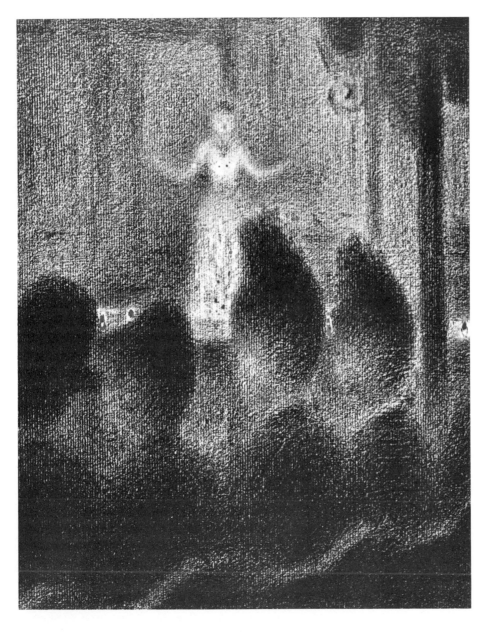

272. Georges Seurat
(1859–91; French).
At the "Concert Européen." c. 1887.
Conté crayon, 12¼ × 9⅜".
Museum of Modern Art, New York
(Lillie P. Bliss Collection).

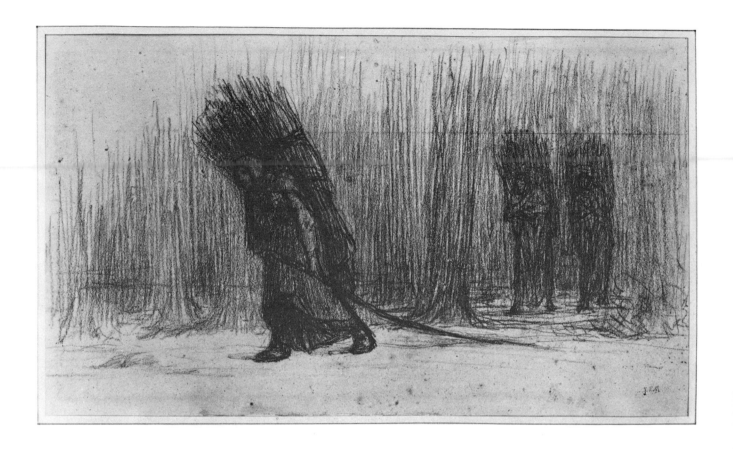

Chalk and Charcoal   The surface quality in Georges Seurat's
At the "Concert Européen" (Fig. 272) derives from the marks of conté
crayon that seem rubbed or forced into the fine, vertical ribs of the
textured paper. This texture breaks down the light into small
particles, and, at first glance, the effect is similar to that in
Seurat's painting, where dots of various colors give an additive
effect (for example, red and blue appear as purple when
seen from a distance). The surface treatment actually produces
a light that seems to be emanating from the white figure at
center stage. Here tool and mark serve naturally the visual drama
of repeated circles in a darkened foreground set against
a lighted background. The vertical bar at right stabilizes the
composition and helps define the space between the heads
and the background space. The tilted, wavy line at the bottom
of the composition defines the frontal plane.

Most master drawings have a tendency to reveal their
tool marks—even in flowing washes—rather than disguising them
by blending. Seurat's work is a rare exception, for the tooth
of the paper takes the role of the mark.

In Jean François Millet's *Fagot Carriers* (Fig. 273) the crayon
marks all are visible, and they produce a broad stage for
groups of sticks. These strokes engulf the figures at right, so that
they become part of the background. The broken light effect,
made by the conté crayon strokes, forms a backdrop for
the central figure, which is presented with the same stroking,
thus keeping the whole drawing in a uniform atmosphere of light.

273. Jean François Millet
(1814–75; French). *Fagot Carriers.*
Conté crayon, $11\frac{3}{8} \times 18\frac{3}{8}''$.
Museum of Fine Arts, Boston
(gift of Martin Brimmer).

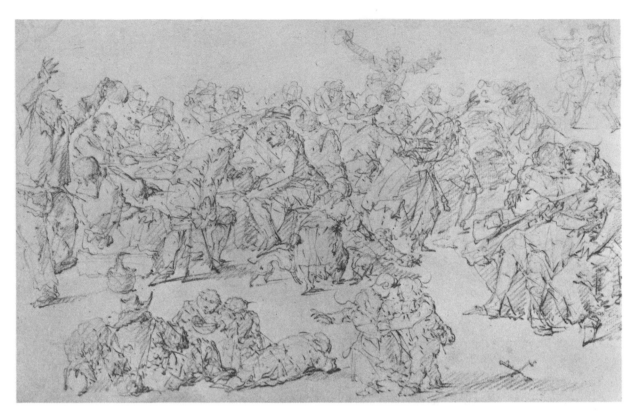

above: 274. Matthias Scheits (1625/30–1700; German). *Peasant Carnival.*
Conté crayon. Kunsthalle, Bremen (destroyed in World War II).

below: 275. Jean-Antoine Watteau (1684–1721; French). Study for *Les Charmes de la Vie.* Black chalk, lead pencil, and touches of red chalk. Louvre, Paris.

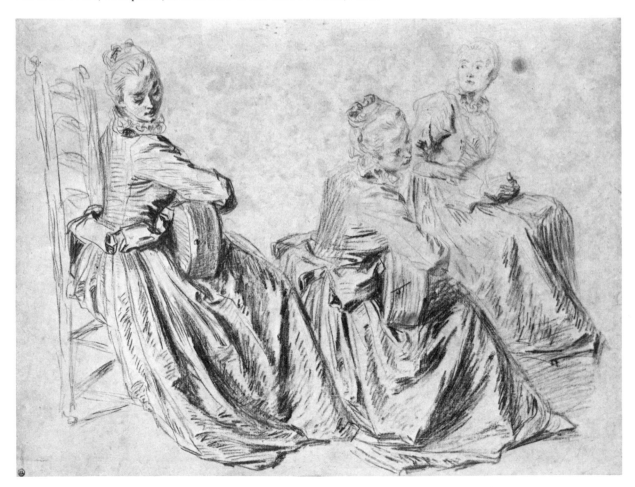

Matthias Scheits' *Peasant Carnival* (Fig. 274) was produced
with the same kind of tool—chalk or conté. In this work the use of
the instrument is clearly dictated by the compositional demands
of the theme; allover activity requires a rapid crisscrossing
of energy and light.

In Watteau's *Les Charmes de la Vie* (Fig. 275) the figures move
across the page in a cinemalike sequence. One postured
gesture blends into another as we read from left to right. The
figures seem to exist in a strong side light, which is kept constant.
This light causes abrupt dark shadows and highlights in the
drapery, and these are depicted with sure, economical marks
that stay in place on the form.

<u>Pen and Brush</u>   Since pen lines cannot easily be erased,
we do not usually connect pen drawings with "searching"—that is,
drawings that may be rehearsals for formal works in other media
or which reveal the quest for the particulars of a form or for
its spatial location. However, there are exceptions to this rule.

In the study reproduced as Figure 276, Pollaiuolo keeps
the contours of his forms open and flexible. The swift, darting
instrumentation of the pen probes the expression and articulation
of limbs. The artist repeats the hands up and down the page
in his search for the exact gesture.

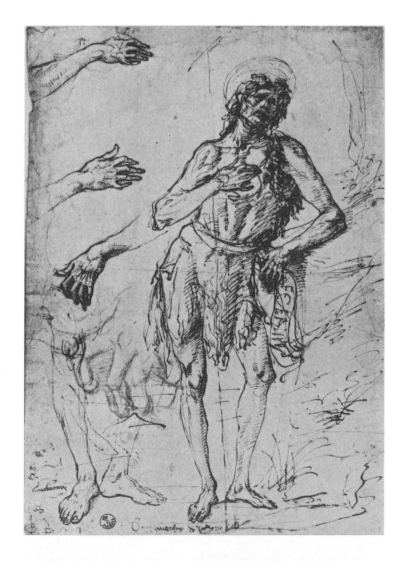

276. Antonio Pollaiuolo
(1431/32–98; Italian).
St. John the Baptist.
Pen and bistre, 11 × 7¾".
Uffizi, Florence.

277. Hans Baldung Grien
(1484/85–1545; German).
Woman with Death as a Partner.
Pen and ink.
Staatliche Kunstsammlungen, Weimar.

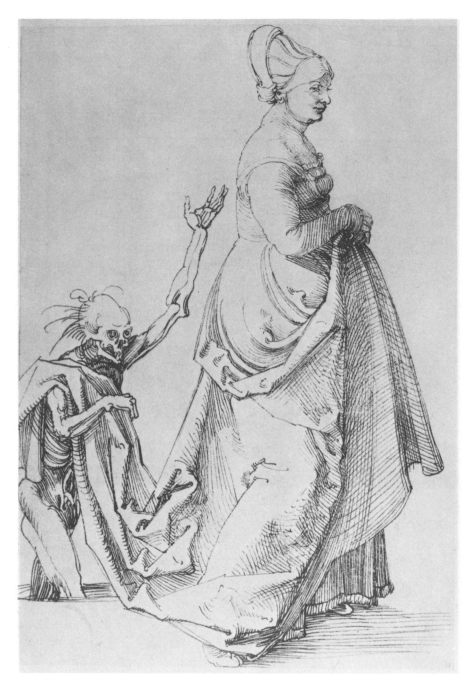

Woman with Death as a Partner (Fig. 277), a steel-pen
drawing by Hans Baldung Grien, suggests another attitude. The
forms are as sharply defined as those of an engraving, with its
demand of total commitment to a line. The image appears
clearly, instantly, making one suspect that there were rehearsals
for this performance. Especially noteworthy is the delicate
line from the nape of the woman's neck, as it travels
down gradually, picking up speed as it reaches the drapery below.
The line is purposely light and broken, for if it were dark
it would close off the space around the figure and allow the white
of the page to separate into nothing but an airless backdrop.

In Figure 278, *Rest on the Flight into Egypt* by an unknown
German master, the instrument, a steel pen, is the same
as that used in the previous illustration, but the weaving groups
of short strokes present a more hesitant performance. The
drapery around the feet is the focal point of the drawing, and the
short strokes that surround this form break the light into
tiny patches of texture. The interweaving of these textured
light patches sets up a peculiar atmosphere that engulfs
the whole spatial surface.

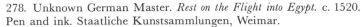

278. Unknown German Master. *Rest on the Flight into Egypt.* c. 1520.
Pen and ink. Staatliche Kunstsammlungen, Weimar.

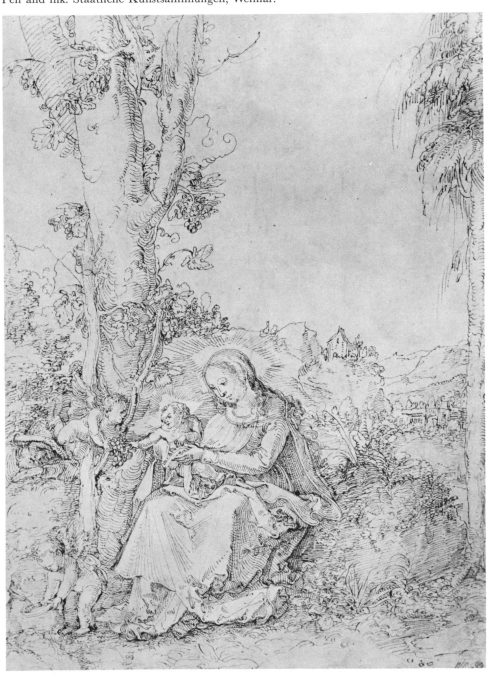

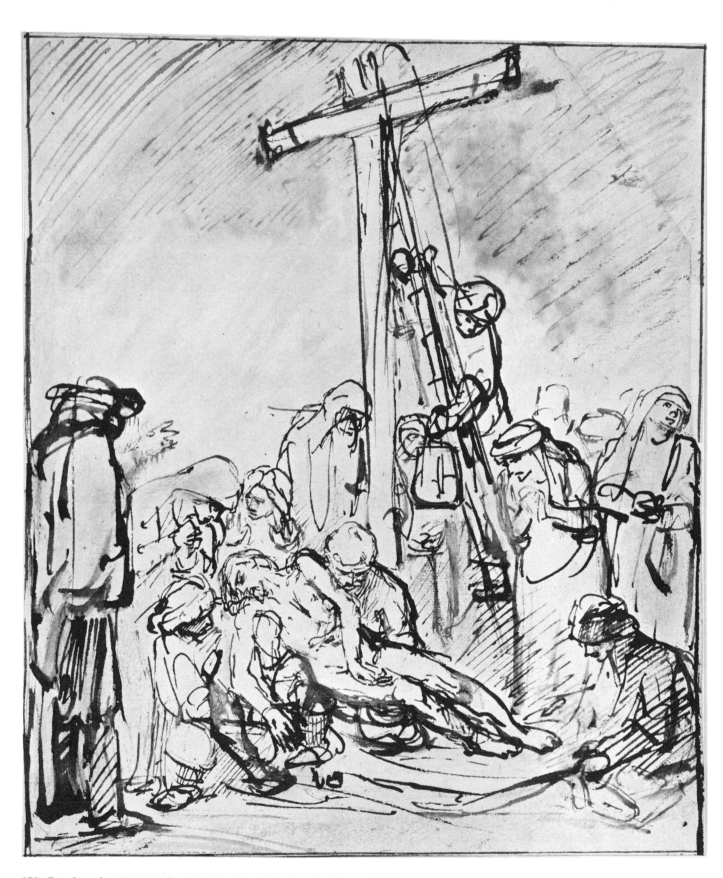

279. Rembrandt (1606–69; Dutch). *The Deposition from the Cross.* c. 1647–50.
Pen and wash in bistre with white body color, $10\frac{3}{8} \times 8\frac{3}{8}''$.
Kupferstichkabinett, Staatliche Museen, West Berlin.

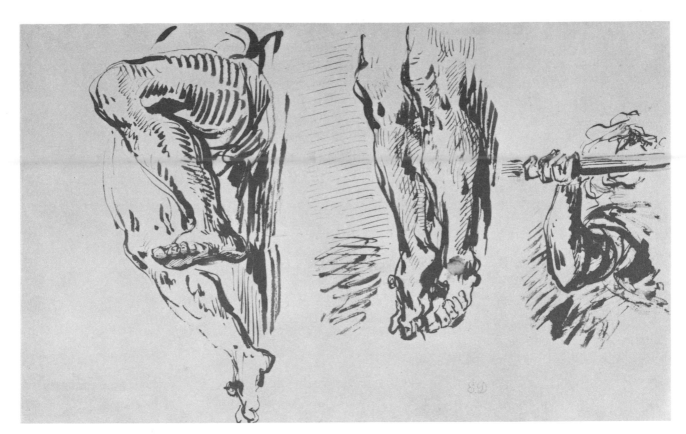

280. Eugène Delacroix (1798–1863; French). *Study after Rubens.*
Reed pen and ink. Whereabouts unknown.

Rembrandt uses a different pen, a quill, and a different
kind of instrumentation in a *Desposition from the Cross* (Fig. 279).
The flowing manipulation of alternately scratchy and fluid,
thick and thin lines sets up a hierarchy of focus. Broad, heavy
strokes create the strongest focus in the heavy columnlike figure
that hugs the left edge and establishes the gravity of the whole
composition. This figure is closest to us and acts as a curtain to frame
the drama. It is balanced by the cross and the triangle below
containing three fairly dark figures. Between these clear
spatial stations the central drama unfolds, in which strong light
created by lighter lines with broken contours seems to melt
the top sections of the main actors. This is a brilliant staging
produced by pen strokes that organize space and direct
the focus rather than calling attention to their own virtuosity.

In Delacroix' reed-pen *Study after Rubens* (Fig. 280)
we witness a strong virtuoso work based on another artist's design.
These sensuous yet functional tool marks are not separate
from the action of the form. The violent round strokes on the
upper leg (far left) force the eye into an upward spiral movement.
The experience of copying, discussed later in this chapter,
is well illustrated here, for the artist is reacting to the forms studied
in order to heighten his own sensation, rather than rendering
the original surface markings.

Magnanimity of Scipio Africanus by Anthony van Dyck
(Fig. 281) returns us to the searching attitude of Pollaiuolo (Fig.
276). This drawing resembles a notebook sketch in which
the artist is testing the positions of shifting and flowing masses
to find the most successful arrangement for a finished work.
We sense this sequence of forms, because the instrumentation
is in turn delicately slow and rhythmically fast. As in all
the drawings reproduced, the instrumentation, beautiful in itself,
is the product of the intention—a search for the clear staging
of the actors.

281. Anthony van Dyck
(1599–1641; Flemish).
Magnanimity of Scipio Africanus.
Pen and ink with wash.
Kunsthalle, Bremen
(destroyed in World War II).

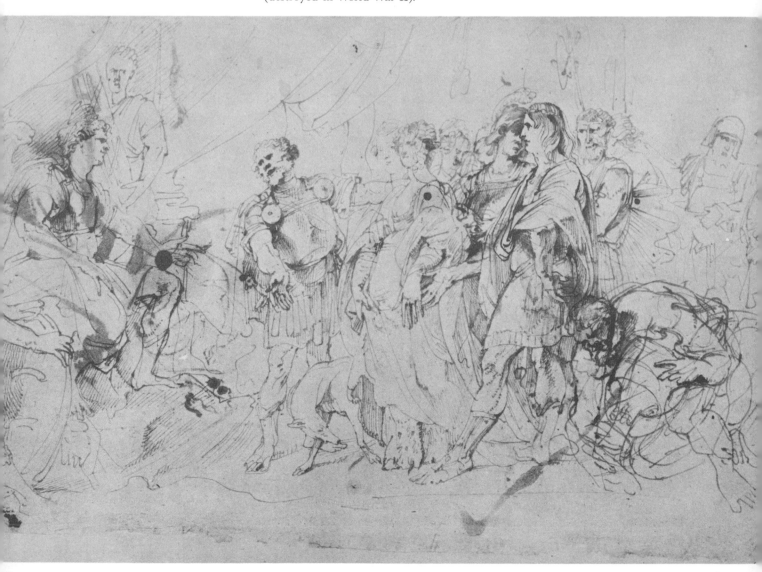

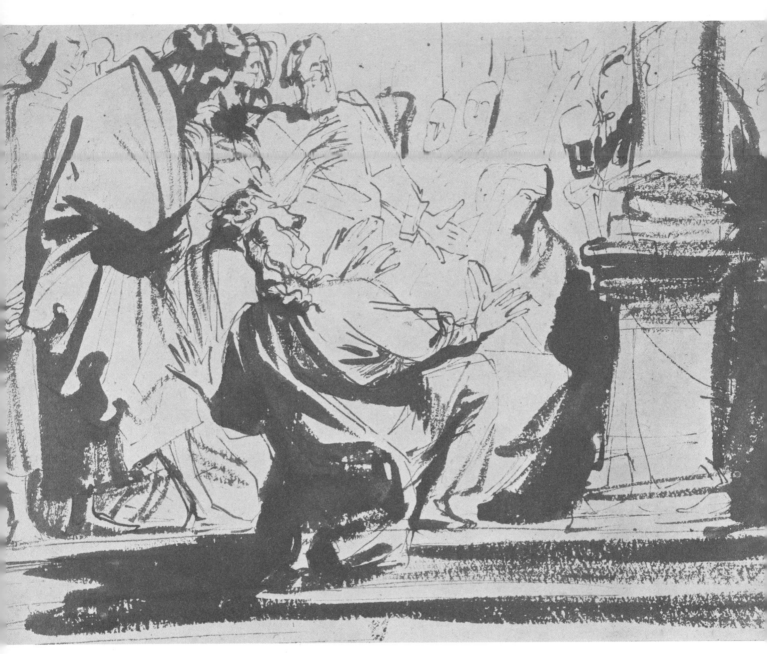

282. Anthony van Dyck (1599–1641; Flemish).
Miracle on the Day of Pentecost. Brush and ink.
Staatliche Kunstsammlungen, Weimar.

Van Dyck's *Miracle on the Day of Pentecost* (Fig. 282)
uses a different tool, a brush, to achieve a different purpose.
The drawing is not tentative. We do not sense the possible shifting
of masses, but it is nonetheless a spontaneous performance.
The brush strokes are sometimes dry and dragging across
the frontal space, sometimes more fluid as they suggest figures
in what seems to be an instant freezing of a dramatically lit
situation. Van Dyck instinctively picked the most appropriate tool
for each concept.

283. Giovanni Battista Tiepolo
(1696–1770; Italian).
Beheading of John the Baptist.
Pen and ink with wash.
Whereabouts unknown.

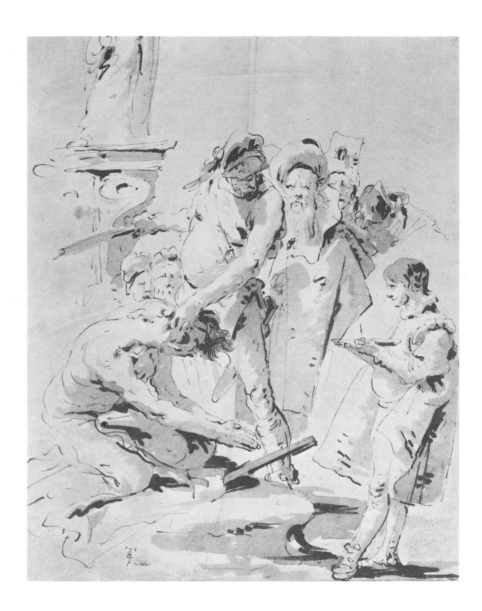

Giovanni Tiepolo's *Beheading of John the Baptist* (Fig. 283)
is also a brilliant performance. Pen lines and dark areas
seem to have been done at the same instant as were the flowing
washes. The action and function of these light washes themselves
are exciting. They do not logically describe the planes of
each figure; rather, they float independently. A wash that covers
the man's hand and sword incorporates the column behind it,
as does the wash at upper right, which covers three figures.
This fluid, watered ink used so skillfully by Tiepolo is the only
material that could create this particular effect.

Copying

As we have implied, one does not acquire a personal handwriting
by emulating a master. The student's goal in copying is not
duplication but understanding, in the hope that this insight will
help to develop a personal handwriting and individual attitudes

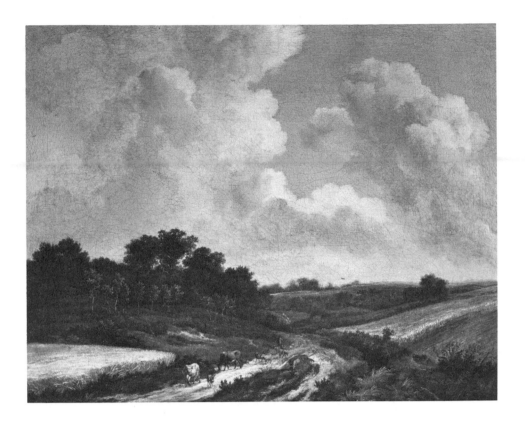

284. Jakob van Ruisdael
(c. 1628–82; Dutch).
Landscape with a Cornfield.
Oil on canvas, 18 × 21½″.
Courtesy Thomas Agnew
& Sons, Ltd., London.

toward form. So it was that Constable did not simply make
a reproduction of a landscape by Ruisdael that he admired (Fig.
284). In the process of developing his own ideas about landscape
form, he transcribed in his sketchbook a few painterly notes
on the spatial divisions, weights, and patterns employed by the
Dutch master (Fig. 285).

285. John Constable
(1776–1837; English).
Landscape with a Cornfield
(after Jakob van Ruisdael).
1819. Pencil, 3½ × 4⅜″.
Courtesy the Executors
of the Estate
of Lt. Col. J. H. Constable.

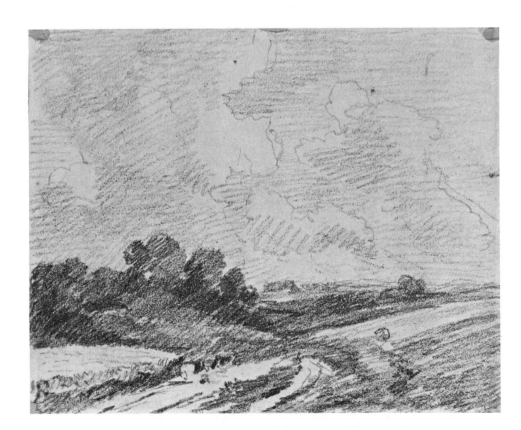

Similarly, in a pen-and-ink study after an etching by Goya, Delacroix translates the original medium into swift, wet washes (Pl. 18, p. 245). This variation changes the tempo of the work and creates a sense of immediacy that forces the viewer to see all the actors at once.

In Plate 19 (p. 246), Jean-Antoine Watteau transforms a head by Rubens by adding his own vibrant punctuation. Instead of a gradual transition from light to dark, Watteau heightens the value range by accenting the features with swift, dark strokes, which combine to form a diagonal axis across the composition.

The intelligent student copyist does not experience a drawing more fully than does the sensitive layman but instead may experience it in a different way. The copyist can perceive the positioning of a particular form in a particular space or divorce a form from its environment for individual study. One may discover, for example, that a seemingly straightforward head in an Ingres drawing is actually a very complicated structure. Copying this head with its special attitude will reveal the uniqueness of its foreshortening and the reasons for the exaggerated tilt in space.

In copying a Tiepolo wash drawing the perceptive student can realize the miracle of suggestion in the master's floating washes, which do not strictly define form in space but, instead, seem to dance from one form to another. Or the copyist can discover the inner pressures of energy in Rembrandt's instrumentation, as these marks simultaneously create light and space for the compositional intent.

Studying the structure of a masterwork is at least as important as understanding its instrumentation. However, the practice of imposing triangles, circles, and S-curves over great works usually leads to oversimplification, if not to complete boredom. Another dangerous method is to cover a work with enforced surface marks. This has led to such bizarre experiments as applying Mondrian's field of plus and minus signs to a drawing by Titian. The idea, then, is not really to copy but to be aware of how the instrument and its instrumentation act as carriers of ideas and attitudes.

Student Response

In the study of masterworks the students were encouraged to use the copying experience directly by first making a free copy and then attempting their own drawings with the same attitude in mind. No specific instructions were given.

One student began by making a copy (Fig. 286) of an Ingres portrait. As a copy it was well done, but the student felt there was little experience extracted. He explained that he had chosen Ingres as a personal challenge, because his own tendencies were quite different. He then experimented with some freely invented studies after Poussin's figure compositions in wash

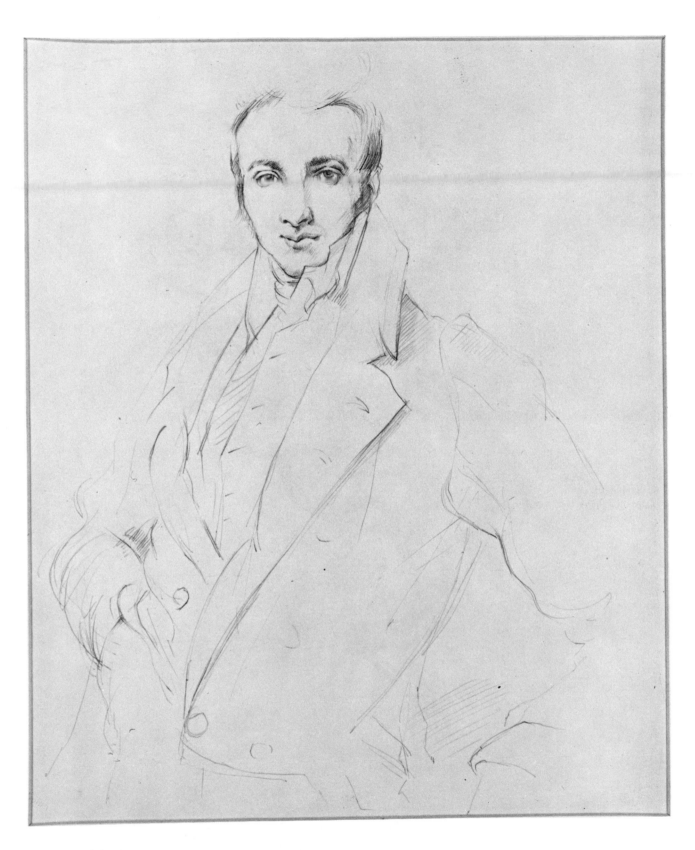

286. Barry Schactman.
Copy after Ingres. 1959.
Graphite pencil.
Collection Yale University Art Gallery,
New Haven, Conn.

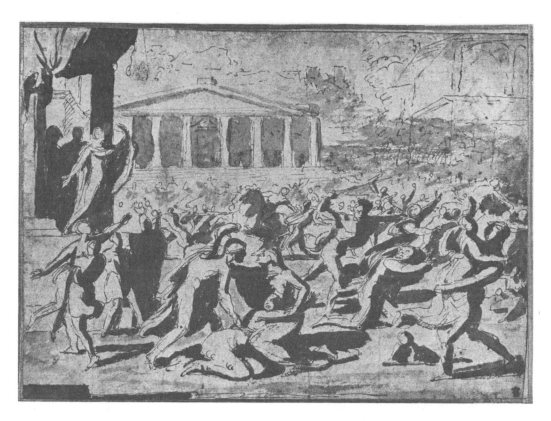

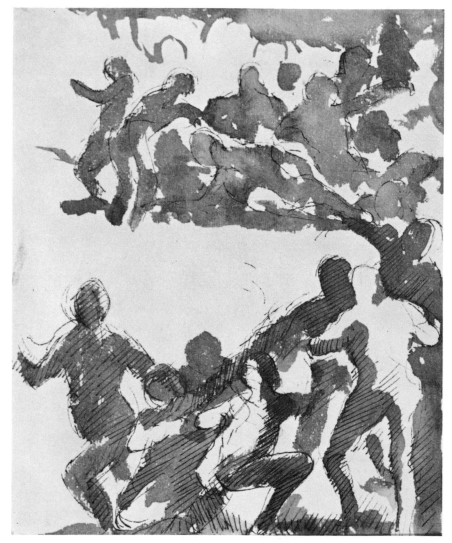

above: 287. Nicolas Poussin
(1594–1665; French).
Study for *Rape of the Sabines.*
Pen and ink with wash.
Devonshire Collection, Chatsworth
(reproduced by permission of
the Trustees
of the Chatsworth Settlement).

right: 288. Barry Schactman.
Study after Poussin. 1959.
Brush and ink with wash.
Collection Yale University
Art Gallery, New Haven, Conn.

264   *The Art of Drawing*

(Fig. 287). These were much more in keeping with his own interests. During the next few weeks he produced a series of reactions to Poussin, of which Figure 288 is an example. This was copying for a purpose. Months later the student's own work, done independently of class study, revealed an interplay of figure and ground—that is, a harmony of interspaces and dark shapes (Fig. 289). In these studies the personal expression forms the composition.

289. Barry Schactman.
Figure-Ground Interplay. 1959.
Brush and ink.
Collection Mr. and Mrs. Richard Lytle,
Woodbridge, Conn.

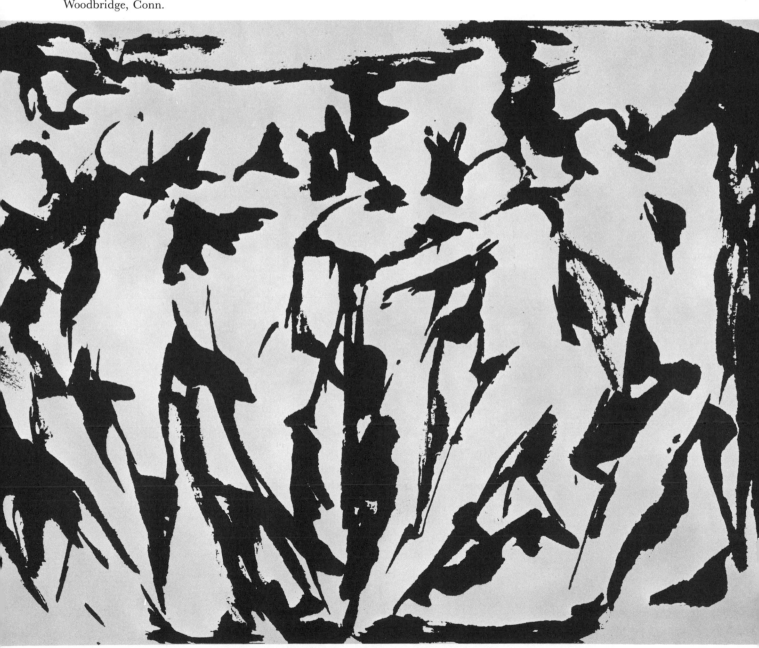

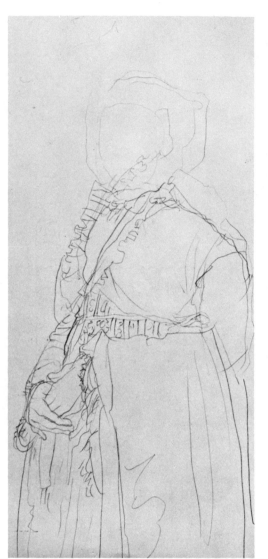

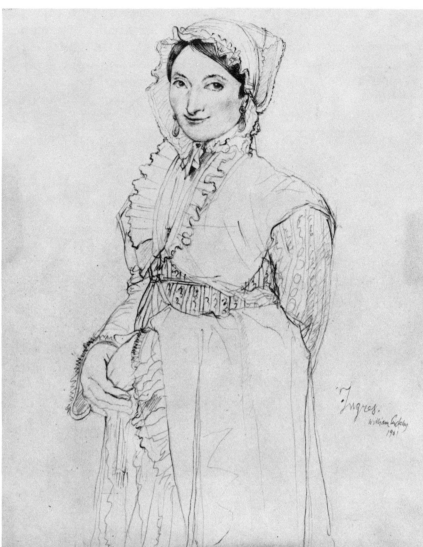

left: 290. William Cudahy. *Study after Ingres.* 1961. Graphite pencil.
Collection Yale University Art Gallery, New Haven, Conn.

right: 291. William Cudahy. *Study after Ingres.* 1961. Graphite pencil.
Collection Yale University Art Gallery, New Haven, Conn.

Two studies after Ingres (Figs. 290, 291) illustrate
different kinds of investigation. In Figure 290 the position of the
figure in space is presented without the main interest—the
head form. In studying these secondary shapes, this almost bland
underpinning, we see Ingres' seemingly sketchy but firmly
stated figure. In the original, with its insistence on the face,
one is hardly aware of the firm structure that supports it.

In Figure 291 the copyist exaggerates the way in which
Ingres stretched the eyes and mouth around the sphere of the head.
This stretching, which we normally associate with a more
sumptuous, "expressive" instrumentation and attitude, is beautifully
understated with a hard yet delicate pencil line. The student
copyist, of course, is studying rather than imitating.

The next group of drawings (Fig. 292), a series of studies
after Rembrandt, presents another attitude. The original pen strokes
are not imitated; in fact, three of the five drawings were
done in graphite pencil. The studies try to reveal the way energy
is directed in the space, rather than imitating the actual
strokes of the original. The strongest form is the violent L-shaped
brush mark surrounding the bent elbow of the lower figure.
This meeting of two planes in opposition creates a kind of visual
noise and causes the form to advance. The secondary emphasis
is the swiftly brushed wash between the two figures, which
both contains and stabilizes them.

292. Sister Mary Frei. *Rembrandt Studies.* 1960.
Graphite pencil (top and center), pen and ink with wash (bottom).
Collection Yale University Art Gallery, New Haven, Conn.

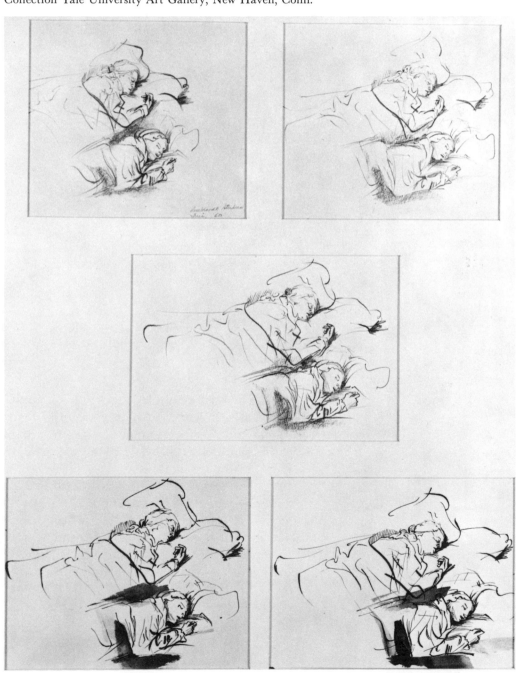

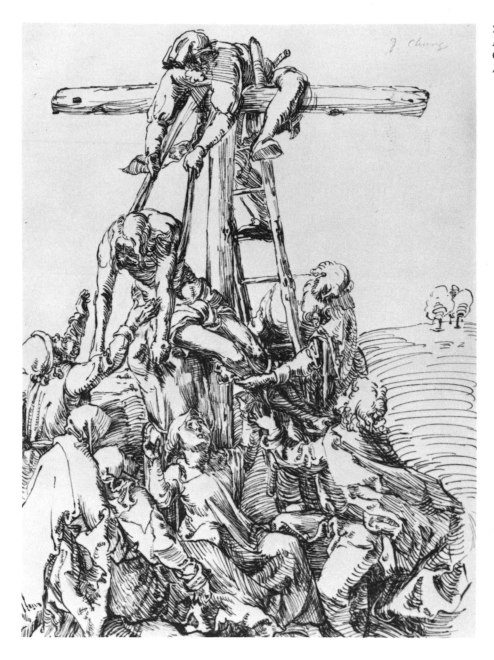

293. Jongsoon Park Chung.
Desposition Study. 1962. Pen and ink.
Collection Yale University
Art Gallery, New Haven, Conn.

The next example (Fig. 293) is a study of the density
and flow of masses in which a group of figures is woven together.
An attempt has been made to simplify the planes, while
at the same time intensifying the baroque play of light and dark
found in the original.

The transfer of form attitudes from one master to another
makes us acutely aware of different modes of perceiving. From a
section of a Rembrandt etching, *Diana at the Bath* (Fig. 294),
one student isolated the turning head of a woman and tried
to capture the attitude of Jacques Villon (Figs. 67, 214).
In Figure 295 the softly modeled and rounded planes of Rembrandt
have been transformed into sharp angles that are gently
stretched in opposing directions.

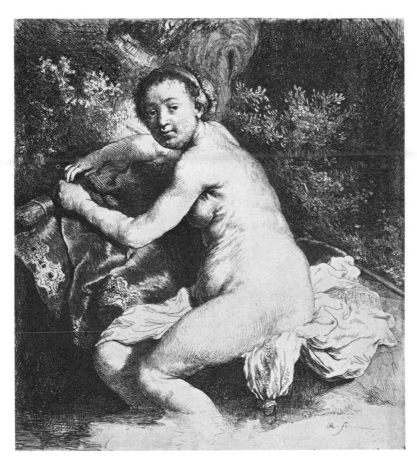

left: 294. Rembrandt (1606–69; Dutch).
Diana at the Bath. c. 1631. Etching, 7 × 6¼″.
Rijksmuseum, Amsterdam.

below: 295. Robert S. Dealey.
Copy after Rembrandt. 1969.
Graphite pencil.
Collection Yale University Art Gallery,
New Haven, Conn.

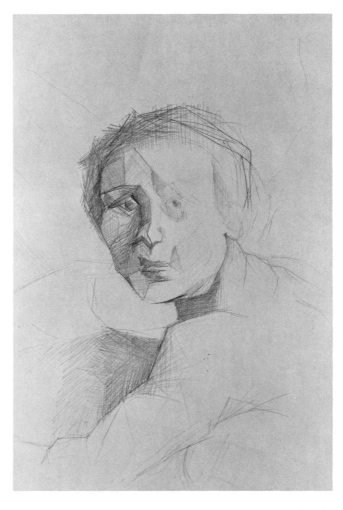

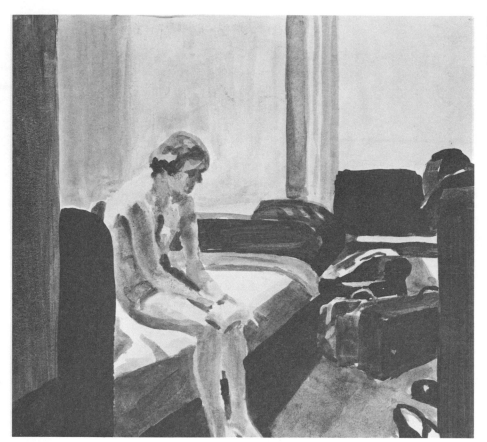

296. Frank Moore.
Study after Hopper I. 1973. Wash.
Collection Yale University
Art Gallery, New Haven, Conn.

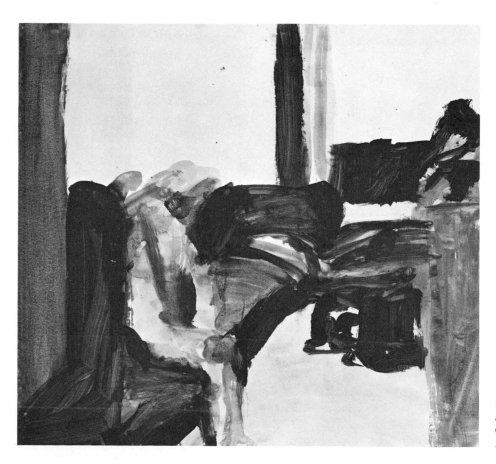

297. Frank Moore.
Study after Hopper II. 1973. Wash.
Collection Yale University
Art Gallery, New Haven, Conn.

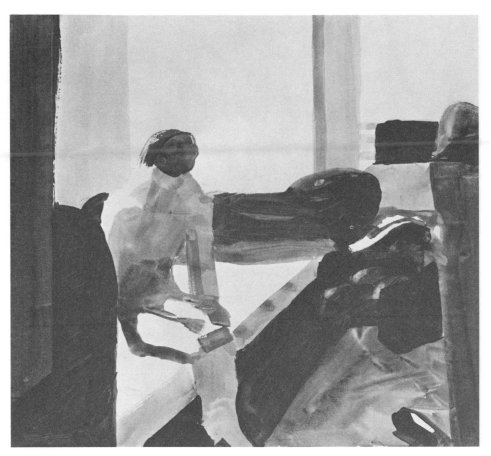

298. Frank Moore.
Study after Hopper III.
1973. Wash.
Collection Yale University
Art Gallery, New Haven, Conn.

The following excerpts are from a student's diary, recording the stages of his analysis through "copying" of Edward Hopper's *Hotel Room:*

"The first study was a direct try at paraphrase, a try at measuring the tempo" (Fig. 296).

"I sought to decompose the composition to determine the weights of the shapes in their places" (Fig. 297).

"Less heavy handed—more in the spirit of the work without imitating. The flow is less clogged, the space a little more measured" (Fig. 298).

In this chapter we have emphasized tool marks and their relationship to form. We have seen that with the same instrument many kinds of instrumentation are possible, depending on the concept and the form attitude. There is beauty in the way marks move to encompass and release forms. The life of lines themselves—their speed, weight, and movement orchestrated in a personal way—is a natural by-product of the search for form.

13 From Drawing to Painting

The transition from drawing to painting is a simple one if we keep within the broad boundaries defined in Chapter 3: Drawing is form without color. Artists in the past have often wished to explore form by means of a black-and-white or monochromatic palette without sacrificing the fluidity and sweep that can be attained with the brush and a liquid medium. Working from a photograph, Edgar Degas copied a fresco by Mantegna in charcoal and white chalk on brown canvas (Fig. 299). Perhaps the best known example of painting without color is Picasso's *Guernica,* a work of commanding size and devastating impact painted entirely in blacks, grays, and white (Fig. 300).

Following the same restriction to black, white, and shades of gray makes for an ideal exercise in the boundary area between drawing and painting. By working in a water-based medium, acrylic, which produces both watercolor transparencies and varying opaque thicknesses—together with a simple support, chipboard—we are perhaps painting and drawing at the same time. At least this medium is calming to the student, who

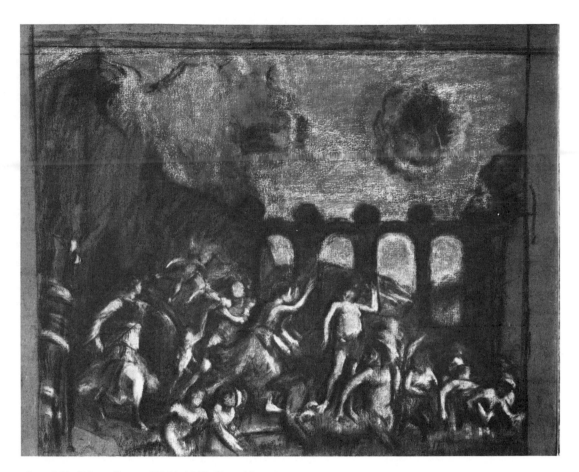

above: 299. Edgar Degas (1834–1917; French).
Virtues Victorious over Vices
(after Mantegna). 1897.
Charcoal and pastel on canvas. Louvre, Paris.

below: 300. Pablo Picasso (1881–1973; Spanish-French).
Guernica. 1937. Oil on canvas, 11′6″ × 25′8″.
On extended loan to the Museum of Modern Art, New York,
from the artist's estate.

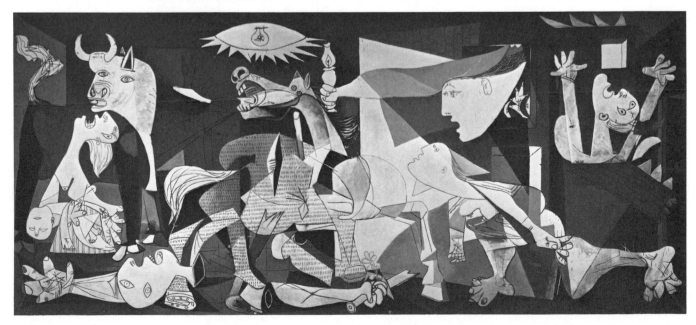

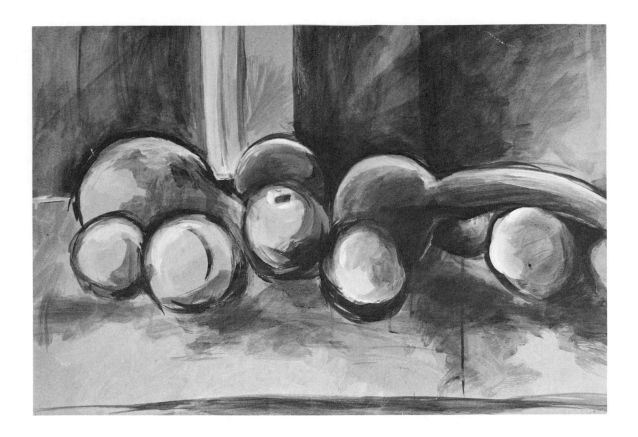

301. Pam Ozaroff. *Still Life.* 1975.
Acrylic on cardboard.
Collection Yale University
School of Art, New Haven, Conn.

does not panic at the thought of the act of painting, with all
its associated aesthetic and technical hurdles.

Acrylic paint does not need much exploration to achieve
a workable control. The brushing—thick and thin applications—
comes naturally to anybody with some basic drawing skill.

The necessary supplies were pint-size jars of black and white
acrylic pigment, chipboard, and a 4-foot-square backboard
or wall board, to which the chipboard was stapled. Also required
were paper peel-off palettes, acrylic gesso (for a ground,
when desired), and four or five brushes ranging from thin watercolor
brushes to 3-inch house-paint brushes. The brushes, support, paint,
and palette are simple, and technical proficiency is no problem.
The students explored this transition, this introduction to painting,
relatively unencumbered with technical problems. In one 13-week
semester they concentrated on just a few broad problems—those
that would give maximum choice to personal attitudes: still life,
masterwork reconstruction, and a combination of the two.

Still Life

We started with objects that could be multiplied—fruits and
vegetables. The only stipulation was that no other kinds of objects
be used, especially the traditional art school props that
frequently add a false note of variety for its own sake. Such variety
tends to weaken or destroy the content and the formal problems
of the exercise. Introducing too many objects that cannot

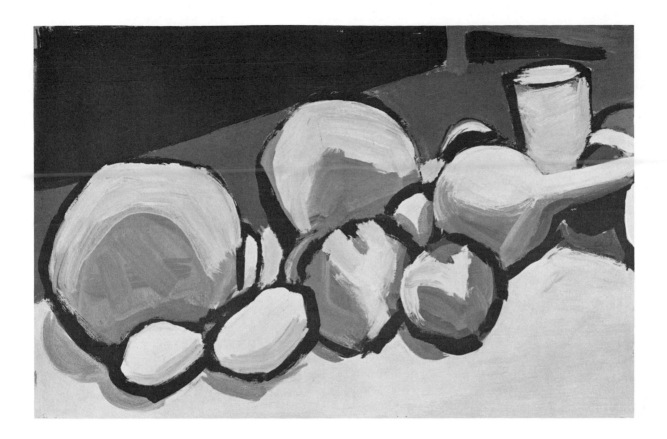

302. John M. Hull. *Still Life.*
1975. Acrylic on cardboard.
Collection Yale University
School of Art,
New Haven, Conn.

be related naturally most often leads the beginner to reproduce
the surface texture of each object and ignore the spatial
effect of the whole page.

Students set up their own arrangements so that personal
preferences in grouping or arranging became immediately evident.
Symmetry and asymmetry, crowding, openness, weighted
pressure—all these sensations and more appeared at the outset
through the placement of forms in a preferred order.

The first and most persistent problem is composition—how
to sustain an orchestrated surface. These exercises are thus about
composing, and their ultimate goal, presented directly in the
last problem, is the discovery that manipulating a physical
sensation, through pressure, overlapping planes, or a desired set
of proportions, is clearly allied—or rather, permanently fused—
with the content.

In Figure 301 the technical approach is almost identical
to a brush-and-wash drawing, for there are few opaque touches.
A liquid fluency is maintained throughout. This technical
fluidity matches the physical effect: a nicely measured, constant
rhythmic pulse is held in place by the weighted verticals.
Although the work does seem to borrow heavily from Cézanne,
its motif is honestly pursued and not merely imitative.

In Figure 302 we encounter vigorously brushed, heavily
contoured forms, enlarged in relation to the page and to the
viewer. This is not the measured beat of Figure 301. These forms
crowd us. The sizes are irregular, as are the brush strokes and

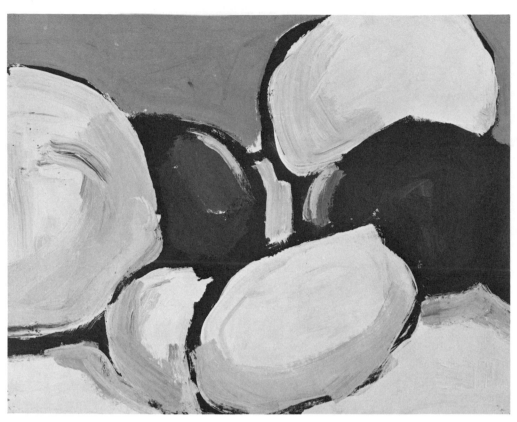

above: 303. John M. Hull. *Still Life.* 1975. Acrylic on cardboard.
Collection Yale University School of Art, New Haven, Conn.

below: 304. Anne E. Heideman. *Still Life.* 1975. Acrylic on cardboard.
Collection Yale University School of Art, New Haven, Conn.

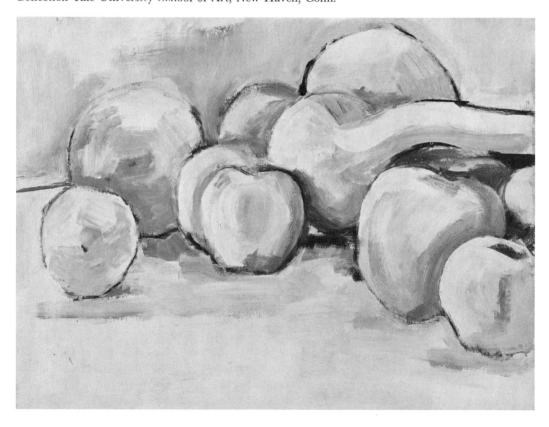

305. Alain Capretz.
Still Life. 1975.
Acrylic on cardboard.
Collection Yale University
School of Art, New Haven, Conn.

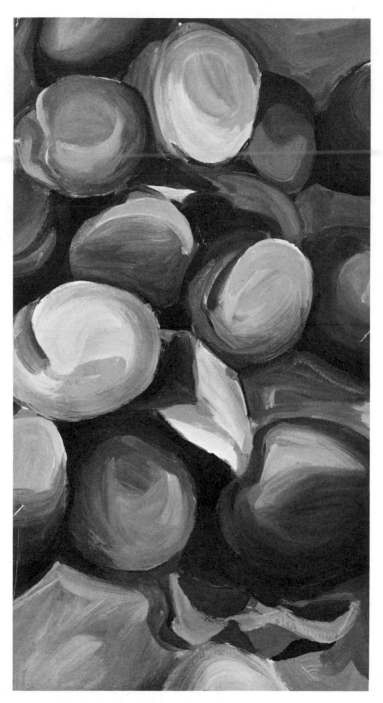

the rhythm. The more enlarged forms in Figure 303, by the
same artist, crowd us even more. The enlargement of these forms
sets up an aggressive scale that makes us feel small. The
forms in both examples loom large and heavy.

The motif of Figure 304 is a blinding white light (more
easily perceived in the original), which is in harmony with the
subtle overlapping of shapes and the gently irregular rhythm.

Crowding is the theme of Figure 305, in which a narrow,
vertical format, with forms cropped on all sides, carries the message
of pressure from left and right—a definite physical effect.

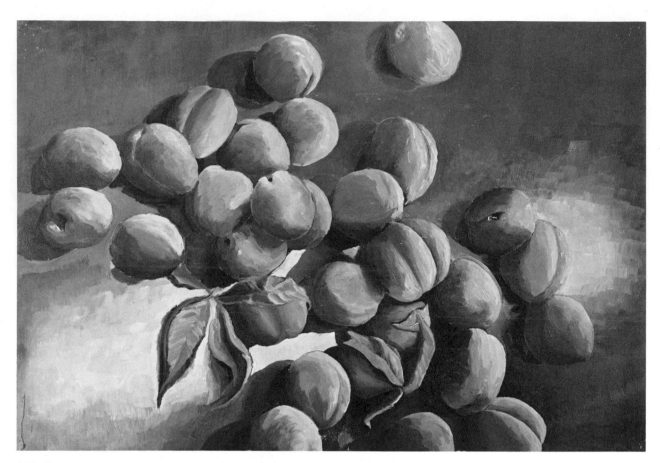

306. Joseph Chambers. *Aerial Still Life.* 1975. Acrylic on cardboard.
Collection Yale University School of Art, New Haven, Conn.

Figure 306 is an aerial view. At a safe distance we hover over the peach forms revealed by a strong raking light. The student is determined to model each sculptural volume with carefully built-up strokes, taking special care to play hard edges against soft edges.

As an extension of this problem students were instructed to set up a still life of their own choosing. In Figure 307 we again see our old friends, the shoes, but this time in a very complicated space. First, the floor plane that houses the shoes is cocked at an angle to the left and tightly held from the back by a vertical mass at the table corner and a diagonal from the far right. In this rigidly held stage, a shoe in the half-light pushes up from the left corner, extending the diagonal. The main shoes seem to be walking, one in front of the other. The brushing, especially of the floor plane, also plays its part in both holding the gravity and surrounding and echoing all the movements. It is a tautly held construction.

Figure 308 comes dangerously close to the academic still life that we warned against. However, it is carried off here by the free, open, loose relationships that tip and lean and have an allover relaxed movement.

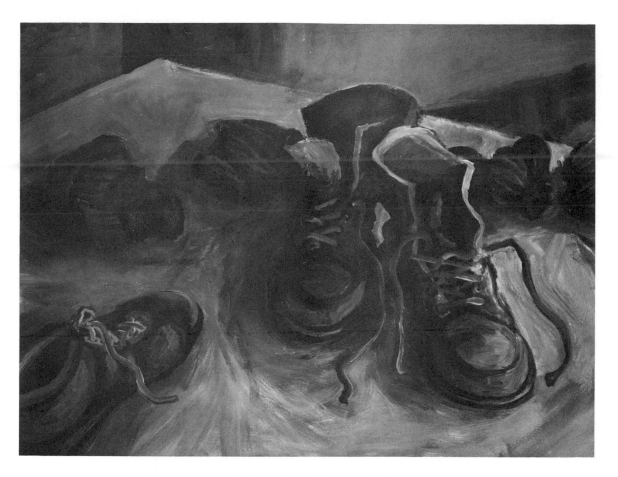

above: 307. Craig Davis. *Study of Shoes.* 1975. Acrylic.
Collection Yale University School of Art, New Haven, Conn.

below: 308. Steven O'Connor. *Still Life with Crockery.* 1975. Acrylic on cardboard.
Collection Yale University School of Art, New Haven, Conn.

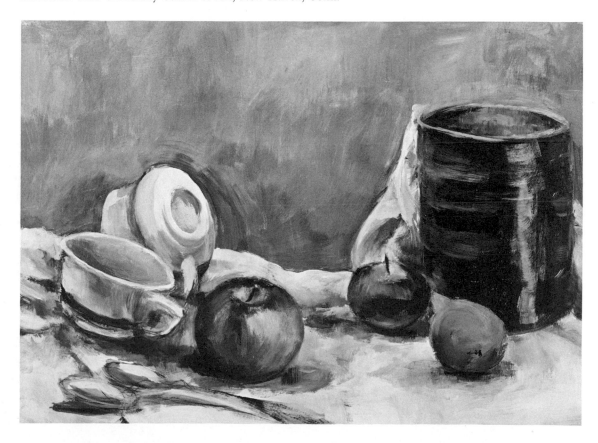

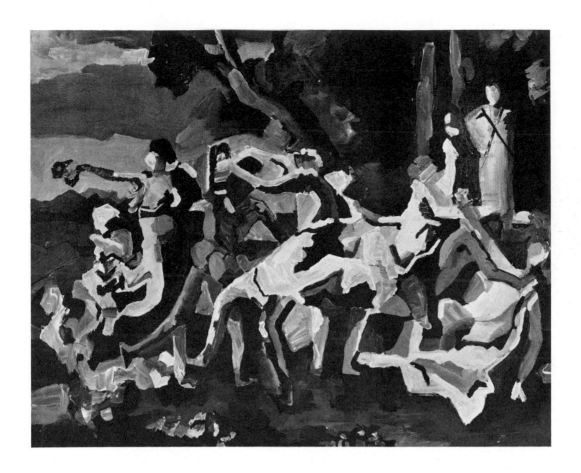

above: 309. Scott Stenhouse.
Study after Poussin. 1975.
Acrylic on cardboard.
Collection Yale University
School of Art, New Haven, Conn.

below right: 310. Nicolas Poussin
(1594–1665; French).
Bacchanalian Revel before a Herm of Pan.
1636–37. Oil on canvas, 33″ × 4′7⅞″.
National Gallery, London
(reproduced by
courtesy of the Trustees).

Masterwork Studies

In the next problem the students chose from a group of clear
black-and-white reproductions of Poussin paintings. Why Poussin?
In Poussin we have certainly one of the great stage managers
in visual drama. Scale and movement are held perfectly
in adjustment, to say the very least. The students were removed
enough from the story content in Poussin to build relationships
in a purely visual manner. The goal, then, was not reproduction,
but the study of these relationships.

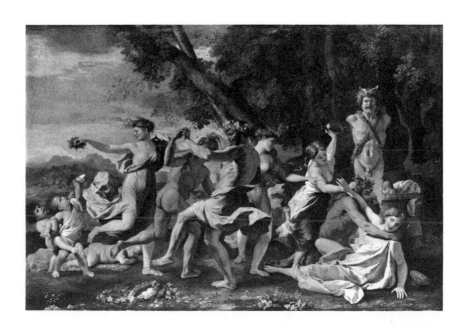

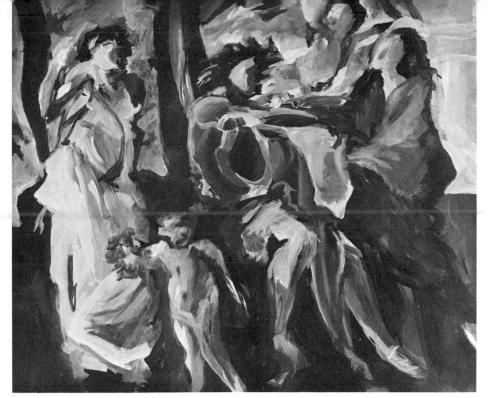

311. Pam Ozaroff.
Study after Poussin. 1975.
Acrylic on cardboard.
Collection Yale University
School of Art, New Haven, Conn.

Even within a seemingly rigid didactic exercise, individual
expression was not lost. Personal preferences for angular planar
relationships or overall baroque movement appeared naturally
as a by-product of reconstruction. The personal handwriting of
forming strokes varied from one individual to the next.

In Figure 309 the student built up coat upon coat of paint
until he could satisfy his own goal of simplifying the masses and
establishing interconnections of shape and pattern. It took constant
shifting and realigning of planes to satisfy his desire of squeezing
out the essence he found in the Poussin composition (Fig. 310).
The result appeared to some of the class as a giant still life.

The artist of Figure 311 analyzes a reduced stage in which
the actors fill the whole frontal plane. The space from front
to back is as narrow as a bas relief. Here the brushing probes and
speeds up the interpenetrating flow of surface movement
found in the "original" (Fig. 312).

312. Nicolas Poussin
(1594–1665; French).
Inspiration of the Poet. c. 1628–29.
Oil on canvas. Louvre, Paris.

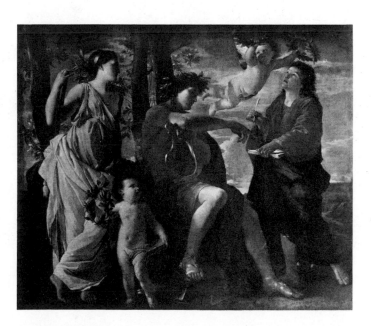

Figure 313 stresses locating and measuring the interplay of planes across the surface and back to the architectural setting, coupled with a concentration on the scale of tonal values. This exercise, like the others in this series, helps make us aware of structure as expression.

By this point the students had gained real confidence in handling the media. We therefore extended the present problem by asking them to select masterpieces of their own choice and, more important, to select visual issues in these works for development in their reconstructions.

A painting by Caravaggio (Fig. 314) was selected by the author of Figure 315, who chose to stress the scale of the gesticulating actors and their relationship to the background. The student developed a direct, flowing brush stroke, which appeared naturally as a personal necessity of form making.

313. Julia Glass. *Study after Poussin.* 1975.
Acrylic on cardboard.
Collection Yale University School of Art,
New Haven, Conn.

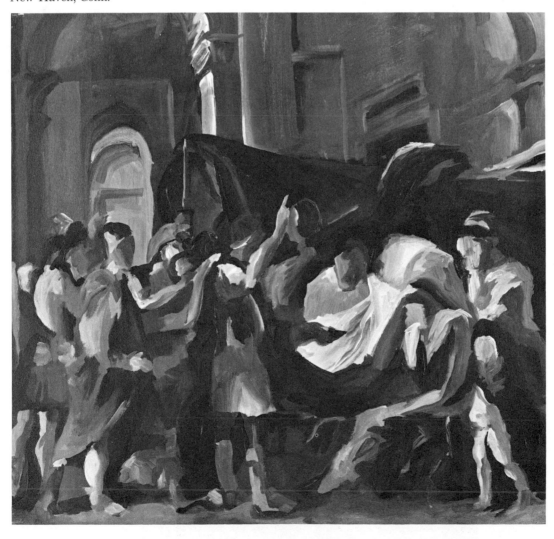

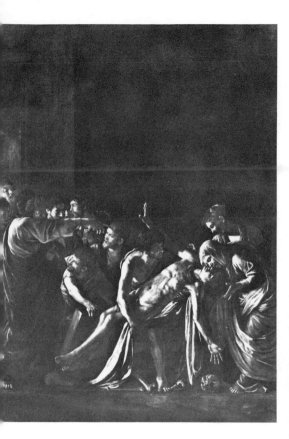

314. Caravaggio (1573–1609; Italian).
Resurrection of Lazarus. 1608–09.
Oil on canvas.
Museo Nazionale, Messina.

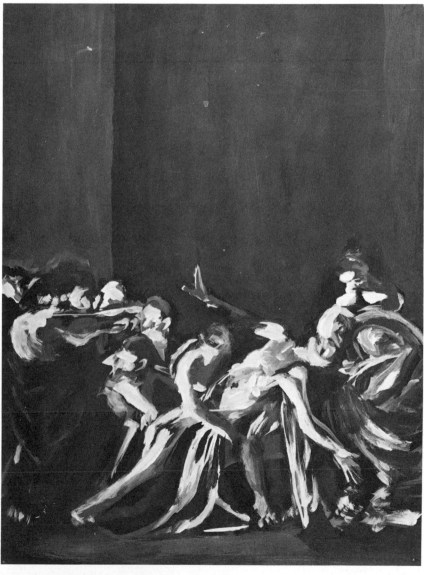

315. Pam Ozaroff. *Study after Caravaggio.* 1975.
Acrylic on cardboard.
Collection Yale University School of Art,
New Haven, Conn.

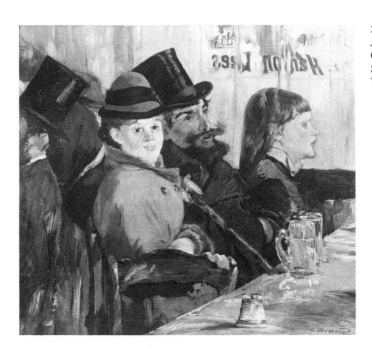

316. Edouard Manet (1832–83; French).
At the Café. 1878.
Oil on canvas, 31¼ × 33½″.
Sammlung Oskar Reinhart,
Winterthur, Switzerland.

The main spatial divisions of a Manet (Fig. 316) were directly indicated in charcoal on bare gray cardboard in Figure 317. The artist captures the strong interplay of triangles and squares, the geometric orchestration, which gives the original its visual life.

A painting by El Greco (Fig. 318) served as the model for a study that radically altered the proportions of the composition (Fig. 319). The student had to continuously rehearse and repeat the large sweep of intervals and dancing white shapes in order finally to reduce the timing to a satisfying essence.

317. Jack Huston.
Study after Manet. 1975.
Acrylic and charcoal on cardboard.
Collection Yale University
School of Art, New Haven, Conn.

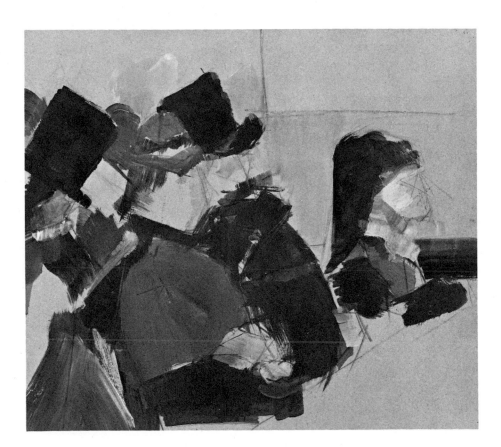

318. El Greco (1541–1614; Greek-Spanish).
The Vision of St. John the Divine. Oil on canvas, 7'4½" × 6'4".
Metropolitan Museum of Art, New York (Rogers Fund, 1956).

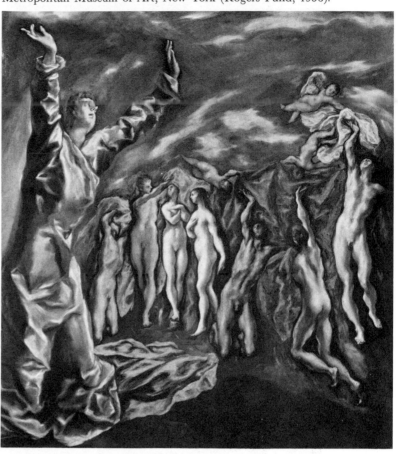

below: 319. Shelley M. Gaffin.
Study after El Greco. 1975.
Acrylic on cardboard.
Collection Yale University
School of Art, New Haven, Conn.

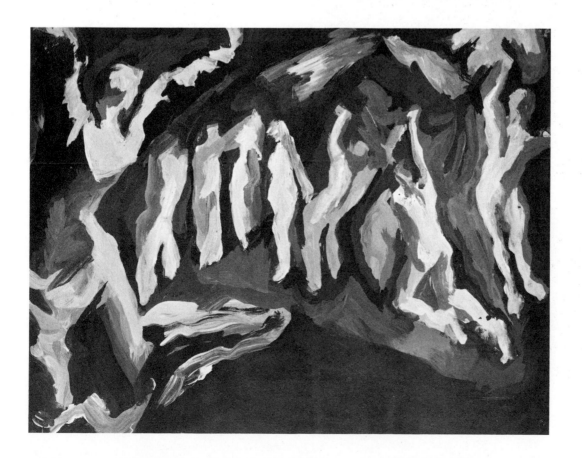

285

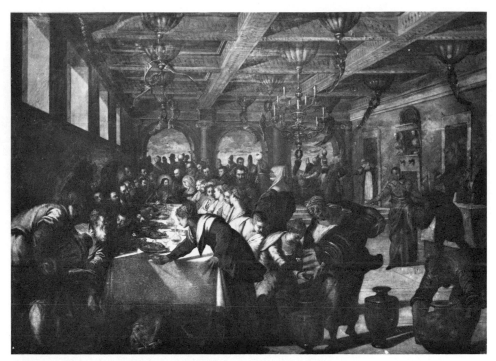

above: 320. Tintoretto (1518–94; Italian). *The Wedding at Cana.* 1561.
Oil on canvas. Santa Maria della Salute, Venice.

below: 321. John Swanger. *Study after Tintoretto.* 1975. Acrylic on cardboard.
Collection Yale University School of Art, New Haven, Conn.

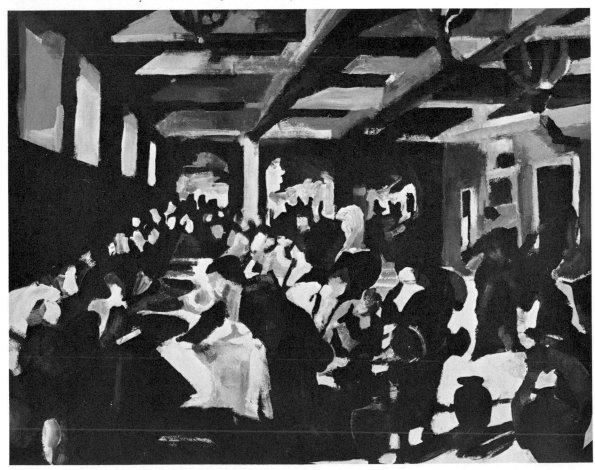

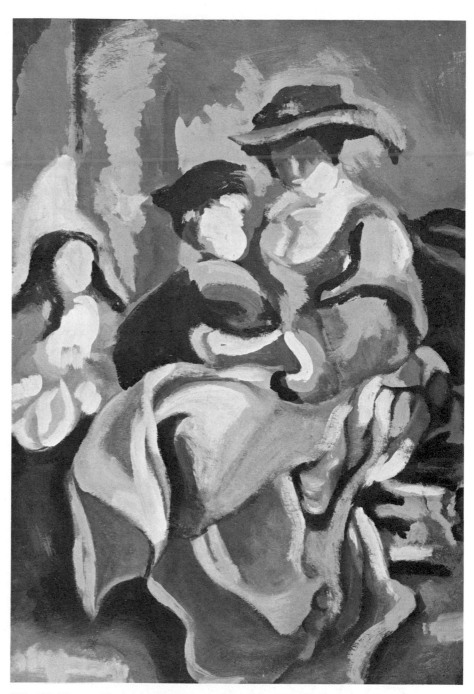

322. Jill Zisman. *Study after Rubens*. 1975. Acrylic on cardboard.
Collection Yale University School of Art, New Haven, Conn.

The positive and negative shapes of a great Tintoretto
painting (Fig. 320) are reinforced in Figure 321. The process
entailed constant change and readjustment to produce the right flow,
the right scale of relationships. The resulting texture was
again a by-product of the trial-and-error search.

Arabesque rhythms are exaggerated in a Rubens interpretation
(Fig. 322), a self-directed study aimed at overcoming a
tendency to produce superfluous detail.

In a painting by John Singer Sargent (Fig. 323), the figures are lifesize. Concentrating on the values but above all on the proportion, the student finally achieved, after four good tries, the correct scale relationships (Fig. 324). This final version, although only 9 inches high in actual size, seems visually very large.

323. John Singer Sargent (1856–1925; American).
Daughters of Edward Darley Boit. 1882.
Oil on canvas, 7'3" square.
Museum of Fine Arts, Boston
(gift of Mary Louisa Boit, Julia Overing Boit,
Jane Hubbard Boit, and Florence D. Boit,
in memory of their father, Edward Darley Boit).

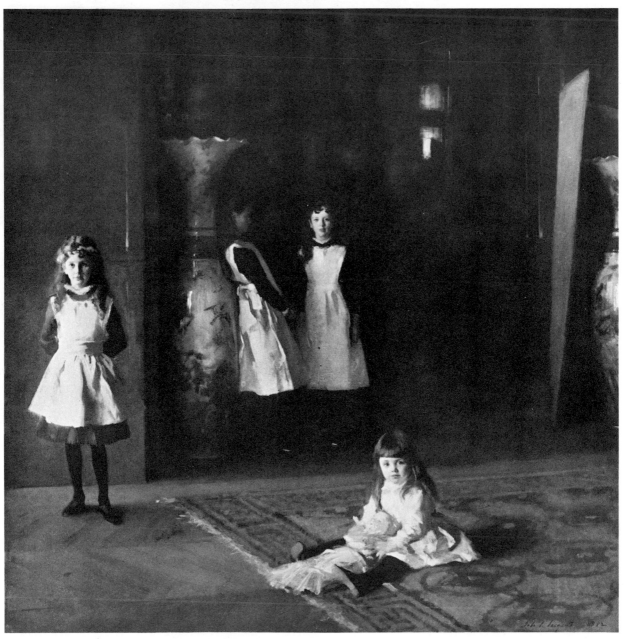

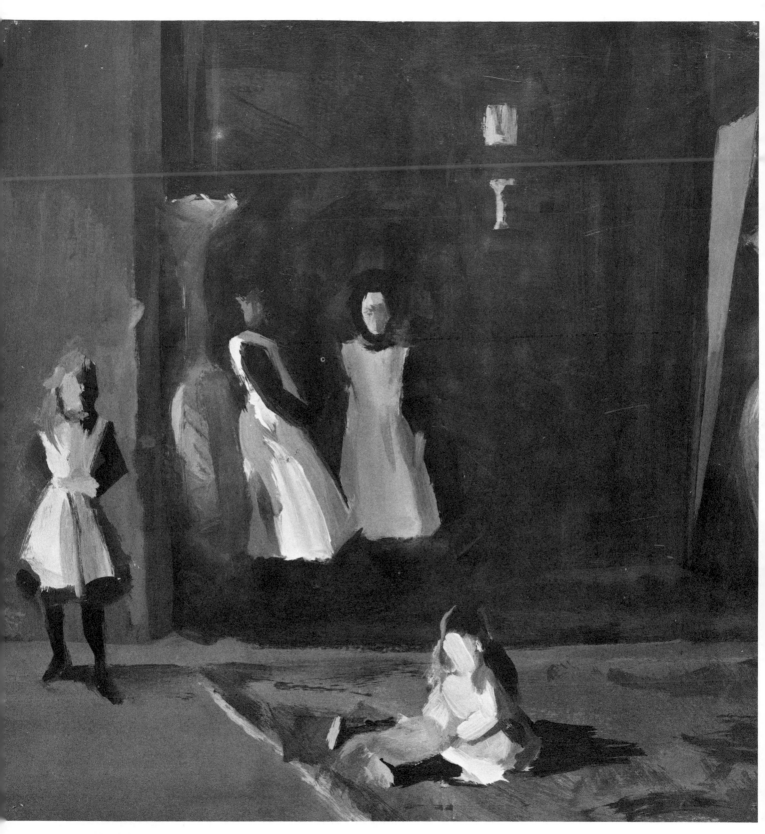

324. Alain Capretz.
Study after Sargent. 1975.
Acrylic on cardboard.
Collection Yale University
School of Art, New Haven, Conn.

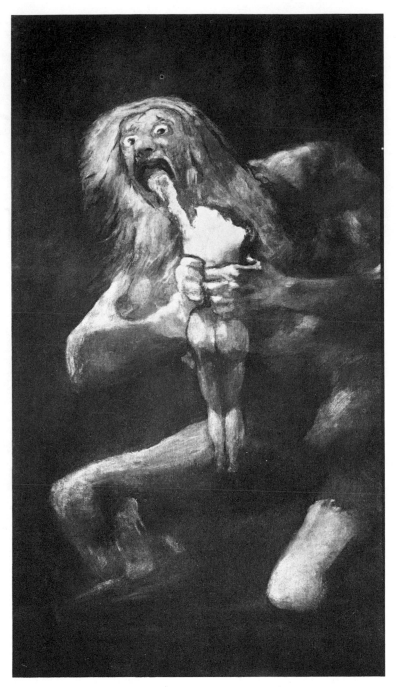

325. Francisco Goya (1746–1828; Spanish).
Saturn Devouring One of His Sons.
Oil on canvas, 4′9½″ × 2′8½″. Prado, Madrid.

Originally drawn to Goya because of the excitement
of dramatic violence (Fig. 325), the author of Figure 326 came to
understand the master's brilliant visual staging. Paraphrasing
the brilliant immediacy of Goya's brushwork, the student focuses
on the stretch and pull of the figure off the stage, rather
than merely cropping the figure. This stretching sensation is
the student's theme; it increases the intensity of the subject.

326. Lee Rudenjak.
Study after Goya. 1975.
Acrylic on cardboard.
Collection Yale University
School of Art, New Haven, Conn.

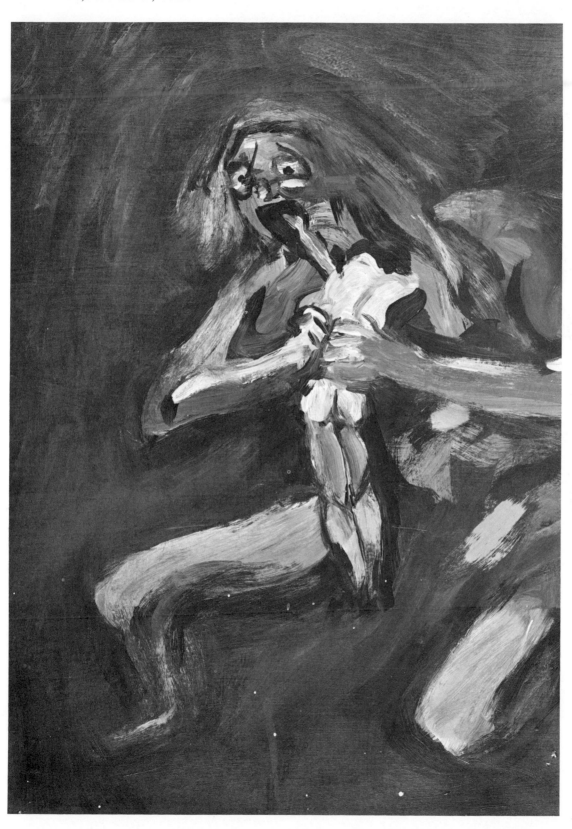

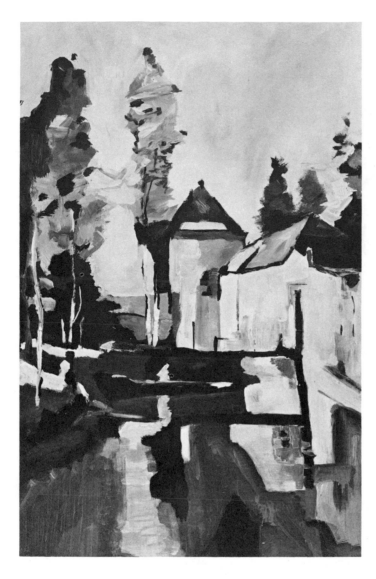

327. Scott Stenhouse.
Study after Corot. 1975.
Acrylic on cardboard.
Collection Yale University
School of Art, New Haven, Conn.

A geometric underpinning is subtly suggested in Corot's landscape works. In the study reproduced in Figure 327, however, the hard edges of the shapes are extremely heightened, and the illumination seems magnified fifty times.

Similarly, two studies after Vermeer paintings focus on some special quality that the student wished to extract. In Figure 328 the allover milky light of the original has obviously been exaggerated, yet the pale ghostlike presence of the original is evoked and preserved as the theme of the exercise. The other study (Fig. 329) concentrates on Vermeer's genius for structuring space and fooling us into thinking he is merely recording reality as a camera does. He fools us by means of naturalistic surface description, but the real form-life is the brilliantly engineered space. The figure pushes into space as part of a perfectly proportional relationship between figure and ground, aided by the inventive use of hard and soft edges. It is this structure, this relationship between figure and ambience, that the student studies.

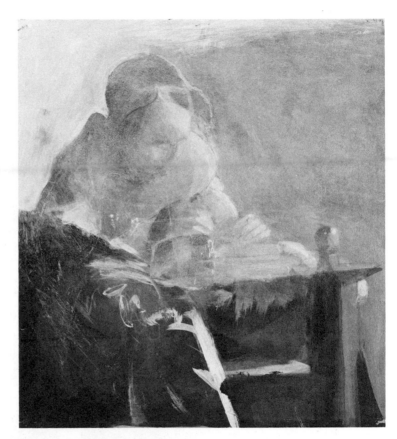

right: 328. Louis Hernandez.
Study after Vermeer. 1975.
Acrylic on cardboard.
Collection Yale University School of Art,
New Haven, Conn.

below: 329. Pam Ozaroff.
Study after Vermeer. 1975.
Acrylic on cardboard.
Collection Yale University School of Art,
New Haven, Conn.

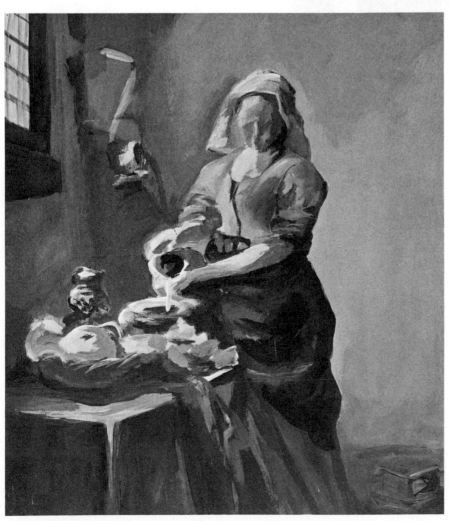

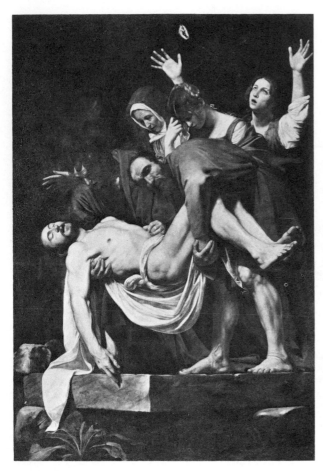

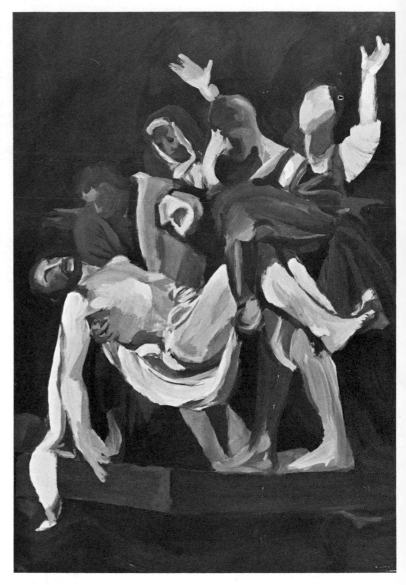

above: 330. Caravaggio (1573–1609; Italian).
The Entombment. 1602–03. Oil on canvas, 12′ × 6′9″.
Vatican, Rome.

right: 331. Alain Capretz.
Study after Caravaggio. 1975.
Acrylic on cardboard.
Collection Yale University School of Art,
New Haven, Conn.

The glaring stage light inherent in Caravaggio's work (Fig. 330) becomes exaggerated through stark, dramatic value contrasts in Figure 331. It is as though the student were X-raying the painting.

In order to reconstruct Manet's *Dejeuner sur l'Herbe* (Fig. 332) the artist of Figure 333 had to reconstruct all the secondary supporting planes as well as the larger, more obvious ones. She also had to make clear all the minor transitions from plane to plane. In this way she was able to discover the underpinning, the interior structure that the master hides.

332. Edouard Manet
(1832–83; French).
Déjeuner sur l'Herbe. 1862–63.
Oil on canvas, 7'3¾" × 8'10⅜".
Louvre, Paris.

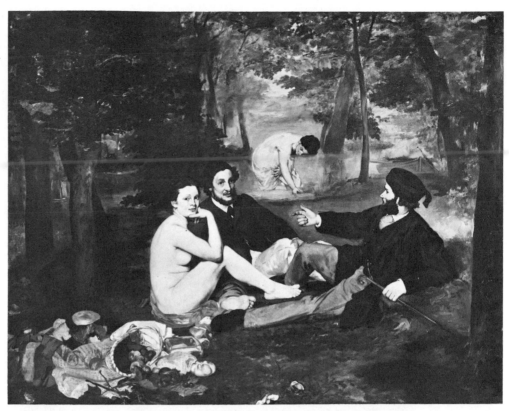

below: 333. Catherine Wehrli. *Study after Manet.* 1975. Acrylic on cardboard. Collection Yale University School of Art, New Haven, Conn.

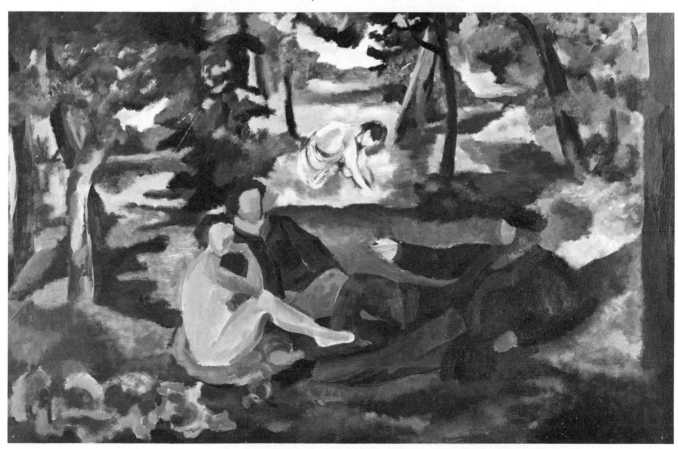

Masterwork into Still Life

The last problem drew upon the masters again to show that proportion, scale, light, composition, and so forth are themselves expressive elements even without a built-in "interesting" subject. The students were asked to set up a still life that would translate the masses of a masterwork into objects, and then to work from this approximation.

A pencil, some cloth, and a collection of small boxes makes a fairly close family resemblance to an original Braque (Fig. 334). The student does not merely imitate the Braque, for he has to follow the flow of his own paraphrased invention, which produces its own problems and intricacies (Fig. 335).

334. Georges Braque (1882–1963; French).
Road near l'Estaque. 1908. Oil on canvas, 23¾ × 19¾".
Museum of Modern Art, New York (given anonymously).

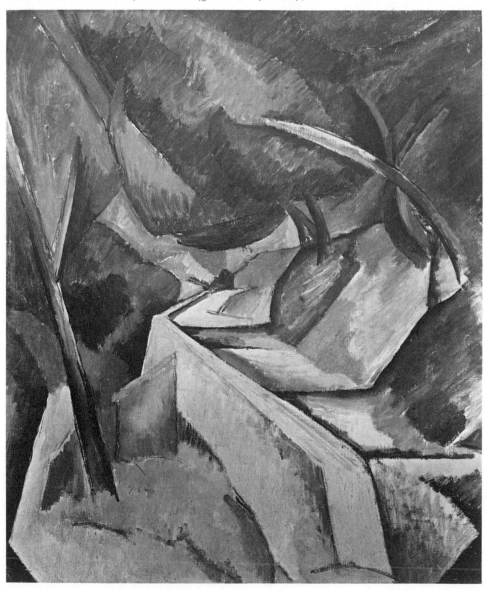

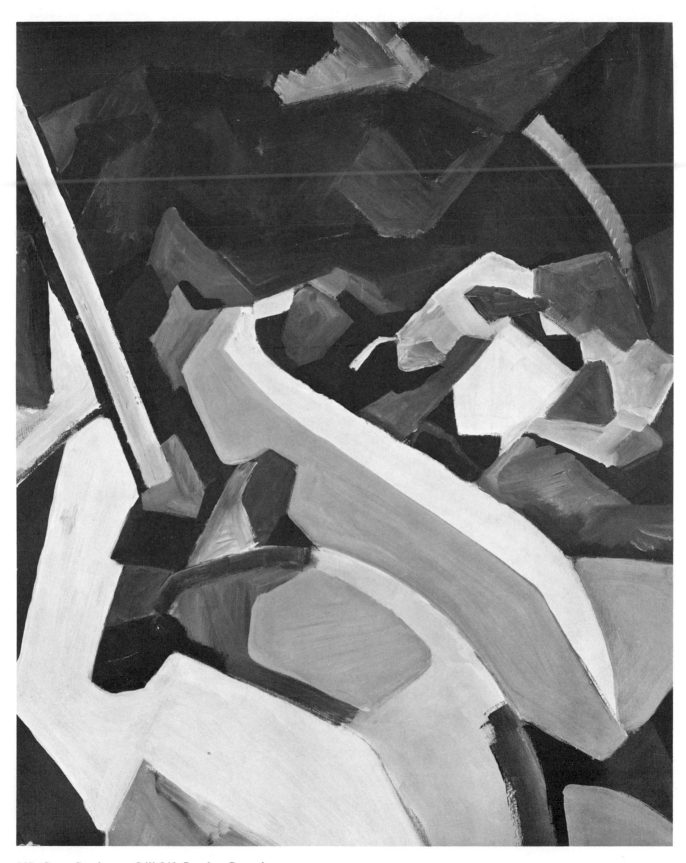

335. Scott Stenhouse. *Still Life Based on Braque's*
"Road near l'Estaque." 1975. Acrylic on cardboard.
Collection Yale University School of Art, New Haven, Conn.

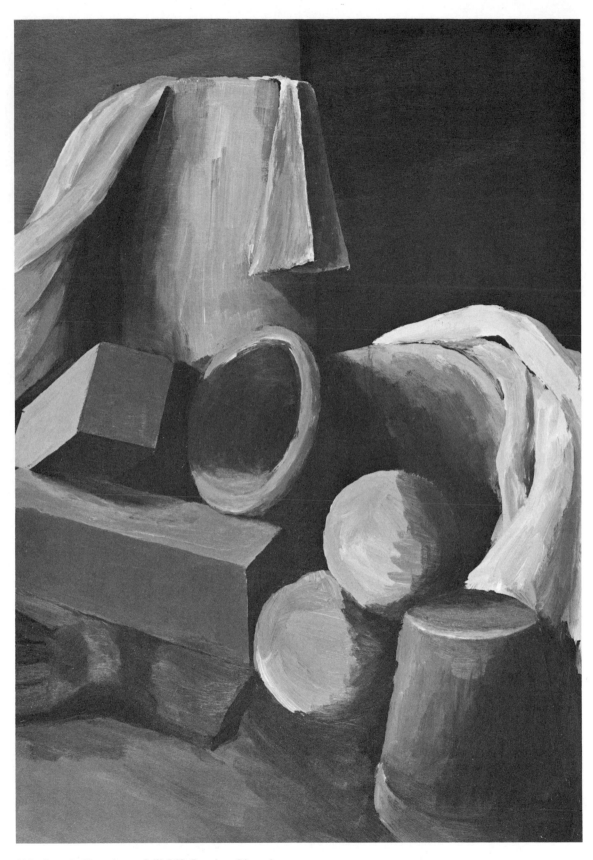

336. Joseph Chambers. *Still Life Based on Picasso's*
"Retrato de Mujer." 1975. Acrylic on cardboard.
Collection Yale University School of Art, New Haven, Conn.

Figure 336 is a very loose translation of a Picasso (Fig. 337). The student chooses a sculptural mode in keeping with Picasso's earlier classical period; the light falls on the tilting, weighted masses in the half-light moving slowly from left to right and culminating in the rounded white drapery.

337. Pablo Picasso (1881–1973; Spanish-French). *Retrato de Mujer.* 1939. Oil on canvas, 25⅝ × 10⅛". Collection the artist's estate.

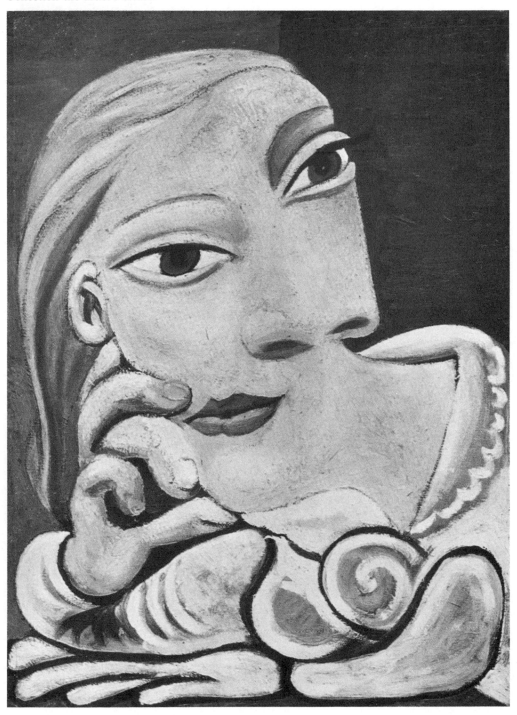

In our final example Manet's *Olympia* (Fig. 338) is brilliantly reproduced by a woman's shoe, an artificial rose, an ink bottle, and some drapery (Fig. 339). Humor aside, this excellent effort presents a freely constructed approximation of the masterwork's original proportions and tonal values.

In this series of black-and-white paintings, planned as a transition from drawing to painting, the energies of the class were focused constantly on what seemed the hardest to learn: the limitless possibilities of personal expression within purely pictorial modes. By this we do not mean that the final goal is abstraction; we must simply remember that a work devoid of visual invention is dull at best. With this ambitious goal in mind, however, technical obstacles of the sort that might be expected, such as putting paint to support, never became an issue. Problems of brushwork and texture "solved themselves" as by-products of building a believable work—an integrated composition.

338. Edouard Manet (1832–83; French). *Olympia.* 1863. Oil on canvas, 4'3¼" × 6'2¾". Louvre, Paris.

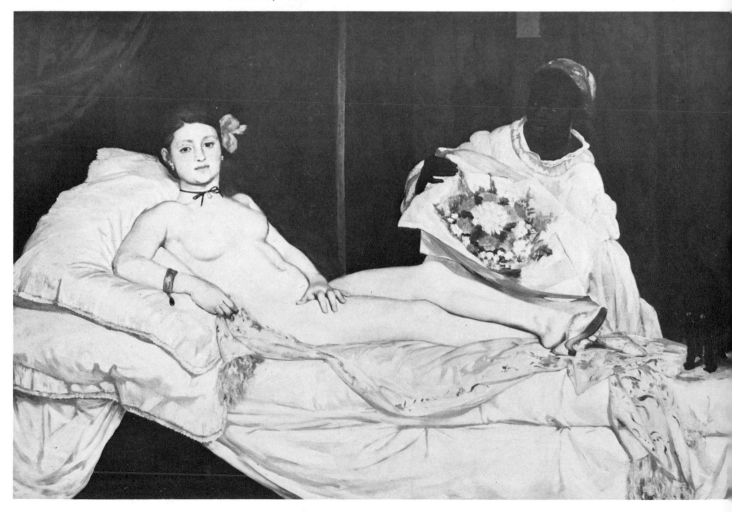

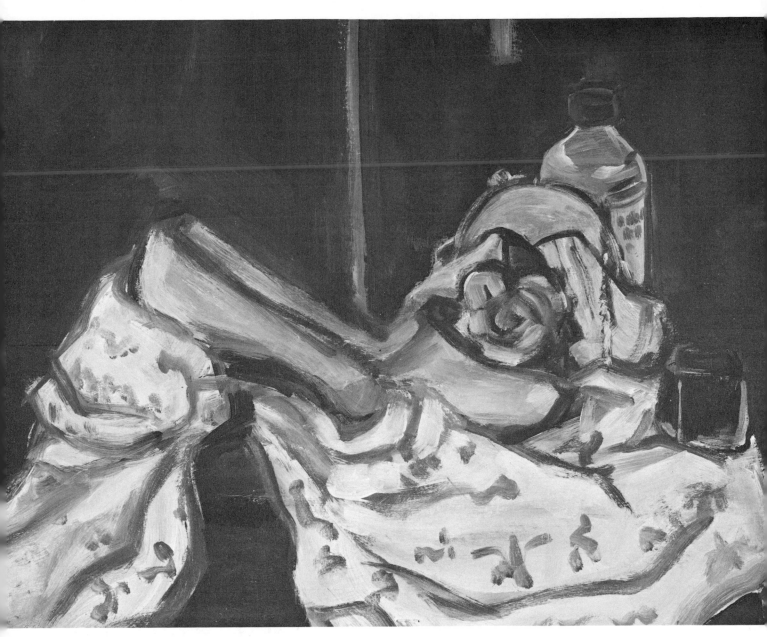

339. Anne E. Heideman.
Still Life Based on Manet's "Olympia." 1975.
Acrylic on cardboard.
Collection Yale University School of Art,
New Haven, Conn.

14 Attitudes and Summary

In this final chapter we shall try to reinforce some of the ideas developed throughout the book, using master drawings as illustrations, and we shall attempt to explore still further the possibilities that exist in the art of drawing.

The first four drawings are concerned with the same subject, a seated or half-length female figure, but each is conceived within a distinct vision that directs the style, the touch, and the spatial arrangement. The purpose gives birth to the idea.

Picasso's straightforward portrait of Dr. Claribel Cone (Fig. 340) is a complete graphic work in itself. It is not, as far as we know, a study that was to be executed in another medium. In this period (1922) Picasso, following Ingres' lead, focused with penetrating clarity on the head, and, in particular, on the facial features. The artist also suggested, in an understated way, the character of the hands, the folds of the dress, and so forth. Yet the whole figure is rather like a

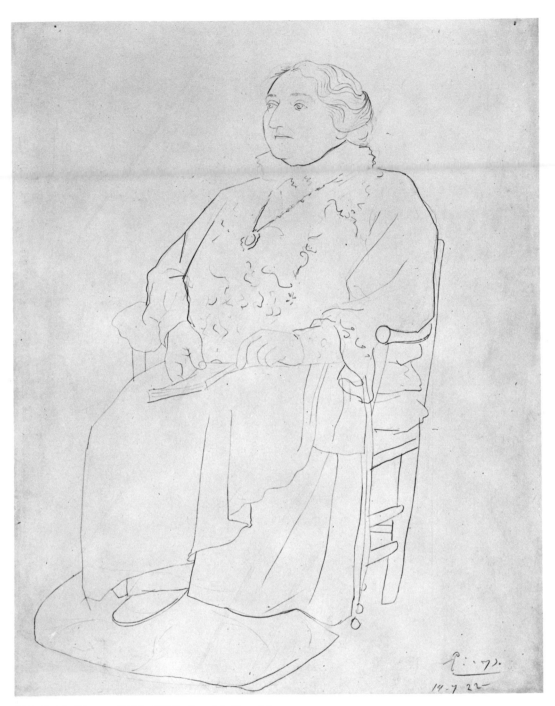

340. Pablo Picasso (1881–1973); Spanish-French).
Portrait of Dr. Claribel Cone. 1922. Pencil, $9\frac{1}{2} \times 8\frac{3}{16}''$.
Baltimore Museum of Art (Cone Collection).

piece of sculpture on a pedestal, seen from one fixed, foreshortened
position. The projection of the skull into three-dimensional space
is clear, as are the transitions from the shoulder to the bust
and from the knee to the pad on the floor. The unified projection
of related forms could be translated into sculpture from this
seemingly offhand line drawing.

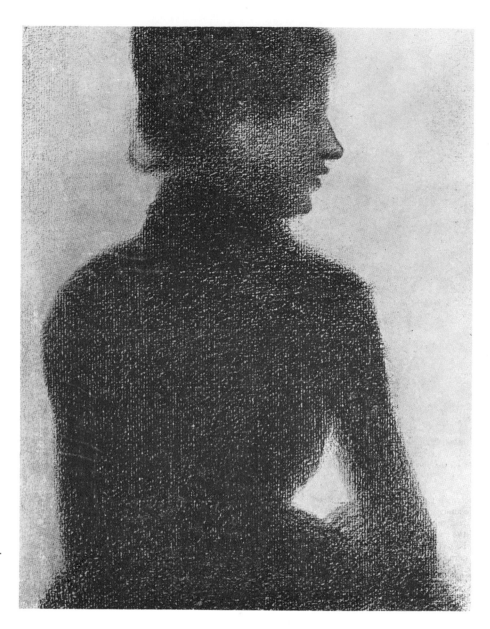

341. Georges Seurat (1859–91; French).
Une Poseuse Habillée. c. 1887.
Conté crayon, 12½ × 9½″.
Destroyed in the fire
at the Gare des Batignolles, Paris.

By contrast, Georges Seurat's conté crayon study for
Les Poseuses (Fig. 341) confronts us with one dark, dramatic
profile, the first impression is of pure silhouette, beautifully
settled on the page. The edges of the drawing, which crop the top
of the head, suggest a window in which the figure is set against
the radiant light of the background. But after we adjust our eyes
to the sharp contrast in the light, we begin to perceive the
character of the head, the slightly open mouth, and the
distinctly formed features. Thus, our initial awareness of one
large shape broadens into an understanding of the particular form.

Holbein's *Portrait of Anna Meyer* (Pl. 20, p. 246) also
presents a silhouette. The figure is set in a softly focused but intense
light, and differences in the texture of skin, hair, and dress are
fully realized. The figure forms a triangle that easily fills
the whole space. The viewer is very close to the transfixed model,

who seems unaware of the intrusion. From this close range, we are directed to study what the artist wants us to see.

Lamenting Woman by Matthias Grünewald (Fig. 342) also forms a triangle, and it fills its space with the same components—hair, skin, and dress. But whereas the Holbein model is immobile, Grünewald's all-encompassing movements of form keep the viewer's eye moving through them. The tightly clasped hands act within these rhythms and connect the bodice to the hair at right. The head, twisting sharply in space, is distorted to make us see what seems impossible—the far side of the face. It is as if these spiraling rhythms, based in the two lower corners, gather momentum as they pulsate to the apex of the triangle, the head. In their speed, they seem to gain pressure and push the forms of the far side of the head toward us.

342. Matthias Grünewald (1470/75–1528; German). *Lamenting Woman with Clasped Hands.* Black chalk with white highlights, $15\frac{5}{8} \times 11\frac{3}{4}$". Sammlung Oskar Reinhart, Winterthur, Switzerland.

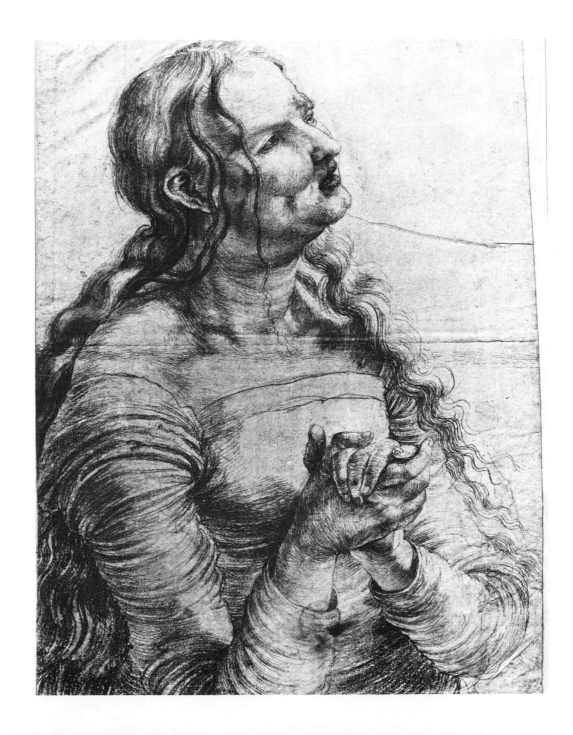

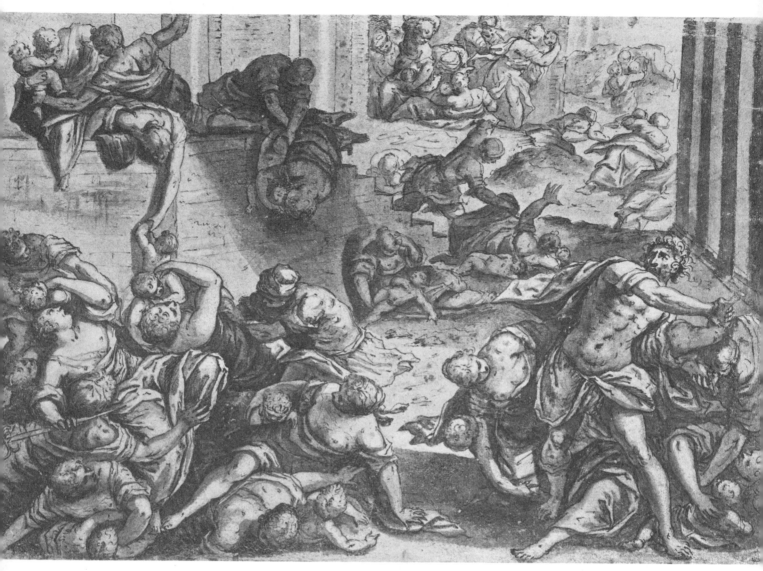

343. Tintoretto (1518–94; Italian). *Massacre of the Innocents.*
Pen, wash, and ink. Albertina, Vienna.

These four drawings, which are all single-feature subjects,
have some similarities, but they reveal how each concept dictates
its own space, rhythms, focus, and instrumentation, all to reinforce
the individual concept. Picasso and Holbein work from a fixed
point with particular models; Seurat constructs one dark shape that
houses a distinctly characterized head; and Grünewald's figure
writhes under pressure from an all-embracing movement.

Tintoretto's *Massacre of the Innocents* in pen, ink, and wash
(Fig. 343) is a study for the painting (Fig. 344). Seeing them both
together, we witness the artist editing his own composition.
First, he reduces the scale of the lower right figure, which in the
drawing dominates the space. He adds to this reduction by
extending the row of vertical columns behind him so he becomes
locked into the space. This action, in turn, makes the artist

pull the figures above closer to the picture plane. In the original
drawing these figures move diagonally into a deeper space.
With the leftover space on top he carves an architectural niche
to hold one group of figures, thereby setting up an additional
compositional vignette. In addition, he makes the lower planes
sharper by reinforcing hard-edge shadows. As a result, the
entire space is compressed, with all the figures locked into strong
planar forces.

The drawing, the initial concept, is a work of art in its
own right. Besides this, it helps us document the steps toward the
realization of the final masterpiece, because we can read
the artist's moves.

344. Tintoretto (1518–94; Italian). *Massacre of the Innocents*. 1583–87.
Oil on canvas. Scuolo di San Rocco, Venice.

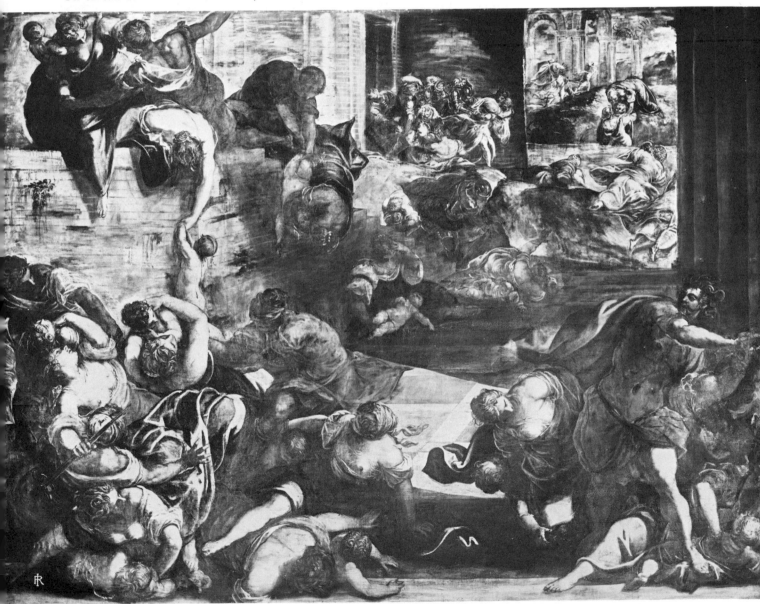

below: 345. Rembrandt (1606–69; Dutch). *Winter Landscape.*
Quill pen and ink with wash.
Fogg Art Museum, Harvard University, Cambridge, Mass.

bottom: 346. Peter Paul Rubens (1577–1640; Flemish).
The Death of Hippolytus. 1608–12.
Pen and India ink with wash, 8¾ × 12¾″. Musée Bonnat, Bayonne.

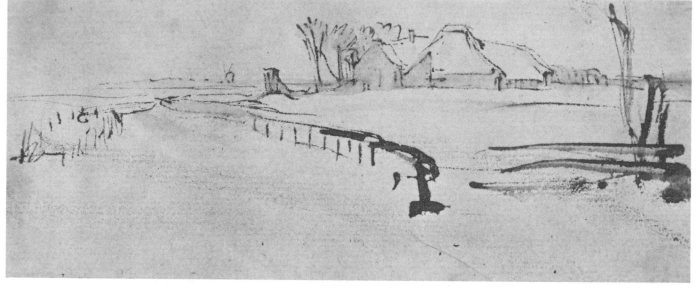

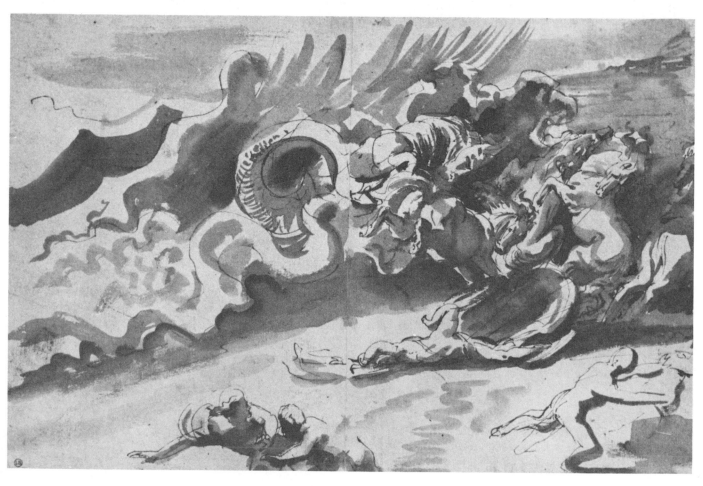

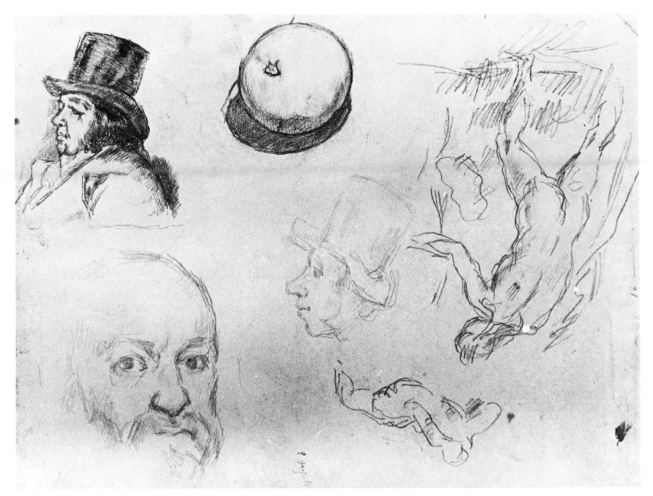

347. Paul Cézanne (1839–1906; French). *Page from a Sketchbook with Self-Portrait.* 1884–86. Pencil on white paper, 19¾ × 12½″. Collection Sir Kenneth Clark, Hythe, Kent.

A more generalized style is that of Rembrandt in Figure 345, a small work in pen and wash. The brief, quickly sketched marks explain the whole space in a miraculous manner. We are pulled into the composition by the dark frontal post of the fence, which then recedes, drawing us even farther into depth. We are returned to the frontal plane by the clash of horizontal and vertical strokes on the right. Here again is a complete artistic statement.

Peter Paul Rubens' *Death of Hippolytus* (Fig. 346) is obviously an invention, and the drawing is composed to complement this concept. The broad, repeating circular rhythm is the main visual theme; when it engulfs and hits the main actors, it creates a tremendous visual noise. This manipulation becomes one with the story line.

Figure 347 is a sheet from Paul Cézanne's notebook. There is no single subject, but rather a kaleidoscopic collection of several of his well-known themes: a self-portrait, an apple, a moving female bather, a study after Goya. We are witness to the master's thoughts—he is thinking, searching, planning.

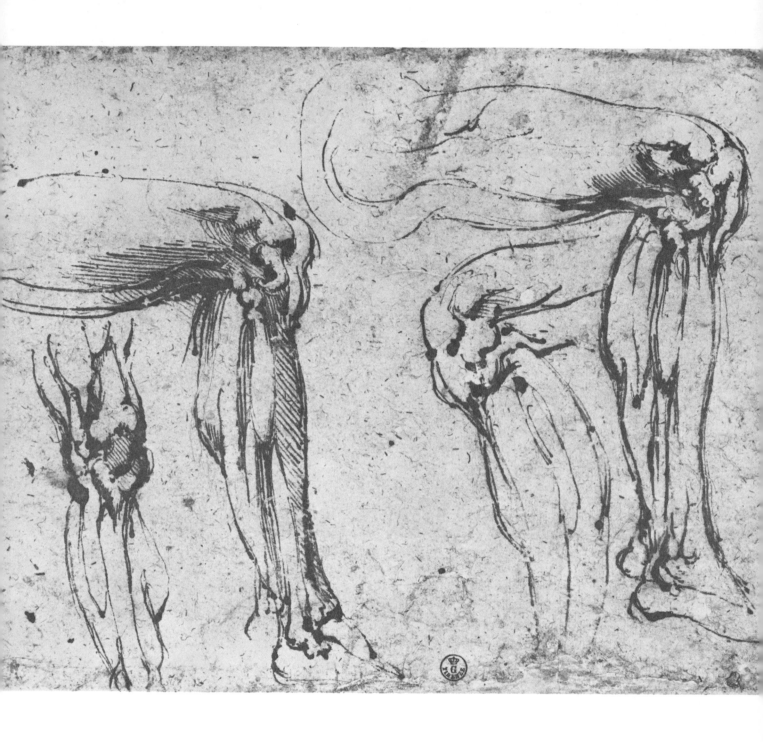

above: 348. Michelangelo
(1475–1564; Italian).
Anatomical Study.
Pen and ink, $8\frac{3}{8} \times 10\frac{3}{8}''$.
Uffizi, Florence.

opposite: 349. Pieter Bruegel the Elder
(1525/30–69; Flemish).
Temptation of Saint Anthony. 1556.
Pen and ink, $8\frac{5}{8} \times 13''$.
Ashmolean Museum, Oxford.

Michelangelo's *Anatomical Study* (Fig. 348) reveals, as
the title suggests, a study of facts. But there is more than
mere structural information in this study. The page, whether by
design or by instinct, is carefully composed. The leg forms
are held in mutual tension, interlocked and interdependent.
The grouping of these forms thus takes on a separate life, distinct
from the problems of anatomical study.

Throughout this book we have emphasized the need to commit
natural, human, and environmental forms to memory as a basis
for individual interpretation. In this context it is appropriate
to reproduce Bruegel's *Temptation of Saint Anthony* (Fig. 349),
a fantasy creation made up of invented and remembered
forms from nature. Discreetly hidden in the lower right,
Saint Anthony becomes part of a vast panorama of whimsical
and grotesque characters.

Goya, too, creates a stage for his invented character, the
"rapacious horse" in Figure 350. The dark horizontal line
at the top and the broken line at bottom set up a narrow stage

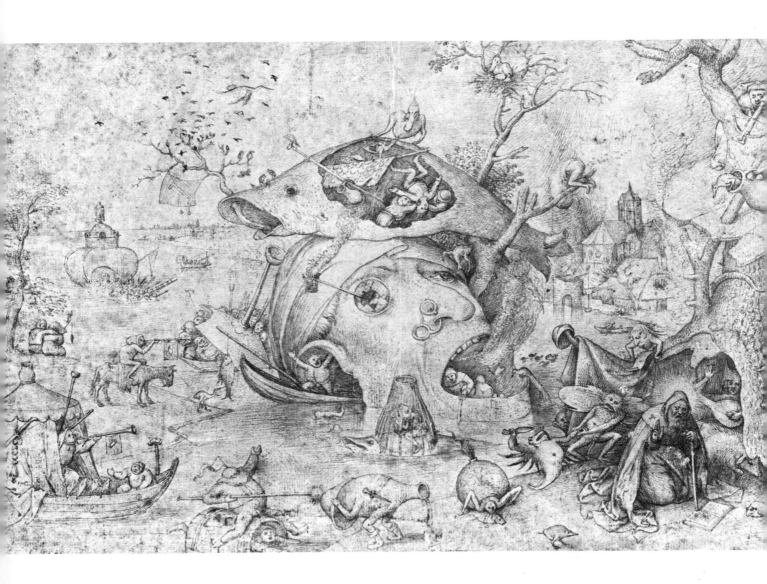

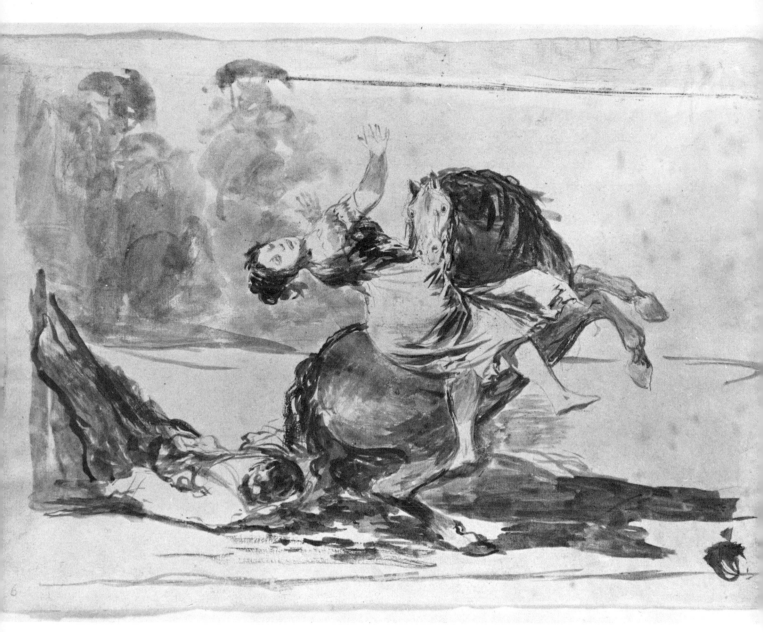

350. Francisco Goya (1746–1828; Spanish).
The Rapacious Horse. 1815–24.
Brush and red ink, $9\frac{7}{8} \times 13\frac{7}{8}''$. Prado, Madrid.

for the violent action. Unlike Bruegel, who makes us see the whole
stage from afar, Goya places us in front row center.

Summary

Compared to other visual media, drawing is a magical act.
In no other medium can we go so directly from thought process
to image, unencumbered by materials or extensive preparation.
We are able, with experience, to refine our thoughts in a
direct way, without complicated techniques. With this immediacy,
drawing can accommodate all attitudes, whether we are reacting

directly to the forms around us, refining forms from memory, inventing new forms, or even planning complicated relationships.

Whether their purpose is the transformation of forms from the environment or inventions for the sake of plastic action alone, great drawings have a built-in economy of conception and performance. This economy is often deceiving to beginners, who may not be aware of the selecting process and the boiling down to essence that gave birth to a particular experience, and who may misread it as simplicity of conception.

The practice of slavishly imitating a master's work leads to frustration and, ultimately, to sterility, for the touch of the master's hand that we admire is the product of natural tendencies—personality, development, and genius. This accumulation of experience and personality builds a unique vision that transmits the message naturally. The young draftsman should, from the beginning, try to experiment with all modes of drawing, constantly trying on different suits to find out what fits before considering the polished technical performance. What we like initially in the masters changes with experience. Even mature artists admire what is not natural to themselves: A "baroque" artist may like Mondrian, or a "minimal" artist may like Rubens. It is important to study rather than duplicate, for understanding fosters natural development, while emulation may lead to a parody of mannerisms.

It is dangerous to use a bit of "master technique" to dress up a work or to conceal a lack of formal invention. What we must extract from the masters is the kind of thinking that was employed and the growth of an ability to select, for we cannot start directly where someone else left off. A lifetime's experience that has developed an attitude cannot be obtained by mere imitation. Still, it is the work of the masters that puts us on the right track, that makes us see the world of forms and our own environment in a new way and inspires us to develop our own ways of seeing, and, just possibly, of inventing our own world of form life.

Forms from our imagination or from the physical environment, which we can call *life forms*—such as a tree in nature or demons in the mind of a Bruegel—are transmitted by the artist's vision and skill to create something new—a *form life*. This cycle from life form to form life begins in drawing when the artist, haunted by an image or an idea, puts pencil to paper.

Index

References are to page numbers,
except for color plates and black-and-white illustrations,
which are identified by figure and plate numbers.

Photographic Sources